EUROPEAN CITIZENSHIP BETWEEN NATIONAL
LEGACIES AND POSTNATIONAL PROJECTS

European Citizenship between National Legacies and Postnational Projects

edited by

KLAUS EDER and BERNHARD GIESEN

OXFORD

UNIVERSITY PRESS

OXFORD
UNIVERSITY PRESS

Great Clarendon Street, Oxford OX2 6DP

Oxford University Press is a department of the University of Oxford.
It furthers the University's objective of excellence in research, scholarship,
and education by publishing worldwide in

Oxford New York

Athens Auckland Bangkok Bogotá Buenos Aires Calcutta
Cape Town Chennai Dar es Salaam Delhi Florence Hong Kong Istanbul
Karachi Kuala Lumpur Madrid Melbourne Mexico City Mumbai
Nairobi Paris São Paulo Shanghai Singapore Taipei Tokyo Toronto Warsaw

with associated companies in Berlin Ibadan

Oxford is a registered trade mark of Oxford University Press
in the UK and in certain other countries

Published in the United States
by Oxford University Press Inc., New York

British Library Cataloguing in Publication Data

Data available

Library of Congress Cataloging in Publication Data
European citizenship: between national legacies and postnational projects/edited by
Klaus Eder and Bernhard Giesen.
p. cm.
Includes bibliographical references and index.
1. Citizenship—Europe.   2. Group identity—Europe.   3. European Union.   I. Eder, Klaus,
1946–   II. Giesen, Bernhard, 1948–
JN40.E825 2000   323.6 094—dc21   00–045292
ISBN 0–19–924120–1

1 3 5 7 9 10 8 6 4 2

Typeset in Minion by
Cambrian Typesetters, Frimley, Surrey
Printed in Great Britain
on acid-free paper by
Biddles Ltd.,
Guildford & King's Lynn

PREFACE

This volume is a product of a year-long collaborative project: the 'European Forum on Citizenship' in the academic year 1995/6 at the European University Institute in Florence. We thank Yves Mény, Steven Lukes, and Massimo La Torre who provided the material and intellectual environment and Kathinka España for her organizational and practical help. For skilful editorial assistance we finally have to thank Sibylle Scheipers.

Klaus Eder and Bernhard Giesen

Berlin Konstanz
1999

PREFACE

CONTENTS

LIST OF TABLES

LIST OF FIGURES

NOTES ON CONTRIBUTORS

Klaus von Beyme, Professor Emeritus in Political Science, University of Heidelberg

Carlos Closa, Professor in Public Law, University of Zaragoza

Bernhard Giesen, Professor in Sociology, University of Konstanz

Dieter Gosewinkel, Lecturer in History, Free University of Berlin

Klaus Eder, Professor in Sociology, Humboldt University Berlin

M. Rainer Lepsius, Professor Emeritus in Sociology, University of Heidelberg

Philippe C. Schmitter, Professor in Political Science, European University Institute, Florence

Wolfgang Streeck, Research Director at the Max Planck Institute for the Study of Society, Cologne

Yasemin Soysal, Professor in Sociology, University of Essex

1

INTRODUCTION

European Citizenship

An Avenue for the Social Integration of Europe

Bernhard Giesen and Klaus Eder

European Integration through Citizenship?

The avenue to European integration as imagined by the founding fathers of the EEC and finally established by the treaties of Maastricht and Amsterdam has led to a common market for goods, labour, and capital and to supranational political institutions. The status of the resulting institutions, however, is far from clear. Although the increasing influence of the European Court of Justice and its claim to supremacy over national legislation and even over the national constitutional courts hints at the growing power of European governance regarding the member states, the status of the European Community has been heavily debated among legal and political scientists as well as among politicians and practitioners of international law. It has centred around the question of whether Europe is a federation created by a treaty between autonomous national governments, as the 'intergovernmentalists' claim, or whether this federation gave rise—intentionally or as an unintended consequence—to strong supranational institutions which reside at the top of national governments and can rightly claim to be based on an implicit constitution. In the first case the European Community is the domain of international law and can dispense with the question of a European demos and of a strong conception of citizenship. Both remain exclusively at the level of nations and their member states. If, however, as the European Court of Justice successfully claims, the Community represents the sovereign centre of governance (at least for a certain range of policy fields, the First Pillar of the Union), then the issue of European citizenship comes to the fore and a debate about its relationship regarding the multiplicity of national citizenship can hardly be avoided.

Even if we accept that there is an undeniable shift of sovereignty to the European centre, the structure of this supranational Leviathan, the 'nature of the beast' is far from having a clear contour. Will the new political institutions of Europe simply copy the institutions of the modern nation-state and its uniform and egalitarian conception of citizenship? Or will it follow the pattern of multinational empires with minority quotas, diffuse frontiers, and political stratification between centre and periphery? Will France be the model for Europe? Or will it be the Habsburg model? Or is there yet another model lurking in the darkness of European history which allows us to make sense of this form of supranational political institution which regulates without a monopoly of power and which represents the Europeans without being elected by them?

The French model (as an ideal typical case of the nation state model) is based on the classic notion of citizenship canonized by T. H. Marshall and has become the meta-narrative of citizenship in Europe: civic, political, and social rights enabling the construction of a free and good society based on as much freedom and equality as possible. In Europe this story of citizenship was born and realized. The Habsburg model enters as soon as a basic assumption of the French model, the collective identity of the nation, is not given. How can a modern society be created when there is more than one nation in the state? The solution then is an aggregation of different nations under one sovereign rule defined as equal (group) subjects with their specific cultural rights. Citizenship in the Habsburg sense is a system of differentiated rights imposed and controlled by an enlightened type of government.

The question of citizenship is not only a question of political control over an emerging European type of governance. It also arises as an effect of this governance on European society, i.e. within the context of the Europeanization of society. The more the legal framework set by European institutions is superimposed on national legislation, the more issues of residence and immigration, welfare entitlements, and the uninhibited move of labour within Europe modify the social conditions of citizenship within the member states. Questions of to whom which rights and which obligations should be granted create conflicts over inclusion and exclusion. In the final instance, all arenas of citizenship politics require a set of rules, rights, and obligations separating insiders from outsiders, i.e. European citizens from non-European aliens.

The institution of European citizenship is an attempt towards defining who is an insider and who is not. It also is an attempt towards defining a demos beyond the nation. European citizenship emerges as a concept that thematizes the problem of the social integration of Europe. European citizenship fulfils—like any other citizenship—two functions: to provide a social basis for transnational institutions and to define what is shared by those included in the social space covered by European institutions.

The debates and politics of European citizenship attempt to create social integration on a transnational and postnational level. Transnationality means citizenship beyond the nation state. Postnationality means citizenship beyond the boundaries of a politically defined ethnic community. The integration of Europe is thus an experiment in building an abstract political community based on a notion of citizenship that abstracts from the ethnic component of being the citizen of a 'demos'. The citizens of Europe become not only the citizens of transnational institutions, but also of a postnational community.

Such abstraction is a necessary prerequisite for citizenship in Europe. Its implication is well demonstrated by the symbolic device of a European passport which is to replace the national passports of the member states. The burgundy-red passport of EU citizens is to replace the national passports which not only represent, but even explicitly verbalize very different cultures. Thus, the British passport refers to travelling citizens and addresses non-citizens abroad when saying: 'Her Britannic Majesty's Secretary of State requires in the name of her Majesty all those whom it may concern to allow the bearer to pass freely without let or hindrance, and to afford the bearer such assistance and protection as may be necessary', whereas the German passport emphasizes the state in distinction to its citizens when declaring that 'this passport is the property of the Federal Republic of Germany'; the Italian passport warns its bearers not to disregard the importance of official documents: 'Anybody who forgets, loses or falsifies the passport will be punished—including imprisonment'; the French passport tries to prevent situations in which the French state is expected to subsidize its citizens abroad: the bearer of the passport should take care that 'he carries with him enough currency'. Obviously the issuing institutions had quite varying expectations regarding critical situations of the bearer and the function of the passport.

Against such national traditions of citizenship a unitary European citizenship has to disregard national legacies. It has to institutionalize the idea of an encompassing citizenship regime which encloses national and local citizenship. Such citizenship is certainly postnational. It will also be transnational because it will still be tied to a system of relations between a limited number of nationally defined political systems.

In order to explore the current issues of an emerging European citizenship regime, this volume will outline the embeddedness of citizenship in different national traditions, describe its impact on transnational social arenas, and investigate the effects on ideals of collective identity when citizenship is put into practice beyond the national realm. This all requires us to strip the notion of citizenship from its historical form and to present a social-scientific conception of citizenship in which cultural traditions and normative definitions of rights and obligations are treated as analytical dimensions.

Three Conceptions of Citizenship

Citizenship is not a clear-cut analytical concept. Like 'democracy', its ideological kin, the concept of 'citizenship', is also a confusing concept—modified in political practices and accommodated to changing historical situations. It is one of the battle-cries in conflicts over boundary construction: it is appealed to by insiders and outsiders in public debates about welfare entitlements and political participation.

Historically, it was brought up as a demarcation of an urban community of equals in contrast to the traditional distinction of masters and servants. As a demarcation of the political community it did establish an egalitarian relationship among those included, but it also strictly excluded most of the population from participation in public affairs, even if they did partake in market exchange or were subject to the authority of the city government, princely state, or empire. The modern conception of citizenship as engendered by the rhetoric of the French Revolution shifted the meaning of citizenship from the exclusive demarcation of a privileged group to the continual inclusion of new groups into the expansive demos. The centre was replaced by the periphery as the authentic source of political will.

Since then citizenship is commonly considered as an interface relating the state and civil society, government, and the people, the territorial political organization and its members. This relationship between both sides—the organization and the individual—can be conceived of in different ways and is described by different models. Most of these models can be subsumed under three major paradigms: the *individualist paradigm* which focuses on legal guarantees for the rational pursuit of individual interests, the *political paradigm* which puts forward the ideal of participation of all in public debates, and the *collective identity paradigm* which links citizenship to a common culture or tradition. The individualist paradigm is historically linked to liberal conceptions of the market and the concomitant idea of market regulation through legal provisions. The political paradigm is similarly linked to ideological debates: to democratic ideas of participation and their republican/communitarian containment. The collective identity paradigm finally is linked to the issue of membership and its intellectual rationalization through ideas that vary from universal to primordial types of belonging.

These paradigms exist not only at the level of intellectual reflection and justification of citizenship, but also at the level of legal institutions and social and political practices. The individualist paradigm, the liberal theory of citizenship, is linked to egalitarian institutions of law, a liberal political practice of inclusion and legal provisions that guarantee these principles. The political paradigm, based on the democratic theory of citizenship, relates a sense of collective project with a legal system of equal obligations and a highly demanding practice of inclusion. The collective identity paradigm, based on a cultural theory of citizenship, corresponds to legal definitions of nationality and to everyday practices of inclusion and exclusion.

The Individualist Paradigm: Between the Market and the State

If citizenship is viewed from the perspective of the state as a formal organization it refers to a set of elementary membership rights which are equal for all individual members and it is insensitive to social, economic, or cultural differences between them. This paradigm disregards political issues or particular historical heritages and restricts citizenship to a formal status enabling individuals to have equal access to the processes of the organization—be it legal rights or education or welfare entitlements.

This paradigm focuses on the liberal idea of providing for everybody the possibility of obtaining access to the social and the political arena. The idea of providing the freedom for everybody to realize their interests is based on the narrative of the presocial state of nature, where everybody fought everybody else, which is to be replaced by an agreement for all to enter a social state. In a contractualist social state—constituted by free individuals—inequality may arise and is even considered to be unavoidable.[1] In order to tame its consequences a strong state is therefore needed which provides the regulatory framework for the market to function. This will not abolish inequality, but makes it legitimate according to criteria of social justice.

The Political Paradigm: Between Democratic Participation and the Republican Community

If citizenship is viewed from the perspective of civil society, it refers to a practice of participation in common affairs and of public debate about political issues. This model considers citizenship not as a matter of formal right or entitlement, but as a practice of active participation in which different individuals engage to a varying degree. Those who participate strongly in the public sphere activate their citizenship, whereas those who do not are—strictly speaking—not full citizens because they are devoid of the constitutive practice. Here the core of citizenship is provided by a strong civil society, by public debates, and by social movements which mobilize supporters, address the government, and intervene in political decisions.

This model of citizenship adds a series of strong obligations to rights. It disregards any reference to an external presocial or anthropological basis such as a state of nature; it rather sees political action as the fundamental source of citizenship. Instead of a Lockean contractualism it refers to a Hegelian idea of politics which emphasizes the public discourse carried by collective actors who constitute themselves by participation in public discourse. Strong institutions are necessary to make participation work, namely a polity which demands loyalty to the common cause to be realized through the participation of all.

French republicanism and modern communitarianism offer historical examples of this type of provision of an institutional frame for the construction of the ideal democratic citizen.[2] There is a clear distinction between the politically active centre and the passive periphery; those at the periphery are strongly invited to participate in the activities of the centre and outsiders are addressed in an inclusive way.

The Collective Identity Paradigm: Between Universalism and Primordialism

If citizenship is viewed from the perspective of collective identity, it refers to the routine practices and rules of solidarity, compromise, and decent behaviour. These rules are considered as self-evident and unquestionable presuppositions of membership. They serve to recognize who belongs and who does not belong to a given people. Citizenship in this sense refers neither to inclusion into markets nor to obligatory participation in the public sphere but to cultural ideas of virtue, icons of good membership, and myths of defending a sense of commonness against some outside enemy. Such cultural constructions of civility and collective identity create a space of shared significations without which civic activities would be at risk of disintegration as soon as strong strategic interests enter the arena. This model of citizenship refers to a prepolitical basis which is not nature, but a consensual constitution of culture and tradition which provide the integrative fundament for the practice of citizenship.

The three paradigms outlined above differ considerably in their requirements imposed on or expected of the potential citizens. The first that which sets free citizenship practices—this is their negative freedom. The second puts obligations on citizenship practices—this is the effect of the positive freedom to constitute oneself as a citizen. The third does not require practical action on the part of citizen; it favours the passive, but emotionally engaging citizen. It demands conformity to collective norms of behaviour and to commonly shared values and convictions, but it neither requires nor demands citizens' critical involvement in public affairs. They also differ in their conception of the legitimacy of a polity. The legitimacy of a polity compatible with these conceptions of citizenship is first that of a polity which provides legal conditions that guarantee the functioning of the market model; it is distinct from the polity which provides opportunities for action on the part of its members, whereas the third requires a steady state of symbolic mobilization of its members through the ritual staging of the political community.

Taking these three conceptions of citizenship as analytical dimensions of citizenship we will be able to address the issue of European citizenship as one of finding a notion of rights, obligations, and identity that abstracts from the nation state but is tied to the emerging social space of Europe, to a European society.

The Spheres of Citizenship

Citizenship is a concept that links the spheres of politics, economy, and culture. The three paradigms described above articulate the different social arenas in which citizenship is enacted. Citizenship is also a concept that covers different levels of citizenship. Models of citizenship differ in terms of practices. They also differ in terms of institutional forms and discursive rationalizations. If we distinguish between practices, institutions, and discourses, on the one hand, and between the three paradigms, on the other, we may cross both dimensions and arrive at the matrix shown in Fig. 1.1.

Citizenship as defined by the social paradigm seems to be the least demanding. It does not ask for more than a homogeneous set of membership rights and clear criteria of admission. This presupposes a legal order and an effective control of legal norms. Whether the citizens make use of their rights and in what way remains unspecified. No commitment to a public cause is required, no common values are presupposed. Citizenship can exist on this level without ever being practised in a public manner by the citizens. Put to the extreme, this model of citizenship can dispense with the active citizen and

	The individualist paradigm: market model; liberal theory and socialist critique	The political paradigm: participation model; democratic theory and republican/ communitarian critique	The collective identity paradigm: membership model; universalist theory and primordial critique
Citizenship as a practice	Individual liberties (negative freedom)	Civic duties (positive freedoms)	Common virtues/values
Citizenship as an institution	Welfare entitlements	Democracy as a strong public sphere	Common culture and tradition
Citizenship as a discourse	Rights	Obligations	Belonging

FIG. 1.1. Three conceptions of citizenship

his or her democratic participation in the public sphere and leave political decisions to the government. Thus, citizens can be reduced to mere consumers of collective goods provided by the government: welfare, education, and entertainment.

Citizenship in the political paradigm is founded on ideas of democratic action and a republican community. It expects citizens to be voluntary and active participants in public affairs. It allows the decoupling of social and political citizenship; the former is granted to every citizen without regard to his or her political activities; the latter covers only those participating in public affairs and politics. Hence, it presupposes and calls for a demos, a common political will of the people generated in public debate and addressed to the government. This puts more demands on the willingness of individuals to engage in public affairs and requires the existence of institutional arenas which give rise to a public sphere. Such assumptions collide, however, with empirical findings. Increasing legalization, bureaucratization, and state control as well as the marketization and commodification of lifeworlds, the globalization and dissolution of locality, the fading away of traditional local and communal ties, all of these processes challenge the project of a sovereign citizenry deliberating public affairs and exerting a political will regarding its own concerns. In addition, the increase in structural complexity and individual mobility (often referred to as 'individualization') has decreased the chance of generating a common political will. This structurally induced weakness of a general political will is more problematical the more the political model does not provide a common culture to which public discourse can refer in order to overcome cleavages and settle conflicts. The cultural foundations that exist are universalist principles. They run into problems facing the rising particularism of ethnic and religious fundamentalism.

Citizenship in the collective identity paradigm solves this problem by considering a common culture to be an indispensable basis for settling political conflicts and generating a common political will. Public debates have to appeal to a common horizon of values, a common historical experience, or common local traditions if they are to arrive at a mode of generating substantive consensus. Assuming a collective identity of the political body is even more important as the structural complexity of a society increases and the chances of a rationally reached consensus decrease. Thus, it was the modern acceleration of change and the modern increase in complexity which had to be compensated by inventing traditions and constructing ethnicity and nationality.

Such collective identities represent an even more restrictive and demanding requirement than the political activities presupposed by the communitarian paradigm. They can hardly be produced by administrative strategies or straightforward instrumental reasoning. Instead, they are the epiphenomena of lifeworld and narrative communication, they are based on myth and ritual

instead of exchange and utilities. Collective identity provides a strong fundament for a strong and most active demos. But it is difficult to construct within
large and structurally heterogeneous organizations like Europe. When Europe
has to cope with strong persistent feelings of belonging attached to nations,
then Europe will have difficulties conveying strong feelings of attachment
projected on itself.

The Prospects of a European Citizenship

Do these models find resonance in actual debates on European citizenship?
Depending on the type of model underlying the idea of a European citizen-
ship, it is possible to discern three proposals for the construction of a
European citizenship.

A minimalist conception is contained in the declarations and intentions of
the treaty of Maastricht reducing citizenship to basic rights. It conceives of
European citizens as a derivative or sum of the member states' citizens. This
conception of European citizenship will allow for mobility of labour within
the European Community, keep the additional amount of legal institutionalization to a workable minimum and will contain the impact of European law
on the national laws of citizenship.

This legal minimalism runs into specific difficulties. For denizens, i.e. non-
national residents, political citizenship, the right to vote and to be elected, is
usually restricted to the communal and local level. The minimalist model
offers access to welfare entitlements for national and non-national citizens in
principle, but these entitlements differ according to nations and are generally
shrinking. The welfare state is under widespread attack and the limits of solidarity are constructed even more exclusively if political community is decoupled from the economic community. Furthermore, strong ties of solidarity
tend to be exclusive whereas large inclusive communities with high structural
complexity such as the European Community will allow for only weak ties.
Only access to educational institutions is open to all European citizens. This
will foster international mobility in the educational field and contribute to the
cultural integration of the European demos. Most probably these effects are
limited and long term; they will not outweigh the disruptive consequences of
different national regimes of welfare and social policy.

A second, more demanding conception of European citizenship is that
suggested by the 'Migrants Forum' which separates European citizenship from
the national citizenship of the member states. Here, European citizenship is
based on territorial residence within the European Community and restricted
to certain basic rights of political participation, welfare entitlements, educational benefits; these rights are complemented by national and local rights

that vary according to the country and region of residence. By decoupling the level of basic rights of access from the national and regional level of citizenship, this model can at least partly avoid the problems resulting from an uneven distribution of citizenship welfare entitlements. It provides chances for an inclusion of resident denizens, but it engenders increasing problems with respect to non-resident aliens at the borders of the European community. The structure of citizenship rights resulting from this second model is multilayered: European citizenship rights reside atop national citizenship; regional and communal citizenship defines lower levels of citizenship. Such a multilayered structure however produces a problematic hierarchy and brings conflicting claims to the fore. In principle, these problems can be settled by muddling through by permanent compromises. The coordination of European-wide problem-solving activities was the main drive for the growth of European integration and this might also hold true for domains like citizenship and immigration. Furthermore, the legal spirit of the European administration backed by the constitutionalist position of the European Court of Justice will most probably thrust for a more principled strategy enforcing the predominance of the European level. Indeed, if European citizenship rights are to supersede national or regional ones, strong constitutional courts as suggested by Weiler are required in order to strengthen and to enforce the European level. But the existence of a strong constitutional court can ensure European citizenship only at the level of rights and will remain indifferent regarding its basis in civic participation or collective identity.

However, this second politicized, often 'constitutionalist' conception of a European citizenry is also problematic. Civic participation in European politics is impeded in several respects. Tensions and conflicts within the Brussels administration result mainly from different national interests and stress the cleavages between the different European nations instead of blurring them. The party system in the European Parliament is not carried and supported by citizen movements, but created by professional politicians at the national level. The Eurocrats in the Brussels administration are in charge of political decisions but still largely beyond the reach of democratic control. Participation in elections for the European Parliament is considerably lower than participation in national or communal elections; the members of the European Parliament are hardly known by the citizens. The nation state, national governments, and national parliaments continue to be regarded as the centres of political power and sovereignty.

Even if citizens could successfully be mobilized for participation, the inclusive thrust of a universalist community (on which this model is based) would produce its risks. In its attempt to overcome the national and regional legacies, Europe cannot simply turn to the inclusive dynamics of universalism which provided the basis for the 'First New Nation' and gave rise to contemporary discourse about human rights. Instead, for various reasons, it has to exclude outsiders for a lack of belonging and this exclusion is difficult to sustain at the level of modern constitutional discourse. It would foster the idea of a fortress Europe defending the interests of its citizens against the rest of the world. The organizational conditions of a European civil society are shaky, and with it the prospects for a universalist conception of a European citizenship. Faced with global intercontinental migration, universalism provides a questionable basis for a universalist conception of a European citizenship.

To overcome these problems a third conception of European citizenship is considered. In order to give legitimacy to the particular interests of the Europeans, a postnational collective identity would be needed to found a European citizenship. Thus, the idea of a collective identity (and this would imply a structural similarity with national citizenship) would be at the centre of the conception of a feasible European citizenship. This third conception refers to the symbolic foundations of a European citizenship. There are elements of such a collective identity, especially the idea of a common cultural heritage. Recalling a common European history, however, reveals a history of conflicts and tensions between nations. There is hardly a common European revolution, a defence against a foreign threat, or a European cultural mission which could be accepted by all Europeans as a common heritage or cause. Neither Christianity nor Enlightenment are unanimously and univocally acclaimed as a special European mission, neither the medieval and early modern defence against Muslim invasions nor the various crusades, neither the heritage of the French Revolution nor the East European uprising against the Soviet empire will today unite all Europeans. The only reference which comes close to a common collective memory of Europeans is perhaps the defeat of Nazism and Fascism but even this is occasionally contested. Instead of recalling a common origin the multifaceted collective identity of Europe reflects rather the diversity of its regions and localities, the continuously changing internal boundaries and the ebb and flow of its Western and Eastern frontiers. This may not provide a strong and marked symbolic representation of identity, but it links the European identity to the formation of a citizenry by a culture of diversity and conflict which is noticed as a precious heritage.

In the debates about a European citizenship, these three conceptions turn out to be the focal codes for imagining European citizenship. The question of collective identity might turn out to be a key to this debate. For it defines the common ground and the boundaries of the people who can hold citizenship rights and duties. By relating the debates on social citizenship and political citizenship to the question of membership, the issue of what makes people members of a community comes to the fore. This is what turns the analytical concept of collective identity into the key to an understanding of the making of a European citizenship. And this makes the different national legacies of collective identities in Europe the clue for an understanding of the dynamics of the making of a European citizenship. When we agree upon who is to be considered a European citizen, then the existing distribution of rights and duties can be criticized according to criteria of justice. As long as such a community of citizens cannot be identified, the dynamics of inclusion and exclusion between competing local and national actors would remain untamed.

The following papers are organized around this idea of how citizenship as a symbolic marker of belonging together (of a 'collectivity') is related to problems of social and civic citizenship, to the issue of a democratic European collectivity, and finally to debates on the national and transnational bases of a collective identity in Europe. The question of a collective identity is at the core of all the contributions. It cannot be sidestepped by policy discourses or political legitimacy discourses. It finally forces taking a stand: to plea for a collective identity as inherited from European history (and eventually learning from this history) or to plea for a collective identity as inherited from the history of competing nation states or pleading for a transnational identity and the construction of the community necessary for such an historical project.

The national legacies of belonging that shape citizenship in Europe are discussed by Dieter Gosewinkel and Bernhard Giesen. The UK, France, and Germany provide the cases that make difference, not unity the basis of European integration. Given such a lack of a common sense of belonging, citizenship in Europe is first of all a question of whether it provides value for some or even all. The question of what is the added value of citizenship rights in the Euro-polity is looked at critically by Klaus von Beyme and Wolfgang Streeck. Both address social citizenship and point to the difficulty a strong version of social citizenship will face in the context of the making of a European market. The proposal to protect national social citizenship and to restrict European citizenship to a minimalist and realist conception of citizenship in Europe find their counterpart in explicit projects for full citizenship in the Euro-polity. Philippe C. Schmitter raises the question of the scope of citizenship in a democratized European Union and offers policy proposals to enhance a sense of citizenship based on a new conception of social citizenship in Europe. Carlos Closa argues for a republican project of European citizenship and discusses the particular requirements of a European public sphere as the core of European citizenship. A final series of papers addresses the project of European citizenship beyond the idea of the nation state. Postnational projects of belonging would give a grounding to European citizenship beyond the rational interests and the democratic impulses of economically well-off European citizens. Is there any feasible project for the construction of a European collective identity? This question—posed in the beginning as a major problem—is addressed by M. Rainer Lepsius, Yasemin Soysal, and Klaus Eder in three quite different ways: the first looking for some common minimal cultural bond, the second generalizing from the experience of minorities in Europe as carriers of a postnational project of citizenship, and finally the idea of a fluid collective identity to be constructed permanently—a *plébiscite de tous les jours* to be generated in a continuous discourse over the past, a permanent writing of a history. In the concluding section, the issue of the social integration of Europe beyond its political integration through Union citizenship is taken up.

NOTES

1. There is, as will be argued later, a certain elective affinity between the liberal egalitarian idea of citizenship and weak primordial constructions of collective identity. Primordial identities consider all members of a community to be naturally equal and refer to an external basis of membership such as nature. In the case of the social paradigm, this is simply human nature.
2. Communitarianism has an elective affinity to universalist codes of constructing a collective identity, an argument to be taken up later.

PART I

National Legacies of Belonging

The Tradition of Citizenship in Europe

2

Citizenship, Subjecthood, Nationality

Concepts of Belonging in the Age of Modern Nation States

Dieter Gosewinkel

Political concepts are concepts of legitimation; this fact is well established. For example, Jürgen Habermas states that the German word for '*citizenship*' or '*citoyenneté*', '*Staatsbürgerschaft*', has been defined to date by lawyers. As a result, the concept has acquired the exclusively legal meaning of a formal, legally defined relationship of adherence to the state, for which the German term is '*Staatsangehörigkeit*.' He observes with satisfaction that this concept recently has been expanded to include the sense of a '*Staatsbürgerstatus*' defined by civil and political rights. He greets this development as an adaptation to a 'Western' (comprising Western Europe and the USA)—that is, republican and constitutional-tradition of the concept of citizenship (Habermas 1993: 638). In Habermas's view, this adaptation would permit an understanding of the core of German '*Staatsbürgerschaft*' as a set of rights intended to secure the political participation and communication of autonomous individuals.

Two conclusions may be drawn from these observations. First, Habermas transfers the legitimacy of a 'Western' conceptualization of citizenship, which is presented as exemplary, to a national conceptualization, which is quite different. Second, however, the historically rooted peculiarity of the national conceptualization of citizenship points to the more general difficulty of finding analogies among concepts across national contexts.

Political concepts reflect political change and shape it at the same time. If this is correct, a nationalization of political terminology has taken place in Europe and the USA in the age of the modern nation state. This fact may justify the following assumption: concepts that once had the same meaning across a variety of national contexts have taken on various particular meanings in different countries.

A survey of European citizenship that focuses on a central concept of modern political language, namely 'citizenship', might tend to presuppose a common framework of concepts for discussing different models of citizenship. It also might analyse shortcomings in the realization of a (presupposed) 'ideal' of citizenship. These assumptions run a double risk: on the one hand, they may absolutize a specific national or historical notion of 'citizenship'; and on the other, they may mistakenly employ a supranational concept of citizenship that is valid across different countries. The universal nature of the ideal of citizenship might be particularly likely to encourage this sort of ahistorical thinking (Somers 1995: 114). However, I would like to take one step backward and recall a historical fact. The Anglo-American term *'citizenship'* denotes a relation of adherence that is variable in a double way: the term has undergone transformation both historically and due to its use within different national contexts. Thus, one must distinguish between the historically changing concept of citizenship and its normative character.

Against this background, I would like to bring together some elements of a comparative history of concepts. In order to demonstrate the historicity of the concept of *citizenship*, I want to sketch its historical development in contrast to the concepts of belonging represented by *subjecthood* and *nationality*. Because of its complexity, the subject must be delimited: in order to prove my thesis of the specifically national character of models of citizenship, I go beyond the Anglo-American terminology and concentrate on the German use of these concepts. To further indicate the specificity of national models of citizenship, I add some observations concerning the Anglo-American and French terminology. Finally, most of the sources for these observations are taken from legal history because legal definitions constitute the foundation of concepts of belonging.

The German Case

1. In the transition to modernity, at the turn of the eighteenth to the nineteenth century, the status of the *'Untertan'* (subject, *sujet*) bore witness to the hierarchical relationship between the state and the individual in Germany. The monarchical states and small territories of the declining medieval Reich did not have constitutions guaranteeing general rights to the *'Bürger'* (citizen). The status rights of (permanent) inhabitants of a state were directed towards the person of the ruling monarch. In this sense, the status of *'Untertan'* (subject) established equality among the subjects, who none the less possessed widely varying rights deriving from their respective legal status. The concept of an *'Untertan'* was linked to monarchical rule as a special type of state. The element of centralizing equality was modern. However, this new equality was not won by revolution and did not entail any participatory rights of the individual. Rather, this form of equality corresponded to a specifically German tradition, that of 'reform from above'. Finally, the element of equality was a pre- or subnational one. It was pre-national in the sense that it did not distinguish between members of different ethnic origin: within the multi-ethnic

state of Prussia before the Congress of Vienna of 1815, no legal gradations existed between German, Danish, or Polish '*Untertanen*' (subjects) of the Prussian Crown.

2. The concept of the '*Staatsbürger*', which nowadays is translated by the term 'citizen' or '*citoyen*' (*Langenscheidt's Enzyklopädisches Wörterbuch der englischen und deutschen Sprache* 1962: s.v. Citizen = *Staatsbürger*) came into use before 1789, when the political triumph of the 'citoyen' was achieved in the 'Déclaration des Droits de l'Homme et du Citoyen'. The political meaning of the concept of the '*Staatsbürger*' was shaped by the ideas of Enlightened Absolutism. In its moral, patriotic, and universalist intention, it was directed against status inequality and monarchical government. However, this egalitarian postulate was not yet accompanied by a democratic claim for participation in the formation of the will of the state (Weinacht 1969: 52 ff.). The egalitarianism of the '*Staatsbürger*' went hand in hand with the persistence of their claims to the monarchical state for protection and care.

The political contents of the word and thus the concept of '*Staatsbürger*' changed under the influence of French revolutionary declarations, especially the 'Déclaration des Droits de l'Homme et du Citoyen' and the Constitution of 1791. The criteria of the 'right to vote in legislation' were taken over from France. It was formulated programmatically by Immanuel Kant and, from then on, became an integral part of the German concept of '*Staatsbürgerschaft*' The status of '*Staatsbürger*'. emerged from the same semantic field but came to signify a clear difference from the older term '*Untertan*'. With the transition to the constitutional age during the first third of the nineteenth century, German legal terminology developed three fundamental elements of the modern concept of '*Staatsbürger*': (1) the fundamental equality of state-members relative to each other; (2) their obedience and loyalty to the law; and (3) their invocation of constitutional rights.

The first element dominated in using the term in the first German constitutions between 1818 and 1848; its egalitarian effect, however, amounted to nothing more than the formal equality of state-members. Because of this, it became approximately equivalent to the status of '*Staatsangehörigkeit*' (see point below). The second element, the legal binding of the '*Staatsbürger*', linked the age of absolutism with modern terminology. Only its reference to individual and democratic rights brought it closer to the concepts and conceptualization of Western constitutional states ('*citoyen*' and 'citizen'). However, to date, the notion of '*Staatsbürger*' in German legal terminology continues to reveal a deficit: its indifference towards the discrepancy between formally granted civil and political rights, on the one hand, and the social and material substance of law, on the other. Indirectly, this explains the virtually total lack of polemics in terms of the history of the concept in Germany. According to the interpretation of Weinacht, the notion of '*Staatsbürger*' was 'so enclosed in the sphere of state that it could remain untouched by reality in civil society [bürgerliche Gesellschaft], especially by the class contrast between bourgeois and proletarian' (Weinacht 1969: 62). Among other reasons, this is why the term '*Staatsbürger*' went into decline in German twentieth century legal terminology. It is not even mentioned in contemporary constitutional law. Thus, at the end of the 1960s, a historical analysis of the notion '*Staatsbürger*' concluded: '*Staatsbürger*' would have to be counted among the 'fictitious historical notions' for its reality would belong to the bourgeois ('*bürgerlich*') nineteenth century and would have passed along with it (Weinacht 1969: 63).

New tendencies towards revitalizing and refilling the notion seem to contradict this prediction, however. One can even go back to the 1967 'Staatsbürgerschaftsgesetz' of the German Democratic Republic. This law, which was merely designed to regulate formal legal adherence to the state (in German: '*Staatsangehörigkeit*', see point 3 below) assumes the historical legitimacy of '*Staatsbürger*' as a democratic concept (Riege 1986: 60). Thus, the reforms intended to overcome the merely formal notion of '*Staatsbürger*' which had already been criticized by Karl Marx. It was to be replaced by the model of 'membership . . . in the first peace-loving, democratic, and socialist German state in which the working class exercises political power in alliance with the class of cooperative farmers, the socialist intelligentsia, and the other working classes'.[1] This was intended as a departure from the historical 'reductions' of the 'bourgeois' nineteenthth century.

As stated, in a very different way (in order to establish a Western concept of a '*Staatsbürgernation*' (citizens' nation), Jürgen Habermas supports expanding the political and participatory meaning of the term thereby trying to overcome its reduction to legal terminology. This is consistent with general tendencies in German political language after 1945, which tried to emphasize and disseminate the egalitarian and democratic meaning of the notion (Weinacht 1969: 61). Recent projects to reform German nationality law no longer differentiate between '*Staatsangehörigkeit*' and '*Staatsbürgerschaft*' but use the concepts interchangeably.[2]

3. Within the semantic field of '*Untertan*' and '*Staatsbürger*', German legal language of the nineteenth century developed the notion of '*Staatsangehörigkeit*'. It departed from the semantic field of '*Untertan*' and emerged later than the word '*Staatsbürger*'. In so doing, it could link the two older concepts and, at the same time, formulate their common core more abstractly. The '*Staatsbürger*' of the first German constitutions in the early nineteenth century and the '*Untertan*' of the Prussian 'Law on the Acquisition and Loss of the Quality of Prussian Subjects' ('*Untertanen*' in the terminology of late absolutism) presupposed the same relationship of adherence to the state. This was precisely denoted by the new word '*Staatsangehöriger*'. It meant the formally and legally defined membership in an abstract state. It also contained a double egalitarian component: first the equality of state-members

in being subject to state power; and second, the equality of members among themselves—according to their rights and duties as members of the state—in spite of remaining differences concerning their social and legal status within society (Grawert 1973: 124).

In the course of the nineteenthth century, the notion of 'Staatsangehörigkeit' underwent a process of legal formalization and substantial standardization. This reflected Germany's transition from a loose federation of territorial states to a politically homogeneous nation state. Moreover, the neutral legal formulation of '*Staatsangehörigkeit*' corresponded with the gradual transition from monarchy to democracy which came to an end in the Revolution of 1918. No longer the '*Untertan*', but—neutrally speaking—the member of the state dominated in this age of transition, in which the abstract state as a legal figure persisted—only its political form changed.

The legal formulation and sharpening of the concept of '*Staatsangehöriger*' was a reflex of German constitutional theory at the height of positivism. Formal conceptual precision with disregard to the social and political substance of law arose from the self-understanding of a legal discipline that wanted to exclude political arguments in order to argue merely 'empirically' on the basis of positive law.[3] With the dominance of this theory, the political notion of '*Staatsbürger*' was gradually reduced to the meaning of '*Staatsangehöriger*'—a process that Habermas pointed out (Habermas 1993: 638).

It was exactly this formal precision and explicitness which led to the success of the concept. '*Staatsangehörigkeit*' can be regarded as the specific German contribution to the semantic field of 'citizenship'. There were even reflections about taking over the notion as a borrowed word into French terminology, precisely because it denotes the relationship between the individual and the state in an unambiguous and exclusive way. In a rational and abstract way it avoids both the democratic promise of '*citoyen*' and the semantic reduction of '*nationalité*' (see 'The English, American, and French Cases', point 4, below).

This should be explained more precisely: the development of the German notion and concept '*Staatsangehörigkeit*' accompanied the rise of the modern nation state. However, this process had no effect on the concept. To date, its use has always been distinct from that of '*Nationalität*'.[4]

Not the notion of '*Staatsangehörigkeit*' as such, but the political and administrative practice of its legislation and administration underwent a process of nationalization. This occurred as a result of the principle of descent (*ius sanguinis*). From the beginning of the nineteenth century this principle exclusively regulated the primary acquisition of German *Staatsangehörigkeit*. Originally, it was to be an institution of modernization and state regulation. At the beginning of industrialization, modern German territorial states faced rising work-migration and poverty. Compared to the fluctuations and contingencies of territorial mobility, the quality of physically rooted descent from state-members seemed to offer the advantage of permanence and unambiguity. However, this state-rational impetus soon came under the influence of nationalist political theory, both in terms of legal science and bureaucratic use. Increasingly, the principle of descent was regarded as the 'true national' (Grawert 1973: 191) principle of belonging to the state. Rogers Brubaker has shown, at that time, German '*Staatsangehörigkeit*' developed into an institution of ethnocultural descent (Brubaker 1992: 119). The practice of naturalization became an instrument to homogenize state membership according to substantial ethnocultural criteria of language, custom, religion, national origin, or even 'race'.

It must be noted that this process of nationalization, at the beginning, happened independently of the strictly legally defined concept of '*Staatsangehörigkeit*', which remained tied to formal criteria and the state. In this sense, nationalization seemed to remain incidental to the concept of *Staatsangehörigkeit*.

Only in one extreme moment did the historical practice of *Staatsangehörigkeit* politics also change the concept. The National Socialist laws of race of 1935 destroyed the abstract, unified model of *Staatsangehörigkeit*. Instead, they distinguished between 'simple' state-members ('*Staatsangehörige*') and a special, privileged class of full citizens of 'German or related blood' ('*Reichsbürger deutschen oder artverwandten Blutes*').[5]

4. This might explain why the concept '*Nationalität*' in German law and politics developed in a different way from England, the USA, and France. The legal use and notion of '*Nationalität*' remained different from the formal relationship of '*Staatsangehörigkeit*'. In domestic law, only the word '*Staatsangehörigkeit*' was used to denote the meaning of the English and French concepts (of) 'nationality' and '*nationalité*'. The term '*Nationalität*' was introduced as a loanword from English and French (Laun 1925), only with reference to international law. In German, '*Nationalität*' was less concerned with the state, being primarily conceived as an (ethnocultural) substance.[6] Finally, it should be pointed out that '*Nationalität*' often appears in the plural form.[7] '*Nationalitäten*' (referring to naturalized immigrant or minority groups) appear as 'other' nationalities in contrast to the one homogeneous German '*Nationalität*', although they have identical relationships with the state.

This terminology emerged and was consolidated at the time of the Weimar Republic after 1918.[8] It reflects the particular political situation of Germany at that time. The German Reich had had to cede considerable parts of its territory and population to newly developing nation states in Central Europe and to France. German minorities in these territories mostly were no longer members of the German state, but they claimed protection by the German 'home-state' as German '*Nationalitäten*' abroad. In analogy to that, non-German

'*Nationalitäten*' within Germany, despite their membership in the unique German *Staatsangehörigkeit* were identified as foreign national minorities. Because of this, the concepts of '*Staatsangehörigkeit*' and '*Nationalität*' became dissociated from one another. Present-day terminology continues and confirms this historical observation. Although the French and English terms of '*nationality*' and '*nationalité*' appear to be converging with the German, this is not the case. Both the legal[9] and the common[10] use of '*Nationalität*' refer to the nation as a pre-political or apolitical category.

These differences reveal the degree of specificity of the entire concept of 'nation'. The German 'nation' did not arise on the basis of an established central state. Although the German national movement in the nineteenth century soon aimed at political unification, the concept of belonging to the nation, was initially based principally on a diversity of cultural and ethnic criteria of adherence. The predominantly cultural concept of 'nation' leads to the persistent identification of divergent national groups within a single nation state. However, this does not correlate with the need for a statewide, rational, and unambiguous definition of who are members of the state. The various notions reflect this.

The English, American, and French Cases

1. The central concept of belonging in the history of the *English* state until recently turns around the concept of '*subject/subjecthood*'. As Holdsworth has shown, Common Law rules up from the thirteenth century began to centre round the doctrine of allegiance. The duty of allegiance, owed by the subject to the Crown, differentiated the subject from the alien (Holdsworth 1944: 72). This feudal principle was both personal and territorial: it is rooted in the feudal idea of a personal duty of fealty to the lord from whom land is held.

As the feudal structure of English law gradually disappeared, the king's power was restrained by the Parliament, which attained political dominance. But the principle of subjecthood has retained its double structure into the era of the modern constitutional monarchy. By focusing loyalty on the person of the monarch in Britain, the ancient doctrine of subjecthood—the traditional and affective notion—helped to hold the British Empire together. It also helped to maintain the territorial structure of the ties of allegiance to the Crown. The traditional principle of *ius soli* was merely modified by the British Nationality Act 1981; it was maintained as a significant rule.

Thus, subjecthood in practice became an element of structural continuity, although its contents—and partly its function—did change. As part of their tradition, the British have often taken pride in being called 'British subjects'

(Dummett 1994: 77). Thus, the word and, to some extent, the concept of subjecthood still carry some legitimizing force.

This might explain why 'nationality'—at least in its legal sense—seems to have kept a neutral (Dummett and Nicol 1990: 268) meaning which took over the function of the word 'subjecthood' in the era of the emerging modern nation state (Salmond 1902: 49). It was the British Nationality and Status of Alien Act 1914, on the eve of World War I, which first codified legal adherence to the British Empire in a systematic way.[11] In terms of the timing of its systematic terminological appearance and its function, the English concept of nationality was placed between subjecthood and another legitimizing principle: *citizenship*. To explain the concept and historical model of the English word citizenship, it is necessary to examine its emergence and central function in the history of the United States.

2. The Declaration of Independence is known to have been a revolution against the ties and obligations of subjecthood to the English Crown. To be a subject was considered to be an inferior, feudal status contrary to the concept of a new republican philosophy. The term and concept of citizenship became synonymous with the ideal of a free, self-determinant member of the state endowed with natural liberties. The struggle of the *American* colonies for independence was accompanied by an incisive change in legal terminology. In the political philosophy of the Early Modern Age, *subject* and *citizen* (*sujet et citoyen*) had not always been sharply contrasting concepts. Some authors, like Bodin, Grotius, and Hobbes used the terms synonymously to some extent. On the other hand, political and legal theory based on Aristotelian concepts established a contrasting distinction between the two terms (Koessler 1946/7: 58).

The American Revolution brought a process of lexicographic delineation to this terminological ambivalence. Within a decade, from its first appearance in the Articles of Confederation (1777) to the enactment of the Federal Constitution (1787), the term 'citizen' came to replace the related words like 'subject' and 'inhabitant'.[12] In a certain parallel to the French conceptualization[13] before the outbreak of the French Revolution, the republican concept of 'citizen/citizenship' marked a political and terminological break[14] with the feudal age. From that beginning citizen/citizenship became core terms of a state order based on democracy and constitutionality. 'Citizen' was a term of the written constitution. It appeared both in the context of the democratic right to vote[15] and relations with other states.[16] The meaning of 'subjects', however, was confined to foreign 'subjects'[17] (obviously with regard to subjects of the British Crown).

Thus, the American legal term 'citizen' was fundamentally linked to political rights and participation in the political body. As a consequence, the jurisdiction of the Supreme Court (in the famous case *Dred Scott* v. *Sandford*, 1857) included the statement: 'The words "people of the United States" and "citizens" are synonymous terms. . . . They both describe the political body, who, according to our republican institutions, form the sovereignty, and who hold the power and conduct the government through their representatives. They are what we familiarly call the "sovereign people" and every citizen is one of this people, and a constituent member of this sovereignty'.

But whom did citizenship include? The other side of the *Dred Scott* (vs. *Sandman*) judgment was the clear exclusion of 'Negroes', descendants of former slaves, from citizenship (Cushman 1957: 702). The intimate connection between democratic rights and the status of citizenship went at the expense of excluding a large group of the population (inhabitants) from the fundamental rights of citizens. The 14th and 15th Amendment to the Constitution as a result of the Civil War, extended the material legal status[18] of a citizen to 'all persons born or naturalized in the United States and subject to the jurisdiction thereof. . . . The right of a citizen to vote shall not be denied or abridged by the United States . . . on account of race, colour, or previous condition of servitude.'[19] With that, the Constitution included blacks as part of the sovereign people.

Taken together, these Amendments combine two aspects of 'citizenship' in an inseparable way, still valid today: the material aspect of citizenship including rights and obligations, on the one hand; and the principle of formal legal adherence to the state, on the other hand. The 14th Amendment thus conferred citizenship on the principle of *ius soli* which itself tends towards extending citizenship rights.

The American nation, from its beginning, was created as a constitutional, democratic, participatory nation state. The needs of an immigrant society and the concept of a politically, but not culturally integrated nation seem to have contributed to affording the American legal term of '*nationality*' a strictly formal and monistic significance. In the legal context 'nationality' refers only to the quality arising 'from the fact of a person's belonging to a state or nation' and 'determining the political status of the individual, especially with reference to allegiance'.[20] Although in this sense nationality is often used synonymously with the formal side of citizenship, it differs from the concept of citizenship in two ways: in contrast to citizenship, nationality denotes a purely formal and abstract relationship between the individual and the state. It does not refer to individual rights and obligations; but rather to a 'man's natural allegiance'. The term denotes 'a relationship between an individual and a nation involving the duty of obedience or allegiance on the part of the subject and protection on the part of the state'.[21] Second, nationality is not significant in domestic law;[22] it is primarily a concept of international law (Koessler 1946/7: 70). In contrast to German legal terminology ('*Nationalitäten*'), the American legal concept of 'nationality' does appear exclusively in its singular form. It does not make reference to ethnocultural aspects of citizenship or even to the existence of a plurality of different nations within the one identified with the state. In inter-state

relations, the American nation state presents its members as a monistic political body—despite ethnic and national groups in its interior. Though, as the
case of the Japanese American nationals in World War II (Daniels 1981) has
shown, the external monism in the concept of American nationality does not
exclude real discrimination within the American citizenry based on ethnic
and national criteria.

However, on the conceptual level, nationality as formal adherence to the
state did more than merely overrule internal differentiation. Specifically, it
contributed to changing the material meaning of the term 'citizenship'. By way
of the Nationality Act of 1940, American nationality was split up into two
categories: American nationality, including American citizenship, and
American nationality, devoid of American citizenship (Koessler 1946/7: 66).
Since then, both national citizens and non-citizen nationals have existed. The
meaning of American national/nationality has become broader than that of
American citizen/citizenship.[23] However, nowadays, the practical relevance of
the conceptual difference is minimal. The category of non-citizen nationals
has been reduced to a diminishing group of former aborigines (Ferid and
Blumenwitz 1975: 26).

3. In *English* (legal) history, *citizenship* has not played any relevant role.[24]
In the Middle Ages, it was used to denote the political status of city dwellers.
Citizenship involved a relationship to a city, and implied certain liberties
(Walker 1980: 220; Dummett and Nicol 1990: 25). But on the state and
national level, the concept of citizenship in Britain has remained 'vague and
fluid' (Dummett 1994: 75). This was the outcome of the substitution of feudal
for Roman concepts in law and politics. The Roman concept of 'citizen' was
replaced by 'subject' (Salmond 1902: 49). Finally, because no written constitution exists, there is no codified set of citizens' rights.

It was not until 1948 that English law, with the British Nationality Act,
introduced the term of citizenship in the sense of nationality consistent with
its use in international law. The Nationality Act, within the framework of a
'British *nationality*', established a new citizenship of the United Kingdom and
colonies alongside new, independent citizenships being created by the self-
governing British Dominions.[25] The strictly formal character of this citizenship (nationality) stems from the fact that it has no rights attached to it
(Dummett 1994: 77). The law of 1948 set up categories of nationality-citizenship in order to regulate the legal consequences of World War II and citizenship of the increasingly independent countries within the British
Commonwealth (Dummett and Nicols 1990: 134). Apart from the practical
need for classification and regulation, however, the concept of citizenship was
intended to introduce a new, participatory equivalent for the feudal term of
subject (Giese 1978: 32). However, the introduction of new terms was not
accompanied by any significant development of the concepts. In 1957, a standard work on 'Nationality and Citizenship Laws' stated: 'The new law of the

Commonwealth, and in particular of the United Kingdom, still does not employ any concept of nationality as such' (Parry 1957: 110, 114). This was confirmed by the terminology of the 1948 Act: the term 'Commonwealth citizen' was interchangeable with 'British subject' or 'British national'.[26]

Finally, in 1981 and 1983, the British Nationality Acts imposed a complicated system, establishing the term 'citizen' for several categories or classes of British nationals according to their geographical origin and immigration status. The change in terminology from 'British nationality' to 'British (British dependent territories/British Overseas) Citizenship'—except the general classification—abandoned the term of nationality; the historical concept of 'subject' remained no more than an incidental category.[27] The establishment of citizen/citizenship as a core term in British (nationality) law first of all makes an effort to standardize modern legal terminology.[28] But, apart from this, there have been other reasons which might be found in the report of 'The Commission on Citizenship' appointed by the British House of Commons. The aim of the Commission was to consider 'how best to encourage, develop, and recognize Active Citizenship within a wide range of groups in the community, both local and national'.

As a point of departure explaining and legitimizing citizenship, the report refers to the 'long tradition of Western thought about citizenship' and the contributions of T. H. Marshall to a 'classical theory' of citizenship ('Encouraging Citizenship, 1990: ix. 4). The report attempts to provide new substance to the notion of citizenship by splitting it up into two main meanings: the first proceeds from the legal interpretation of citizenship as nationality implicit in the British Nationality Act of 1981, as the 'external manifestation of the relationship between individuals and the State to which they belong'. Material citizenship rights (civic, social, and political rights) derive solely from this legal basis, which remains formal in itself. This is called 'nationality-citizenship'. The second model of citizenship, apart from nationality, is based on universal human rights and comprises a set of civil, political, social, and economic rights.

The clear intention of the report is to take the notion of citizenship in positive law as a basic reference, isolate it from the compulsory precondition of nationality, and fill it with the entire range of revolutionary (Dummett 1994: 76), participatory tradition and pathos. The aim is both political and pedagogical: to lend more legitimacy to an entire material set of fundamental rights and duties which are summed up in the concept and ideal of citizenship. Thus, in the course of the twentieth century, British legal terminology denoting adherence to the state has gradually replaced the traditional concept of subjecthood with the concepts of nationality and citizenship; as such, the English legal terminology has been modernized and given additional substance. At the same time, by introducing 'citizenship' in the 1948 Act and 'encouraging citizenship', it approximates the legal concepts of other Western democracies.

4. In *French* history, the eighteenth century marks a break in concepts of belonging. Until the middle of the century the use of the words '*sujet*' and '*citoyen*' had coexisted without any confrontation (Rétat 1988). '*Sujet*' had its origin in feudal ties of allegiance to the monarch. But it did not exclude the quality of '*citoyen*' as long as the subjection to monarchical power was a legitimate one and power was not exercised arbitrarily. Although the concept of citoyen/citoyenneté was increasingly linked to liberty, social utility, and even democracy (Montesquieu), it was basically still compatible with the political framework of a moderate monarchical regime. However, the Philosophy of Enlightenment and the change of mentality among the elite of the *ancien régime* were reflected by changes in the political language. An ideal of '*citoyen*' developed, which referred to general virtues of man in society, his public utility, as well as perfection of his individual, moral, and practical potential. The '*sujet*', on the other hand, was pejoratively viewed as a timid, passive person oblivious to any rights he may possess.

The French Revolution cut the former ties between the concepts of *sujet* and *citoyen*. In an abstract way, both reflected concepts of equality: the immediate subjection of the individual to the concentrated and unified power of the state—whether a monarchy or a republic. But the Revolution idealized the active, autonomous individual—'*citoyen*'—as the centre of the newly established revolutionary nation.

The political term '*sujet*'[29] was delegitimized and abandoned in a process comparable to that in the American revolutionary nation state. Only in terms of international law is '*sujet*' still in use. It means someone who is personally and permanently subject to the authority of a state and enjoys its protection.[30]

From the beginning of the first revolutionary Constitution in 1791, '*citoyen*' had a double meaning: in its constitutional sense it referred to the active member of the political community with political rights, thus determining the nation as a political body. Apart from that, the quality of being a '*Français*' is regulated in civil law.[31] To be a '*citoyen*' in the sense of the Constitution, on the other hand, means to adhere to the political community. Since 1791, the Constitution defined as citizens those who accepted the political programme embodied in it (Grawert 1973: 163; Rétat 1988: 19).

Thus, *citoyenneté* in this sense was a genuine political, participatory, and potentially assimilationist concept. It was open to transnational interpretations in the international socialist movement, to its expansion on the local level, and to societal rights. The other aspect of '*citoyenneté*', the definition of 'who is French', underwent a process of 'nationalization'. This was indicated by the introduction of the term '*nationalité*' in French legal language.[32] '*Nationalité*' in France before the French Revolution—like the English word 'nationality' (*Robert, Dictionnaire historique de la Langue Française* 1992: 1307)—had the (vague) meaning of national feeling or patriotism.[33] In the first half of the nineteenth century, in a period of rising national ideas and movements throughout Europe, nationality took on the meaning of a principle defined according to groups, customs, language, and history (*Grand Larousse universel: Grand Dictionnaire encyclopédique* 1865: 855). At that time, nationality in France often was used in the plural form to denote the political 'principle of nationalities' and their struggle for independence. Within the second half of the century, '*nationalité*' in scientific use primarily took on a legal meaning (*La Grande Encyclopédie: Inventaire raisonné des Sciences, des Lettres et des Arts* 1899: 835). The new Nationality Code of 1889, which contained a systematic definition of French nationals underscored this development. From then on, the legal meaning of 'legal assignment of a person to the population constituting a state, while this quality can only be assigned [*conférée*] by a sovereign state which is acknowledged in international law' (*La Grande Encyclopédie* 1975: 8399) became the core meaning of nationality in broader encyclopedic use, as well. In doing so, the singular form of 'a' French nationality came to dominate again, while the plural form was reduced to the historical 'principle of nationalities'(*Grand Larousse Encyclopédique* 1963: 679). The French legal term 'nationalité' was precisely synonymous to the German word '*Staatsangehörigkeit*'. In contrast to the latter, however, it preserved the political affinity between state and nation because a political concept of the French nation—as will be shown—gained the upper hand over ethnocultural tendencies.

In the legal sense of adherence to the state, '*nationalité*' came to be used as a synonym to '*citoyenneté*'.[34] The nationalization of citizenship, however, had a second aspect: during the second half of the nineteenth century, the concept of citizenship was influenced by ideas of national homogeneity and cultural community (Brubaker 1992: 98). But—in spite of ethnocultural overtones in the neologism of 'nationality' (Brubaker 1992: 99)—the semantic linkage between nationality and citizenship was restricted to a formal, legal meaning. It illustrated the limits of nationalizing citizenship: the contractual, political aspect in '*citoyenneté*' survived and French national thinking put more emphasis on common memory, ideas, and interests than on language and race.

Until 1946,[35] '*citoyenneté*' (as the set of rights and duties of a 'full citizen') and '*nationalité*' were never completely congruent[36] in French history. However, as has been pointed out, there is a historical tendency of mutual rapprochement, which has made the national-citizen a model up to the present. On the other hand, as this conceptual survey has shown, neither the nationalization of '*citoyenneté*' in France nor the use of '*nationalité*' (necessarily) mean a depoliticization or adaptation to pre-political, ethnocultural criteria of belonging. The singular use of 'nationalité *française*', without identifying any other '*nationalités*' within the French nation, still makes reference to the '*nation une et indivisible*'. It, too, emphasizes the political core and nexus contained in the double meaning of '*citoyen*'. Thus, the French movement for the dissociation (de Wenden 1995: 88; Weil 1991: 442) between *nationalité* and *citoyenneté* will have to take this political—that is, republican and democratic—nexus into account.

Concluding Remarks

The four cases considered reveal a common development: the historical transition from the concept of subjecthood to citizenship and nationality/nationality-citizenship.

There is a conceptual core of citizenship common to these four cases. It goes back to the Philosophy of Enlightenment with its ideal of the autonomous individual and equality as opposed to feudal status rights.

The concepts differ according to their participatory elements. The American and French citizen/*citoyen* connotes the formation of state will by the citizens for the citizens. In contrast to that, the German concept of *Staatsbürger*, since its inception, was more closely related to the sphere of state than to society. This observation is confirmed by different concepts denoting the formal, legally defined adherence to a state. While the German term *Staatsangehörigkeit* exclusively refers to the abstract state, the broader English and French words citizen and *citoyen* include a participatory, democratic element.

Different historical relations between state and nation seem to have shaped different concepts of nationality. In English, American, and French history, the state developed before or at the same time as the nation. In these cases, the concept of nationality—at least in terms of its legal meaning—always maintains a reference to the state. In Germany, however, the concept of nation developed before the establishment of a central state. Given that historical background, nationality preserved a pre-political, pre-state meaning; underlying the monistic conception of the modern state, an element of diversity has been preserved. This element, rather than being limited to the state-building nation, always preserves the potential of different national groups within the nation state.

The legitimizing force of the concept of citizenship/*citoyenneté* varies, depending upon whether it has been introduced and put through in a revolutionary or evolutionary process. While the American and French concepts of citizenship/*citoyenneté* still include the idea and pathos of individual autonomy and republicanism, in England and Germany this tradition was weak from the outset or has weakened with time. At present, a double process seems to be underway. On the one hand, the ideal of citizenship is being contested. On the other hand, there is a trend towards its revival on the conceptual level. The legitimizing force of 'Western' revolutionary citizenship has returned to England and Germany.

In the course of general revaluation of the participatory concept of citizenship/*Staatsbürgerschaft*, citizenship has been (re)introduced into English legal and political language on the state level. Its legitimizing force has been transferred to the formal status of adherence to the state by replacing the term 'nationality'. Parallel to this, German projects to reform nationality law intend to replace the purely legal term *Staatsangehörigkeit* with the broader concept of *Staatsbürgerschaft*.

Decolonization and the establishment of democracy after World War II in all the countries considered have contributed to making legal adherence to the state (nationality, *nationalité*, *Staatsangehörigkeit*) and the status of citizenship rights (citizenship, citoyenneté, *Staatsbürgerschaft*) more and more congruent. As a consequence of convergence in real politics, the difference between the concepts of belonging—nationality and citizenship—is fading.

NOTES

1. Gesetz über die Staatsbürgerschaft der Deutschen Demokratischen Republik (Staatsbürgerschaftsgesetz), 20 Feb. 1967, preamble.
2. Draft of a reform bill introduced to the German Bundestag by the Green Party, Deutscher Bundestag, 13. Wahlperiode, Drucksache 13/423, p. 5 (motivation: 'die Staatsbürgerschaftsfrage. Ihr kommt eine entscheidende Bedeutung im Rahmen des demokratischen Gefüges der Bundesrepublik Deutschland zu').
3. As a classic example: Paul Laband (1964: 158): he reserves '*Staatsbürgerschaft*' to the federal states of the German Reich and treats it as completely equivalent to '*Staatsangehörigkeit*', thereby deliberately rejecting the French concept of *citoyen*; Max von Seydel (1896: 303) denies the autonomy of '*Staatsbürgerrecht*' as a legal concept according to the state law of Bavaria.
4. On the tendency towards convergence, *Brockhaus Enzyklopädie* (1971: 220); *Meyers Enzyklopädisches Lexikon* (1976: 780).
5. Reichsbürgergesetz vom 15. September 1935 (Reichsgesetzblatt I S. 1146).
6. The 'Handwörterbuch der Rechts- und Staatswissenschaft' (Posener 1909: 157) did not even mention '*Nationalität*' as an independent legal term. The article on 'territory' implicitly used the ethnocultural meaning of '*Nationalität*' in the statement: 'Territory and nationality are not congruent.'
7. Article 'Nationalitätenstaat' (Strupp and Schlochauer 1961: 570).
8. As an example: Rudolf Laun (1927: 182) in his article on 'Nation und Nationalitätenrecht' states that the concept of '*Nationalität*' is common in state law and international law. But its criteria in domestic law, according to him, are language and national self-identification, whereas in international law it refers specifically to minorities. Fritz Hartung (1923: 167) in his article on 'Nationalität' defines '*Nationalität*' either as an affiliation to a nation or a term for little nations which do not constitute independent states.
9. Wegener (1984: 866–81) defines '*Nationalitätenstaat*' as a state comprising bigger

groups of people of different '*Nationalität*' (in the meaning of ethnic origin, 'Volkszugehörigkeit').

10. On the background of a persisting ambivalence between an ethnic group and the state, Article 'Nationalität' (*Der Große Brockhaus* 1932: 205; *Brockhaus Enzyklopädie* 1971: 220): 'Membership of a nation; in English and French terminology equivalent to "Staatsangehörigkeit" (legal membership of the state). Also often used in German in the sense of "Staatsangehörigkeit" '; Article 'Nationalität' (Meyers Enzyklopädisches Lexikon 1976: 780): 'In domestic law synonymous of membership of a people ['*Volk*'] or [!] state.'

11. *Fransman's British Nationality Law* 1989: 40.

12. For examples of the overlapping use of 'subject' in international treaties (Koessler 1946/7: 58).

13. See below, point 4.

14. Still to be seen in the contemporary distinction between citizen and subject: 'Subject is not merely the British English equivalent of the American citizen. A citizen is a person from a country in which sovereignty is believed or supposed to belong to a collective body of the people, whereas a subject is one who owes allegiance to a sovereign monarch' (Garner 1995: 156).

15. Art. I, sect. II(2); Art. II, sect. I(5) of the Constitution.

16. Art. IV, sect. II(1).

17. Art. III, sect.I (1).

18. Evident in the definition of citizenship in Chandler, Enslen, and Renstrom (1987: 585): 'One's status as a person who owes allegiance to the United States and is entitled to all the rights and privileges guaranteed and protected by the Constitution'; 'In other words "citizenship" carries with it the idea of identification with the state and a participation in its functions. As a citizen, one sustains social, political and moral obligation to the state and possesses social and political rights under the constitution and laws thereof' (Garner 1995: 156); 'The privilege of membership in a political society, implying a duty of allegiance on the part of the member and a duty of protection on the part of the society; the status of a citizen with its respective rights and duties' (*Ballantines Law Dictionary* 1969: 202).

19. 14th Amendment, sect. I; 15th Amendment, sect. I.

20. 'National' as used in the phrase a 'national of the United States' is broader than the term citizen (*Black's Law Dictionary* 1990: 1024).

21. *Corpus Iuris Secundum*, vol. 65 (New York, 1966), 52.

22. Treatises on American constitutional law often do not even mention the word nationality in the index.

23. Immigration and Nationality Act 1952 (66 Stat. 163; 8 USC 1101, 1484), Title I, sect. 101a(22): 'The term 'national of the United States' means (A.) a citizen of the United States, or (B.) a person who, though not a citizen of the United States, owes permanent allegiance to the United States'.

24. In the classical œuvre of Holdsworth on the *History of English Law*, it is not even mentioned in the index. Citizen/Citizenship is not even mentioned as a legal term in some recent law dictionaries: *Osborne's Concise Law Dictionary* (1976); *The Layman's Dictionary of English Law* (1984); *Words and Phrases Legally Defined* (1988).

25. British Nationality Act 1948, Part I, 1.

26. The British Nationality Act 1948, Part I, 1(2); *Fransman's British Nationality Law* (1989: 57).
27. Part IV. British Subjects.
28. An amendment to declare that all the three kinds of citizen defined in the Bill had the status of 'British nationals' was refused on the grounds that the concept of British national is not something known to our domestic law and additional words would generate confusion Dummett/Nicol (1990: 249).
29. In spite of several efforts of revival after the decline of the First Republic and at the time of Restoration.
30. *Dictionnaire de la Terminologie du Droit International* (1960: 587); comparable to the English use: 'Parfois syn. de national (spéc. dans les pays à régime monarchique: ex. Sujet britannique. Comp. ressortissant, citoyen)' (Cornu 1987: 787).
31. According to the tradition of the Code Napoléon, affirmed by the reintegration of the chapter 'De la Nationalité Francaise' (Act of 22 July 1993) into the Civil Code after a period of distinct regulation in several codifications beginning with the Nationality Act of 11 Aug. 1927.
32. In a treaty of International Private Law in 1843 (Wihtol de Wenden 1994: 85); according to *Le Grand Robert de la Langue Française* (1988: 694), nationality as a legal definition in international private law appears first in 1862.
33. Used by Rousseau in this sense in 1778 (*Trésor de la Langue Française* 1986: 7).
34. Articles *citoyen/citoyenneté*: 'Usuel: . . . pour désigner la nationalité' (*Trésor de la Langue Française* 1977: 854).
35. Pursuant to the law of 7 May 1946, the difference between citizens holding all political rights and 'simple nationals' (French subjects in the colonies) was abandoned.
36. One can be a national without being entirely a citizen (especially in 19th-cent. French history; for example, the lack of voting rights on the part of women and inhabitants of French colonies, etc.). One could also be a citizen without being a national (see e.g. the French Constitution of 1793 and during the 'Commune' of 1871), Withol de Wenden (1994: 87).

REFERENCES

Ballantine's Law Dictionary (1969). San Francisco.
Black's Law Dictionary (1990). St Paul, Minn.: West.
Brockhaus Enzyklopädie (1971), vol. 13 (17th edn.). Wiesbaden: Brockhaus.
BRUBAKER, W. R. (1992). *Citizenship and Nationhood in France and Germany*. Cambridge, Mass.: Harvard University Press.
CHANDLER, R. C., ENSLEN, R. A., and RENSTROM, P. G. (1987). *The Constitutional Law Dictionary*. Santa Barbara, Calif.: ABC-Clio Informations Services.
CORNU, G. (1990). *Vocabulaire juridique* (2nd edn.). Paris: Presses universitaires de France.
CUSHMAN, R. F. (1957). *Cases in Constitutional Law*. Englewood Cliffs, NJ: Prentice Hall.

DANIELS, R. (1981). *Concentration Camps, North America: Japanese in the United States and Canada during World War II*. Malabar, Fla.: Krieger Publications.

Dictionnaire de la Terminologie du Droit International (1960). Paris: Sirey.

DUMMETT, A. (1994). 'The Acquisition of British Citizenship: From Imperial Traditions to National Definition', in R. Bauböck (ed.), *From Aliens to Citizens: Redefining the Legal Status of Immigrants*. Aldershot: Avebury, 75–84.

—— and NICOL, A. (1990). *Subjects, Citizens, Aliens and Others: Nationality and Immigration Law*. London: Weidenfeld and Nicolson.

'Encouraging Citizenship' (1990). *Report of the Commission on Citizenship*. London.

FERID, M., and BLUMENWITZ, D. (1975). *Das Staatsangehörigkeitsrecht der Vereinigten Staaten von Amerika*. Frankfurt: Metzner.

Fransman's British Nationality Law (1989). London: Fourmat.

GARNER, B. (1995). *A Dictionary of Modern Legal Usage*. New York: Oxford University Press.

GIESE, H. (1978). *Das Staatsangehörigkeitsrecht von Großbritannien*. Frankfurt: Metzner.

La Grande Encyclopédie (1975), vol. 14. Paris: Larousse.

La Grande Encyclopédie: Inventaire raisonné des Sciences, des Lettres et des Arts (1899), vol. 24. Paris: Société Anonyme de la Grande Encyclopédie.

Grand Larousse Encyclopédique (1963), vol. 7. Paris: Larousse.

Grand Larousse universel: Grand Dictionnaire Encyclopédique Larousse (1865), vol. 11. Paris: Larousse.

Le Grand Robert de la Langue Française (1988), vol. 6. Paris: Robert.

GRAWERT, R. (1973). *Staat und Staatsangehörigkeit*. Berlin: Duncker & Humblot.

Der Große Brockhaus (1932), vol. 13 (14th edn). Leipzig: Brockhaus.

HABERMAS, J. (1993). 'Staatsbürgerschaft und nationale Identität', in J. Habermas, *Faktizität und Geltung*. Frankfurt: Suhrkamp, 632–60.

HARTUNG, F. (1923). *Nationalität*, vol. 2. Leipzig: Koehler.

HOLDSWORTH, W. (1944). *A History of English Law*, vol. 4. London: Methuen.

KOESSLER, M. (1946/7). ' "Subject", "Citizen", "National", and "Permanent Allegiance" '. *Yale Law Journal*, 56: 58–76.

LABAND, P. (1964). *Das Staatsrecht des Deutschen Reiches*, vol. 1. Aalen: Scientia.

Langenscheidt's Enzyklopädisches Wörterbuch der englischen und deutschen Sprache (1962), vol. 1. Berlin: Langenscheidt.

LAUN, R. (1925). 'Nationalitätenfrage einschließlich des Minderheitsrechts', in K. Strupp (ed.), *Wörterbuch des Völkerrechts*, vol. 2. Berlin: de Gruyter.

—— (1927). *Nation und Nationalitätenrecht*, vol. 4. Leipzig.

Layman's Dictionary of English Law (1984). London: Waterlow.

Meyers Enzyklopädisches Lexikon (1976), vol. 13 (9th edn.). Mannheim: Bibliographisches Institut.

Osborn's Concise Law Dictionary (1976) (6th edn.). London: Sweet & Maxwell.

PARRY, C. (1957). *Nationality and Citizenship Laws of the Commonwealth and of the Republic of Ireland*. London: Stevens.

POSENER, P. (ed.) (1909). *Rechtslexikon: Handwörterbuch der Rechts- und Staatswissenschaften*, vol. 2. Berlin: Weber.

RÉTAT, P. (1988). 'Citoyen—Sujet, Civisme', in R. Reichardt and E. Schmitt (eds.), *Handbuch politisch-sozialer Grundbegriffe in Frankreich 1680–1820*, vol. 9. Munich: Oldenbourg, 75–105.

RIEGE, G. (1986). *Die Staatsbürgerschaft der DDR*. Berlin: Staatsverlag der Deutschen Demokratischen Republik.

Robert, Dictionnaire historique de la Langue Française (1992), vol. 2. Paris: Robert.

SALMOND, J. W. (1902). 'Citizenship and Alligiance'. *Law Quarterly Review*, 18: 49–63.

SOMERS, M. R. (1995). 'What's Political or Cultural about Political Culture and the Public Sphere? Toward an Historical Sociology of Concept Formation'. *Sociological Theory*, 13: 113–44.

STRUPP, K., and SCHLOCHAUER, H.-J. (1961). *Handbuch des Völkerrechts* (2nd edn.). Berlin: de Gruyter.

Trésor de la Langue Française (1977), vol. 5. Paris: Gallimard.

Trésor de la Langue Française (1986), vol. 12. Paris: Gallimard.

VON SEYDEL, M. (1896). *Bayerisches Staatsrecht*, vol. 1 (2nd edn.). Freiburg: Mohr.

WALKER, D. (1980). *The Oxford Companion to Law*. Oxford: Clarendon Press.

WEGENER, B. W. (1984). 'Nationalitätenstaat', in A. Erler et al. (ed.), *Handwörterbuch der deutschen Rechtsgeschichte*, vol. 3. Berlin: Erich Schmidt.

WEIL, P. (1991). *La France et ses étrangers: L'Aventure d'une politique de l'immigration de 1938 à nos jours*. Paris: Calmann-Lévy.

WEINACHT, P.-L. (1969). ' "Staatsbürger": Zur Geschichte und Kritik eines politischen Begriffs'. *Der Staat*, 8: 41–63.

WIHTOL DE WENDEN, C. (1994). 'Citizenship and Nationality in France', in R. Bauböck (ed.), *From Aliens to Citizens: Redefining the Legal Status of Immigrants*. Aldershot: Avebury, 85–94.

—— (1995). *l'Europe et toutes ses migrations*. Brussels, Éd. complexe.

Words and Phrases Legally Defined (1988), vol. 1 (3rd edn.). London: Butterworth.

3

National Identity and Citizenship

The Cases of Germany and France

Bernhard Giesen

Introduction

Citizenship has become one of the central issues of contemporary debates where politics, public law, and social science meet. The controversial character of these debates not only is a matter of conceptual diversity but results from the nature of the issue itself. Regardless whether we conceive of citizenship as a legal status or as a practice, as a foundation in a communitarian perspective or as rights in a liberal perspective, as a matter of welfare entitlements or of political participation, it is publicly debated, claimed, and challenged. It requires justification. These public debates are engendered by the tension between the inclusive thrust of universalism and the fact that citizenship can never avoid exclusion.

The following analysis starts with an outline of Enlightenment universalism, which claims categorical validity and is therefore unable to construct political actors and citizenship. The main part of the paper deals with different modes of justifying claims on citizenship by appealing to constructions of collective identity. Collective identity is taken for granted by those who appeal to it; in fact, however, it is not naturally given but socially constructed and publicly staged. I will present a typology of three different codes of collective identity, which provide different strategies of inclusion and exclusion with respect to a particular historical situation. The second part of this article reconstructs German and French national identities with reference to these codes of collective identity. In contrast to common accounts of national identities in France and Germany, I will argue that neither can the German construction of national identity be reduced to primordialism nor can the French one to universalism; instead primordialism, traditionalism, and universalism are part of both nations' cultural repertory. Which code of collective identity prevails in a given historical situation depends on the challenges of demarcation and the responses provided by different social carrier groups.

Natural Rights and Civic Exclusion

The Categorical Universalism of the Enlightenment

Tracing back the idea of universal inclusion leads inevitably to the philosophy of the European Enlightenment. The community of mankind as seen by the Enlightenment was bound to missionary expansion and inclusion. No longer were the prince and his court, the privileged aristocracy, and the dogma of the Church viewed as the sources of truth, legitimacy, and authenticity, but rather the periphery, the common sense of the citizens, and the natural reason of mankind unspoiled by the distortions of particular interests and prejudices. The imagined community of humankind transcended the barriers of class, confession, and locality and included all those who in principle were able to rise from their self-induced serfdom by the use of reason. The particularity of privilege was replaced by the universality of reason, in which every human being partakes regardless of his or her descent and origin.[1]

Contemporary debates on the universalist basis of civic inclusion, however, tend to ignore that the universalism of the Enlightenment aimed less at a practice of citizenship than at a categorical basis for historical analysis. The paradigm for the universality of reason was not of citizenship but mathematics and geometry. As mathematics abstracts from concrete forms of real things, the universal categories of reason too transcend any particular empirical events. They claim categorical validity, because without them the empirical events could not even be perceived. In a similar way we cannot conceive of the history of mankind and of society as based on contract if we do not presuppose all members of the human species to be endowed with a capacity for moral judgement and natural rights. These presuppositions are valid even if real individuals are not aware of their natural rights and ignore their capacity for moral judgement.

As mathematical relationships cannot be refuted or verified by empirical events, natural rights are also independent from particular decisions and traditional privileges. They cannot be questioned or denied, traded or transferred. Most philosophers of the Enlightenment—Voltaire, Rousseau, Diderot, Grotius, and Kant, as well as Locke and Montesquieu—were ethical rationalists in this sense. Assuming the categorical validity of natural rights, they constructed a transcendental basis for a new universal community of mankind that extended far beyond the territorial boundaries of the state or the historical realm of European Christianity.[2]

In contrast to the transcendental idea of universal community, the practice of inclusive citizenship is a relatively recent achievement. The Enlightenment philosophers still combined the categorical universalism of reason with a highly exclusive praxis of discourse (Wuthnow 1989). In the society of the Enlightenment, exclusion by privilege and birth was replaced by a new pattern of exclusion based on education and participation in the public sphere (Giesen 1993). Not everybody who was naturally endowed with reason, but only those who had overcome traditional superstition and had already proved their competence as reasonable persons, were admitted to the public sphere.[3] The intellectuals and their educated audience were the carriers of this public sphere. Neither peasants and servants, nor women and workers were included. They were thought to lack the necessary education (Conze and Kocka 1992) (and most of them were indeed illiterate) or the economic independence required for the proper use of reason (Haferkorn 1974).[4]

In this respect the Enlightenment philosophers continued the practice of civic exclusion, which in the ancient Greek polis was the official programme of citizenship: slaves and *barbaroi* could never be included in the citizenry. The Enlightenment, however, combined this practice of exclusion with the categorical universalism of natural rights. This, inevitably, engendered tensions and problems for the modern conception of citizenship.[5]

The Problem of Civic and Political Exclusion

The categorical universalism of natural rights opened up an infinite horizon of inclusion that was unable to cope with the cleavages of politics. Political interaction presupposes the existence of at least one political opponent who is also endowed with reason and who is also included in the universal community of humankind. Political coalitions as well as social solidarity always engender the exclusion of outsiders; otherwise they would be meaningless. The inclusion of all humankind can therefore refer only to the most general and universal aspects and must abstract from empirical and historical differences. Hence the categorical universalism of the Enlightenment engendered a new problem: below the universality of reason and natural rights, collective actors must be constructed who can engage in effective political action and who thereby have to exclude others.

This problem increases in salience as collective actors take off from the level of simple contractual relationships between a few individuals and encompass a multitude of different people who cannot conceive of their relationships as a mutual contract. On the most general level, this construction of political actors amounts to the demarcation of citizenship. Citizenship is a legal status with respect to political participation. It defines individual persons as members of a political community, and by this very definition it has to exclude others who are part of the categorical community of humankind. This unavoidable exclusion from citizenship rights can be tacitly accepted and routinized. For instance, few objections will arise if people who are not concerned by decisions of a political community and do not live on its territory are excluded from political participation. If, however, exclusion from citizenship overlaps and intersects with existing social ties, it may be challenged and will require justification. Thus, citizenship can be regarded as a regulatory interface between civil society and the polity.

Exclusion from citizenship becomes a debatable issue, especially in democratic systems that claim open access to political participation for all members of the societal community. Here the problem of defining the boundaries of the societal community cannot be avoided: it is by reference to this communal foundation of markets and states that exclusion from citizenship can be justified and challenged. Thus, in modern democracies the question of collective identity comes to the fore.

The Public Construction of Collective Identity

Debates about citizenship appeal to collective identity because collective identity appears as taken for granted, as a pre-political fundament, as the 'people' whom democratic politics should represent. This seemingly stable fundament is not naturally given, but socially constructed and subject to historical change. In the next chapters we will outline some cultural codes that are used for this construction and hint at some historical shifts in the relationship between citizenship and national identity in Germany and France.

The main arena, in which national identities are staged, constructed, and appealed to, is, of course, the public sphere. Most public debates assume and occasionally refer openly to a collective identity that unites the audience, imagines an invisible community, and constructs a bond between the speaker and the anonymous (and mostly non-present) others addressed by public communication. These assumptions of collective identity are, however, strongly influenced by the perspective of the speakers, who try to imagine the encompassing collective identity according to their own situation.

Strategic interests in the mobilization of public resources may move social groups to proclaim risks and dangers threatening the collective identity or to couch themselves as the true representatives of it. Identity entrepreneurs or identity brokers may even appeal to the latent identity of social categories whose members are not yet aware of their commonality and turn them into a politically valuable clientele. In these cases the strategic actors do not have to believe in the collective identity they are trying to construct, but they do have to hide their strategic interests in order to convince others.

Collective identity exists only if some people believe in it and adopt it as their 'true' and 'real' identity. If all involved are motivated exclusively by strategic interests, no collective identity can emerge. Hence the process by which individuals accept an encompassing identity as 'their own' takes on special importance. Images of collective identity are adopted by individuals as true and real if these patterns correspond to the central parameters of their life-world and cultural frames—that is, to their taken-for-granted perspective on the world.

The basic mechanism of this process is analogical reasoning: the invisible and unknown realm is imagined according to the visible and well known. This immediate plausibility of analogical construction, however, will not necessarily be transferable to other groups with different lifeworlds and cultural frames. These groups will be more ready to adopt a collective identity from outside if structural cleavages are breaking down as a result of revolution, war, rapid social change, increasing immigration, or imperial expansion of the state. Here the spread of a new idea of national identity responds to new challenges of demarcation and boundary construction: old patterns of collective identity are devalued and new orientations are requested.

A second and even more important way of spreading a pattern of collective identity is based on the institutionalization of public discourse. The public sphere provides an arena where the social cleavages between groups recede into the background and communication has to appeal to values, images, experiences, and narratives not specific to particular groups. Here patterns of collective identity have to be presented in publicly accepted cultural frames, and new elements of identity have to be embedded in old and well-established ones. In these attempts, the original lifeworld is frequently transformed in accordance with the systemic exigencies of public debates: professional advisers and identity brokers take over, the media rephrase the issue in order to catch attention, and so on.

As always in the course of professionalization, the original issue is blurred and subjected to a new logic of professional interests and professional problem-solving. The original carriers of collective identity are turned into a useful clientele or into consumers of identity offers in postmodern markets. This clientele of professional identity brokers accepts and supports the process of public staging and phrasing because it promises public recognition.

Participation in public affairs presupposes the recognition of actors as relevant, autonomous, and self-determined, and representation in the public sphere conveys the impression of being recognized as relevant. This recognition presupposes the existence of an audience that is not moved by strong personal interests, but intends to consider the issues impartially. The distinctive logic of the public sphere would fade away and public discourse would be dissolved into market exchange if all actors were exclusively pursuing their own interests. Recognition of collective identity in the public sphere does not always engender a corresponding legal status of citizenship. Public communication can respond quickly to new situations, whereas the change of legal institutions follows a much slower pace. Tensions between the construction of civility and social solidarity, on the one hand, and the lagging legal definition of citizenship, on the other, may arise and be publicly debated with respect to shifting ideas of national identity. Sometimes patterns of national identity that are centred in the public debate and supported by the cultural elites fail to get majority support or are rejected by the political elites and are therefore never turned into citizenship laws.

Three Types of Collective Identity

Conflicts and debates about citizenship refer to tacit constructions of collective identity, that is to boundaries between those who are included on the basis of some fundamental similarity and others who are viewed as different, as strangers or outsiders. Following the ethical rationalism of the Enlightenment, the difference between insiders and outsiders should be based on contingent reasons that do not affect the categorical presupposition of natural rights. But because these boundaries are to justify civil exclusion, they also cannot be based on shifting political decisions. Instead they have to be regarded as pre-political, unquestionably valid, and exempt from the range of strategic action.

The very perception of political affairs as malleable and of history as progress required a stable and unchanging background against which the accelerated pace of history and the fluidity of social processes could be discerned. Thus, the modernization of society was compensated by the construction and imagination of communities, which were assumed to be ahistorical and timeless, and the emphasis on individual self-determination was counteracted by the demand for collective identities, which could be taken for granted and which provided binding commitments.

If the construction of collective identity has to provide a stable point of reference for civic exclusion, but also was not to affect the level of universal rights, then only a limited set of options was available. The following outline will present these options in a threefold typology (Eisenstadt and Giesen 1995; Giesen 1993).

Primordialism

The first mode of constructing and reinforcing the boundary between inside and outside refers to embodied distinctions that are empirically given and cannot be changed by voluntary action. We call these distinctions primordial. By relating collective identity to empirical conditions like territory or kinship, climate or ethnicity, codes of primordiality provide a firm and stable basis beyond the realm of voluntary actions and shifting involvements. Below the universality of reason there was the realm of empirical contingencies perceived by the senses and imprinted into the body.

As long as these primordial boundaries are crossed by the universality of reason, no barrier will impede understanding between primordially different individuals. Both the universality of reason and the primordial variation of real individuals were considered to be mutually related, like categories and empirical objects or moral judgement and voluntary decisions. This was the position of the Enlightenment from Montesquieu to Herder.

If, however, the universality of reason is questioned, primordial differences become fundamental cleavages. This departure from the Enlightenment duality started with certain strands of the German romantics and became central in the naturalism and racism at the end of the nineteenth century. Here crossing the boundaries is impossible, because it would ignore a fundamental natural cleavage.

The question of purity and pollution takes on paramount importance and the internal homogeneity of a group is ensured by rituals of purification, which extinguish the traces of the outside in the members of a collectivity (Gennep 1960; Turner 1969). Especially in modern patterns of collective identity, the focus on purity becomes central. Striving for purity of style or ethnic purity exhibits the same pattern of boundary construction in modern societies. Primordialization consists not only of a special way of constructing the inside, but also of a particular way of mapping others outside the collectivity. The relationship of primordial collectivities to their environment is not a missionary one. The 'outsiders' cannot be converted and adopted, educated, developed, or even understood. If primordial attributes are not counteracted by universalism, they demarcate an insurmountable difference, and this difference conveys inferiority and danger at the same time. Hence, outsiders are frequently seen as demonic, endowed with a strong and hostile identity that threatens the existence of primordial communities. Mapping the environment by primordial codes results therefore in a pressure to keep a certain distance for security, or if this is impossible, to prepare for war.

Primordiality naturalizes the boundary between inside and outside (Barth 1969; Douglas 1986). Hence, the unity of the collectivity itself becomes a basic natural similarity of its members. There is no personal representation of collective identity apart or above this natural similarity; primordial codes reduce the identity of the whole to the sum of its elements, and these elements are conceived as similar and equal. Therefore primordial codes question hierarchies and entail a tendency towards majority principles of democracy and egalitarian distributions of entitlements. This egalitarian tendency and the sharp and distinct boundaries of primordial collectivities have an elective affinity to citizenship in the ethnic nation states. From the second half of the nineteenth century onward primordial constructions of national identity were therefore considered to be more modern than traditional references to princely rule and territorial boundaries. They foster the institution of rela-tively wide package deals of access to resources and public goods by all members of the national community and refuse access and entitlements to outsiders. Citizenship is here ascribed and linked to descent and natural ties; it cannot be acquired by appealing to common convictions or the merely incid-ental fact that people are living on the territory of a state and under the rule of a constitution.

Primordialization allows for the exclusion of denizens and immigrants who are declared to be ethnically different. It reinforces boundaries under conditions of rapid mobility and close contact with outsiders. But it also offers a strategy for defending the collective identity of a minority against majority pressure for assimilation and even for claiming an independent and separate political community. Even if the minority were willing to ignore the differ-ence, the primordial boundaries would resist to any attempt at assimilation.

Universalism

A second type of constructing boundaries remains within the universalist project of the Enlightenment but tries to bridge the gap between the ideal of universal inclusion and the practical inevitability of exclusion: it links the constitutive boundary between 'us' and 'them' not to natural conditions, but to a particular relation of a collectivity to the transcendental realm of reason and perfection. A particular social group claims privileged access to the tran-scendental sphere, based on a historical mission, on a special awareness of universal reason and progress. In distinction to outsiders, they have already realized the transcendental ideal. The central axis of distinction in this respect is time and history.

In contrast to the primordialist code that naturalizes the boundaries, universalist codes temporalize the boundary between inside and outside. While stressing the universality of reason as a timeless transcendental idea, they profoundly temporalize access to the transcendental sphere and the embodiment of reason. Some social groups get it earlier than others. The avant-garde of reason demarcates itself from the backward masses, which are still confined by traditional superstition and narrow-mindedness, but may eventuality be converted to the new faith in reason, emancipation, and progress. Hence, the historical realization of reason and natural rights presup-poses a rupture between past and future; it has a tendency to devalue past experience and to open up the future for utopian orientations.

Universalism therefore engenders a missionary orientation towards outsiders. In contrast to primordial codes, universalism invites every outsider to cross the boundaries by acquiring learning and education (Eisenstadt 1987). Those who resist the mission are not only different and inferior, but

Bernhard Giesen

mistaken and erring; they have to be converted even against their own will, because they are not aware of their true identity. Here, outsiders are considered to be natural objects requiring cultural formation and identity.

The openness of boundaries in universalism, however, is frequently compensated by a graded and stratified access to the centre and by complicated rituals of initiation; the toils and inconveniences of learning and education have to be overcome in order to approach the centre of a universalistic community. Between the virtuosi and the laity is an internal boundary within the community.

The expansive movement at the periphery of universalistic collectivities is therefore counteracted by stratification and internal ranking within the community. This stratification between teachers and pupils is accepted by the inferior groups as long as they can regard it as a temporally limited inequality (Eisenstadt 1987). Although the roles will never be reversed, education will finally turn pupils into teachers for new generations of outsiders.

Universalist coding is the appropriate strategy through which a majority or a powerful centre can exert pressure for assimilation and integration without risking the central authority. On the basis of cultural superiority, outsiders can be educated and converted even against their own intention and will. If citizenship is based on universalistic constructions, access to basic rights is available for all those who commit themselves to a particular cultural project—to Christianity, to enlightenment, to socialism, to secular humanism, etc. This opens up the boundaries for a *transnational citizenship* based on a universal culture and excludes all those who clearly oppose this universal culture even if they are ethnically tied to the majority of a state, live on its territory, and obey its laws. Universalistic collective identities engender the focus on internal outsiders who resist to the mission of universalism and reject fiercely any attempt at cultural assimilation. The existence of committed opponents disturbs and challenges the inclusive thrust of universalism. Citizenship cannot be entirely denied to these internal opponents of universalism but a temporal restriction of citizenship rights can be declared in order to increase the pressure for conversion.

In between the group of respected citizens who are faithful to the universalist project and the internal outsiders, there are 'marginal people' who are obviously not adherents of the universalist culture but who do not oppose it. These people at the boundary are usually treated as pupils who need education and tutelage in order to become full members of the community. Whereas universalist constructions can easily dispense with internal enemies, they need this group of marginal people in order to maintain the dynamic and tension of the inclusive boundary. Universalist conceptions of citizenship therefore favour immigration and multi-ethnic citizenship as long as the migrants can be regarded as potential members of the cultural community. They are incompatible with strong cultural or ethnic movements that refuse to acknowledge the superiority of the universalism, insist on insurmountable differences, and reject any attempt at assimilation.

Traditionalism

Because of their close affinity to the universalist project, the Enlightenment rejected the codes of boundary construction that we may call 'traditional'. This code is constructed on the basis of familiarity with implicit rules of conduct, traditions, and social routines (Shils 1981). Here collective identity refers to temporal continuity, to the recurrence of social practices, to a *habitus* (Bourdieu 1984). These routines and rules are difficult to separate from the praxis of acting and participation in everyday life. On a daily level they tend to be exempted from argumentation, communication, and debates. Attempts to question them, to ask for instructions with respect to proper behaviour are the mark of the outsider. The insider is familiar with the rules, even if he is unable to name and explicate them.

Here the boundary is only an undefined and diffuse frontier. The only way to be accepted as a member of a traditional community and to partake of its collective identity is to participate in the local practices and institutional arrangements and slowly to adopt the local customs and routines. Considering the implicitness of most of the rules and routines, any special instruction and education will fail.

Traditional constructions of collective identity maintain the boundary by not mentioning it. They conceive of inside and outside in a symmetrical way and depict the outsider as the stranger who is simply different and extraordinary without attributing particular—positive or negative—charismatic qualities to him. Because the stranger is unfamiliar and different, his actions are difficult to understand and his behaviour is difficult to account for; the logic of interaction itself requires a certain caution and distance. In a sense, the traditional code of collective identity can be regarded as the most fundamental of any such constructions. It refers to its own continuity and has some similarity to Weber's concept of 'tradition'. In the public sphere, traditional forms of collective identity are frequently based on commemorative rituals and the representation of the past, of continuity, routine, and tradition in particular people, places, and events. Hence, the traditional identity of a nation is not only embodied in special virtues and recurrent practices but also related to mythical origins, to founders or historical events, like revolutions or migrations.

Tradition can provide a particular basis for the justification of citizenship: only those who observe certain rules of conduct, who revere the traditional virtues and display the right manners, will be accepted as citizens. Obviously these criteria are more difficult to monitor than ethnicity or commitment to a universalist culture. If states do not provide special institutional agencies for examining candidates for citizenship (as Switzerland does), they can only focus on some basic features of civility, on respect for the law and the constitution. Citizenship rights are granted to all those who are competent to act as regular citizens without further assistance and who have respected the norms of civil behaviour for a certain time.

Traditional constructions of collective identity do not provide special tutelage for immigrants: in contrast to universalism, nobody is invited to apply for citizenship, but if an applicant succeeds in proving his or her civility for some time, access cannot be refused regardless of descent, origin, or cultural conviction. This citizenship by competent participation can maintain its boundaries mainly by controlling the time during which the applicant has to make proof of his or her civility (by not violating the law).

National Identity and Citizenship in Germany

Although the contemporary public debate in Germany aims to disconnect citizenship from primordial attachments, the legal status of German citizenship is clearly based on primordial grounds. The idea of the *ius sanguinis* allows immigrants from Eastern Europe provided they can prove their German descent even if they are unable to speak German and are largely alien to the culture of modernity. Some absurd consequences of the German *Staatsbürgerschaftsrecht* were frequently noted in contemporary public comments and provoked marked oppositions between the primordial identity of Germany and the universalist identity of France.

In contrast to this common view, I will argue that primordial and universalist elements can be found in French as well as in German public discourses on national identity and that differences in citizenship laws between both nations are mainly due to the particularities of the historical situations in which they were established: German history as well as French history has produced three distinctive projects of national identity: a primordial, a traditional, and a universalist one. Even today public debates and everyday knowledge refer and appeal to these projects in order to construct national identity, to exclude outsiders, and to justify different patterns of citizenship.

Germany as the Natural Nation (*Naturnation*)

Usually Herder is considered to be the intellectual architect of a primordial construction of German identity, but even more important were the German romantics. Their movement started as an ambitious aesthetic movement and later engaged in the war of liberation against the French occupation. The German romantics assumed a deep, unique, and natural individuality of the German nation beyond the vain affairs of commerce and politics.

This identity could not be touched by superficial reasoning. It could not be described or compared, exchanged or alienated; it was considered as a dark natural essence that could be approached only indirectly by aesthetic rituals. The purity of this natural identity had to be defended against intruders from outside like the Napoleonic occupation.

On the basis of this primordial German identity, culture is reduced to nature and the nation is constructed in basically apolitical terms. Political action can be conceived of only as an extraordinary charismatic event, such as defence against a threat from outside, or rebellion against an unnatural order. This defence of natural purity constituted a German primordial identity that underwent considerable historical transformation but hardly changed its basic pattern. This pattern contrasted nature and society, saneness and sickness, rural life and urban life, poets and politicians, work and money, the natural simplicity of the people and the artificial system of modern life. History was seen as an attempt to overcome the alienation of modern society and to return to a timeless community living in accord with nature.

The romantic longing for a natural ground of national identity was later replaced by intellectually less ambitious ideas about harmony between man and nature, represented and embodied in German art and literature and embodied in the German poet and the German peasant. The rapid modernization, urbanization, and industrialization of north Germany in the second half of the nineteenth century was compensated by a defence of its 'natural roots'. At first this primordialism continued to be couched in aesthetic terms, and aesthetic rituals (Richard Wagner's Theatre) were of central importance for the intellectual construction of national identity. At the turn of the century, however, the primordial identity was rephrased in a new, seemingly scientific terminology of racism and anti-Semitism. The purity of the German race was to be defended against the increasing influence of other races, especially the Slavic peoples (who in the case of Poles were actually living under Prussian German domination and were to be excluded from full citizenship in the Reich) and the Jews, who after their emancipation were accused of controlling business and banks and of being favoured by Bismarck and the German Kaiser. Again the primordialization of boundaries reacted to social mobility and rapid changes in the social structure and took a clearly anti-modern turn. In these decades of rapid modernization, between 1871 and 1913, German citizenship law took its basic form. It responded to a situation that had clearly changed since the middle of the century: after the failure of the revolution of 1848, many disappointed liberals left Germany and the German authorities tried to prevent emigration by returning to a territorial citizenship; after some years abroad, Germans lost their citizenship rights. In the last decades of the century, however, Germany changed into an immigration country that attracted many Polish workers in particular. The attempt to exclude Polish denizens was complemented by offering citizenship to Germans who lived abroad and could not return, on the basis of *ius soli*. Even if the law of 1913 did not refer to the concept of race, it was certainly influenced by the prevalence of primordial elements in the intellectual discourse about national identity at the turn of the century. The reluctance to engage in an purely ethnic foundation of citizenship resulted from the requirement to justify the exclusion of Austria in the so-called '*kleindeutsche Lösung*' of the new German empire. Several decades later, Nazi legislation turned what were previously the racist ideas of intellectuals into a racist law of citizenship.

After the holocaust and the end of Hitler's Germany, racism was evidently banned from the construction of the new national identity of the Germans. But primordial elements and the idea of German descent still remained part of the concept of citizenship. Citizens of the GDR and refugees from Eastern Europe were to be included into the citizenry, although they obviously were not born in the territory of West Germany. Ethnic definitions of citizenship provided a more flexible and more acceptable solution than a shift to the *ius soli*, which would have deprived Germans in the former eastern parts of their German citizenship or would have had to recognize two different German states and citizenships.

Even later, in contemporary German discourse about collective identity, primordial patterns can be discovered. The particular German preoccupation with '*Waldsterben*' and other ecological issues and the impressive political success of the German Greens compared to those in other European nations cannot be explained by the extraordinary severity of the problem in Germany, but were certainly fostered by primordial patterns of identity construction that assumed a special German relationship to nature. This project of the German ecological *Naturnation*, however, is indifferent to citizenship issues.

In contrast to this subtle primordialism on the left, the new youth movement of the extreme right pushes violently again for primordial criteria of exclusion. According to them, foreigners (*Ausländer*) should not only be excluded from citizenship and welfare entitlements but also be expelled from German territory. Members of this primordialist movement frequently come from groups in marginal situations or in downward mobility: jobless youngsters in depressed areas in East Germany, for example. But they use primordialism not only in order to exclude competitors; primordialism also provides an aggressive identity for a new generation in a society that has banned primordial arguments from the public sphere.

The range of transformations of the German primordial identity may appear to be vast: from the ambitious aestheticism of the Romantics via the racism and anti-Semitism of the turn of the century to the ecological fundamentalism and the vulgar xenophobia of contemporary youth movements.

But all these different brands of German primordialism are united in their reference to nature as the basis of national identity. We will see that the French version of primordialism takes a different frame of reference.

The German Virtues

Political constructions of a German national identity have always been and still are comparatively weak. This weakness of political traditions is particularly striking with respect to commemorative rituals or *lieux de mémoire* (Nora 1992) of national identity. Certainly since the *Reichsgründung* by Bismarck there have been strong movements and attempts to invent and to establish commemorative rituals, to construct monuments, and to restructure history with respect to the re-foundation of the German *Reich*: the celebrations of Sedan victory, the cult around Bismarck or—on an intellectually more ambitious level—the famous Sybel–Ficker debate about the misleading orientation of medieval German emperors towards Italy. All these constructions of a traditional national identity started late and did not last long. The German defeat in World War I as well as the seizure of power by the Nazis and the start of the new federal republic devalued in each case the preceding constructions of traditional political identity and required new commemorative rituals and a new founding myth.

Therefore in post-war Germany strong constructions of traditional identity emerged not on the level of the nation state but on the level of national virtues, commensural rituals, and regional folklore. Evidently the nationalist traditions were radically devalued and any vision of a future nation state was blocked. On this basis Turkish workers who had lived in Germany for many years were included, in contrast to refugees or ethnic Germans from Russia, who were regarded as aliens because they did not speak German and were unfamiliar with local traditions. Central to this traditional construction of German national identity is the idea of German virtues like duty, plainness, honesty, loyalty, natural simplicity ('*Der reine Tor*' was praised), industriousness, reliability, and efficiency. According to this code of virtues, non-German outsiders were labelled as dishonest, artificial, lazy, unreliable, and arrogant.

The code of German virtues changed its focus according to historical and institutional changes, but its core remained fairly stable: in the Prussian army the focus was on duty and obedience, the expanding bureaucratic administration and industrial system in the Bismarckian *Reich* added reliability, loyalty, and industriousness.

The original carriers of these virtues were neither the aristocracy nor the commercial bourgeoisie, but the petit bourgeoisie in small towns and the *Beamten* in the public service. Their lifeworld as praised by the German classics centred on work and duty and was based on their distance from underclass vagabonds and servants, on the one hand, and aristocratic leisure and luxury, on the other.

In contrast to the French focus on individuality and distinction, the German code of virtues fostered compliance and conformity with the norms of modern functional organizations. These virtues took on a special importance for the construction of national identity after World War II, when the political history of the nation state did not provide any chance to identify with a positive tradition. The German *Wirtschaftswunderidentität* was centred on an economic interpretation of German virtues that allowed integrating several million refugees and displaced persons after the war. Membership in West Germany's civil society was defined not by primordial and ethnic ties or by a common history but by continuous participation in the common task of reconstructing the German cities and developing the German economy. With respect to the '*Wirtschaftswunderidentität*', prospects for effective and relatively frictionless integration into the German economy had to be considered as the core criterion for social solidarity and legal citizenship. On this basis, '*Gastarbeiter*' who had lived in Germany for many years could be included. Participation in celebrations of local associations, beer drinking in local pubs, speaking the local dialect, and joining the working habits of the locals allows inclusion of people who are obviously of non-German origin. This traditional or folkloric inclusion cannot be used as a clear criterion for legal citizenship, but it provides an important basis for a common civil identity.

Abroad, the traditional identity of the German economic and technical virtues was symbolized by the strength of the German currency. Hence, the Maastricht prescription of a unified European currency is seen as a direct threat to the traditional German identity—more important than European citizenship or the free movement of labour and capital within Europe.

The German Cultural Mission (*Die deutsche Sendung*)

In contrast to some historical reconstructions (Greenfeld 1992), German national identity from its very beginning in the eighteenth century contained some strong universalist elements. The enlightened patriotism of the educated bourgeoisie (*Bildungsbürgertum*) in the second half of the eighteenth century was carried by a missionary movement of inclusion that did not differ much in its rhetoric from the ideas of the French and British philosophers.

Even the early German romantics—although opposed to the universalism and rationalism of the Enlightenment—occasionally conceived of Germanhood (*Deutschheit*) in universalist and missionary terms and laid the ground for what later on was called the German cultural mission (*deutsche Sendung*).

The German educational bourgeoisie was the main carrier of the liberal national movement in the first half of the nineteenth century; faced with the scattered political map of the German states, it imagined the German nation as created by culture and education, as an intellectual power in contrast to the political idea of the nation represented by France. In particular the Hegelian philosophers contributed to a German self-consciousness based on intellectual and cultural superiority. They pressed for emancipating the repressed nations and changing radically the course of history by ideas and concepts. After the *Reichsgründung*, when the cultural idea of the nation was turned into the powerful political reality of the new German empire, universalist and inclusive patterns, however, lost their attractions for the public discourse on German identity. They were replaced by primordialist ideas, which were able to exclude even those who were ready to be educated and to adapt to German culture.

The idea of the cultural nation with a universalist and missionary drive was revived in post-war Germany when the prospects for a unified German nation state were blocked by the German partition and the recent history of Nazi Germany fundamentally devalued any attempt at political nationalism. The holocaust provided the turning point of German history; it urged a radical departure from the past and demanded re-education and conversion of the German population towards a new political culture. Again this internal cultural mission was led by intellectuals and carried by the educated bour- geoisie. It renounced political nationalism and the narrow-minded tradition- alism of the *Wirtschaftswunderidentität* and thereby it perpetuated the disdain of the nineteenth-century *Bildungsbürgertum* for the world of power and money. Instead it gradually claimed a leading position in international social and intellectual movements (student movement, Third World movement, ecological movement, feminism, peace movement, etc.) because the new German identity was based on a particularly radical rupture between past and future. A special German cultural mission for world peace was proclaimed and imposed on other nations even if they had decided otherwise in their own internal affairs.

This new German identity, as promoters of global missionary movements, had strong implications for contemporary citizenship debates. Obviously it does not allow for exclusion on grounds of ethnic differences or unfamiliarity with traditional virtues. The borders are to be opened to refugees from all over the world, and help is to be offered to all those who are fleeing the economic misery of Africa or other depressed regions.

This opening of boundaries for inclusion clearly differs from the univer- salism of the Enlightenment: it requires not only a categorical recognition of natural rights but also material solidarity, the transfer of scarce goods, and even entitlements to citizenship. The global extension of welfare entitlements advocated by the new German social movements usually provokes resistance from those who have to pay and to share; today public debates about the limits of solidarity arise and right-wing populism gains supporters.

Usually the praxis of universalism sets limits to this inclusive movement by a stratification between the core members of the citizenry, on the one side, and the immigrants and refugees crossing the boundary, on the other. In contemporary cases, however, this stratification mostly extends only to the difference between victims applying for help and their advocates engaged in a public crusade in order to raise welfare funds and support civic entitlements. The increase of non-European immigration into Germany and the populist reactions to the alleged privileges of these immigrants led to administrative restrictions on access for non-European immigrants and refugees. German universalist and humanitarian movements in their turn strongly opposed these restrictions by appealing publicly to the dark legacy of the German past. In light of the history of nationalism in Germany and in marked distinction to French universalism, they challenge the importance of territorial boundaries and of nationality for citizenship in general; instead they favour the idea of a European citizenship with porous borders: whoever has succeeded in entering European soil should be entitled to basic economic support and rights of political participation. The idea of a transnational citizenship linked to mere presence on the territory avoids the hardships of exclusion, but it also engenders problems that are brought to the fore by the supporters of a traditional or primordial grounding of citizenship: either mobility across the boundaries is hampered, or citizenship has to be restricted to second- or third-generation immigrants. Otherwise the rapid turnover of citizenship status will decouple political decision making from the people who, later on, are affected by these decisions.

National Identity and Citizenship in France

La France de Charlemagne

Although French conceptions of citizenship are commonly presented as tied to universal political participation, there have been also strong primordialist positions in the public debates about French national identity since the nineteenth century. Although the political success of legitimist anti-republicanism was quite limited and the attempts to change the *ius soli* into the seemingly more modern *ius sanguinis* in the second half of the nineteenth century were never successful, primordialism was prominent in the public sphere. French anti-Semitism was among the strongest and most militant in Europe at the turn of the century. It divided the nation into two irreconcilable camps. From the Dreyfuss scandal via the Action Française in the 1930s to the OAS in the late 1950s and the Front National of contemporary France, there has been a continuity of primordial constructions of national identity.

Although the carriers of this defensive identity and its organizational forms varied considerably, the core ideas remained fairly stable: the French are seen as the descendants of the Franks and France is imagined as the noble defender of Latin Christianity against tides of Semitic, Muslim, or simply foreign invasions. Although Charlemagne and Jeanne d'Arc are revered as founding heroes, although the medieval knight and the sacred kingdom of France represent the paradigmatic core of this French identity, its primordial elements are far stronger than its traditional ones. The discourse of cultural purity and pollution, the focus on the 'blood of France' as represented in the lineage of the king and the French nobility, the defensive orientation against a strong enemy who has invaded the sacred country, and a sharp and exclusive boundary construction show the primordial core of the French identity. Even religion is mostly interpreted in a primordial way. Being a Muslim or a Christian (and here Christian means Catholic) is less a matter of confession and conviction than a cultural *habitus* acquired by birth. Joining a crusade to liberate the Holy Land or defending the nation of the '*roi très chrétien*' against heretics and protestants required the sword and not the argument. This focus on embodied culture is at the core of French primordialism. It differs in that respect from the German focus on nature. In contemporary French debates, too, primordial exclusion refers rather to enculturation and ethnicity than to hard biological racism or to special natural foundations of the French nation.

Evidently this primordial construction of Frenchness has strong implications for the idea of civic inclusion and citizenship: immigrants from non-European (i.e. non-Christian) countries should not be entitled to apply for citizenship and welfare support and should get only limited access to French soil. As in the case of Germany, the public resonance of primordialism grew in times when the influx of foreign immigrants increased or was thought to be increasing, when a war was lost, or when colonies were given autonomy. Hence, it is hardly surprising that supporters of this primordial identity can be found mainly among groups that have experienced or expect downward mobility and are afraid of new competitors.

Le Château et le village: The Civilization of Distinction

A second important pattern of French national identity refers to special manners that convey distinction in contrast to uneducated and uncivilized people: the cult of dining and wining (*raffinement*), ways of dressing (*bon chic, bon genre*), knowledge of French literature and French history (*érudition*), playful irony, gallantry, and entertaining conversation (*esprit*), etc. This French *habitus* is certainly acquired by education and enculturation, but it is never promoted in a missionary way. Those deplorable people who unfortunately

lack the essential marks of distinction and civilization will not be invited to
educate themselves but kept at a distance. Silence and mockery are the typical
ways of referring to them.

The civilizational identity of the French presupposes the existence of uneducated outsiders. Only the contrast to them conveys distinction. But the civilizational exclusion of outsiders is never based on primordial boundaries;
Léopold Senghor was included as a highly distinctive member of this civilizational community although he was African. The civilizational *habitus* of
France has the unmistakable features of a traditional identity; it centres
around rules and manners, which cannot be improved but are transmitted
from generation to generation less in schools than in families.

Although today the bourgeoisie is the carrier of this traditional French
identity, it still shows the marks of its origin in the French aristocracy. Here
the traditional line of distinction runs between the chateau and the village.
From the sixteenth century on, the absolutist state decoupled the French
nobility from their bases of power in the provinces, deprived them largely
of their military functions, and assembled them at the court of the *Roi
Soleil*.

Without their traditional basis of distinction, the nobility at the royal court
cultivated a special *habitus* in contrast to the rude and plain behaviour of
peasants and other ordinary folk. They despised the bourgeois concern with
function and profit and turned conversation and social life into an art of its
own that was difficult to imitate even if outsiders tried hard. Civilizational
refinement constructed traditional boundaries because it was based on pure
distinction, and apart from that it was useless.

In the second half of the nineteenth century, however, this aristocratic
identity started to diffuse into the bourgeoisie, which in turn insisted on
distinction from the rising working class. Today this civilized distinction is
regarded and recognized from outside as the traditional identity of France.
Its direct effects on citizenship issues are mild. Because distinction is the
core motive, this identity allows (if not requires) the presence of non-civil-
ized others in the citizenry. The chateau needs its counterpart, the village.
But if the uncivilized villagers forget the distance and invade the chateau,
angry reactions may arise. The neighbourhood should be homogeneous and
civilized.

Non-French civilizations should be admitted to France, but they should
never be permitted to take a dominant position. The civilization of distinction
is benevolent with respect to the diversity of villages, but it will not allow
questioning its own dominance. If the authority of French civilization is seriously challenged, even the authority of the state is urged for its defence.
Restoring the dominance of French language and culture in France and
banning foreign—in particular American—cultural influence is therefore
today at the core of this traditional identity of France.

La nation révolutionnaire: France as the Avant-garde of History

French conceptions of citizenship are frequently seen as based on the universalism of the Enlightenment and the *ius soli*. Every person born on French territory is entitled to citizenship regardless of descent, and the nation is imagined as an inclusive political community participating in public debates and decisions.

This inclusive idea of national identity and citizenship was born in the French Revolution. The programme of the revolution promised abolition of old privileges and a new equality of all citizens, and the praxis of the revolution created the new agency of the nation, storming the Bastille and liberating the prisoners of the *ancien régime*. Riots and *émeutes populaires* were not new, but the great revolution successfully constructed a republican state on the reversal of the class/periphery relationship: it was the people at the periphery of the traditional society who seized the power, devalued the centre, decapitated the king, and persecuted everybody suspected of ties to the old centre. A new inclusive idea of the nation emerged: the revolt of the periphery against the old centre had opened boundaries for everybody who could claim to be a member of the people or a victim of the Old Regime.

This inclusive movement could not stop at the old boundaries of the state: the revolution released a universal mission of emancipation and liberation carried by the French armies as the avant-garde of progress. The conquered and liberated nations were to be incorporated into the French state and their peoples turned into French citizens. In contrast to German cultural universalism, the French programme of assimilation was decidedly political and centred on the state: outsiders should be included by turning them into French citizens. The process of inclusion was conceived as the expansion of French territory. Although the holy alliance of conservative governments succeeded in stopping the wave of revolutionary conquests after two decades, the pattern of avant-garde identity established by the great revolution has persisted. *La France révolutionnaire* imagined itself as the historical avant-garde of humanity, as the seedbed of European (and later global) movements of liberation and emancipation, as the guardian of universalism and progress.

French identity is here not defined as the continuation of the past but as a radical departure from the past. Because *La Grande Nation* is privileged as the frontrunner of history, it has to teach the message of progress to the world and to take special responsibility for the victims of repression and persecution in more backward nations.

This *gauchiste* identity of France opens up the horizon for universal inclusion not only on the level of categorical assumptions but also for the politics of citizenship. Immigration from other European countries in the nineteenth century and from the Third World today does not challenge this pattern of identity but rather reinforces and strengthens it.

Citizenship itself is not restricted to political participation but also includes welfare entitlements and education. In particular the project of a centralized and comprehensive system of education rose to paramount importance for the equality of citizens and the politics of assimilation. It is education that converts outsiders into Frenchmen and it is education that decides about individual careers. The price the immigrants have to pay in exchange for citizenship rights is abandonment of their strong religious traditions.

The universalism of *la France révolutionnaire* is anti-traditional and strictly laic. Only if the constitutive cleavage between past and future is emphasized and only if religion is decoupled from the state and reduced to a private folklore can the *gauchiste* project of universal inclusion and assimilation succeed. Today the problems of religious fundamentalism in a laic republican state can occasionally be blurred if the orthodox faithful can be presented as a persecuted minority or as the victims of underdevelopment in need of advocates and assistance. As soon, however, as religious fundamentalism attracts a strong followership and insists on public respect and representation, the identity of the lay nation is directly challenged.

After two centuries this identity itself has been strongly traditionalized. *La nation révolutionnaire* celebrates its achievements and commemorates its history with elaborate public rituals, monuments, and political addresses. The original carriers of revolutionary universalism, the working classes, have partly abandoned the project and joined the ranks of defensive primordialism, whereas members of the public service and the education system support a watered-down version of it as their official ideology. Their contemporary clientele, the non-European immigrants from North Africa, frequently reject the assimilationist programme of French universalism. They claim a universal right of freedom of confession in order to be fundamentally different, and they inevitably come into conflict with the legacy of laicism.

Concluding Remarks

The commonly accepted thesis of a universalist construction of French national identity in contrast to a primordial construction of the German one cannot be accepted with respect to the public sphere and civil society: primordialism, traditionalism, and universalism can be found in the history of both nations. In contrast to the public debates on national identity, the legal institutionalization of citizenship differs more clearly between Germany and France. The Code Civil could resist a public turn towards the seemingly more modern idea of an ethnically based citizenship, whereas the German

Staatsbürgerschaftsgesetz could not. Reasons for this difference can be found in the problems of boundary demarcation that both nations had to face when their citizenship laws were established.

French revolutionary expansion differed clearly from the historical setting in which—almost a century later—Germany established its laws of citizenship. Based on a well-established territorial nation state, France could start a revolutionary mission, whereas Germany could not build its national identity on a comparable political tradition and firmly established territorial boundaries; instead it had to refer to a cultural heritage or to primordialism in order to construct a unifying bond between its citizens. Furthermore, the impact of primordialism on the public sphere was weak at the beginning of the century when the French citizenship laws were written, whereas it was relatively strong at the end of the century when German citizenship was legally institutionalized. Differences between national identities do not result from dark and unchangeable essences, but are constructed from cultural traditions, depending on structural situations and moved by public debates and strategic interests.

NOTES

1. This shift towards inclusion not only could borrow from a secularized version of Christian universalism, but also was fostered—in an unintended way—by the efforts of absolutist states to subject their citizens to uniform administration, taxation, and legal control regardless of local differences and traditional privileges.
2. Exotic peoples at the periphery of the known world, like the Indians, or ancient civilizations before the advent of Christianity, like the Chaldeans, were discovered as the embodiments of natural reason and natural morality.
3. Public communication inevitably has to be selective with respect to the speakers: not everybody can talk and expect to get an audience, there must be a coordinated focus of attention. Today this problem is solved by a clear differentiation between the speakers, who are few, and the audience, which includes almost the entire population. The public sphere of the Enlightenment, however, was also highly exclusive with respect to the audience (Brewer 1995; Koselleck 1973).
4. Occasionally their ignorance was not considered to be a contingent and deplorable lack of education, which could be removed in the course of progress, but a matter of principle and civil order. Voltaire, e.g., did not want his wife and his servants to enjoy the pleasures of the Enlightenment. Instead they should believe in a '*dieu rémunérateur et vengeur parce que je ne veux pas être conçu ni volé*'.
5. During the reign of the *sans-culottes* in the French Revolution, radical thinkers like Marat and Baboeuf turned the categorical universalism of the Enlightenment into a programme of citizenship: the periphery of society was now defined as the

sovereign nation; economic independence and education were ruled out as a condition for inclusion; active participation in the revolution became the only basis of citizenship; cleavages of privilege and class were replaced by those between parties and movements.

REFERENCES

BARTH, F. (1969). *Ethnic Groups and Boundaries: The Social Organization of Culture Difference*. Boston, Mass.: Little, Brown.

BOURDIEU, P. (1984). *Distinction: A Social Critique of the Judgment of Taste*. Cambridge, Mass.: Harvard University Press.

BREWER, J. (1995). 'This, That and the Other: Public, Social and Private in the Seventeenth and Eighteenth Centuries', in D. Castiglione and L. Sharpe (eds.), *Shifting the Boundaries: Transformation of the Languages of Public and Private in the Eighteenth Century*. Exeter: University of Exeter Press, 1–21.

CONZE, W., and KOCKA, J. (eds.), (1992). *Bildungsbürgertum im 19. Jahrhundert, Teil 1. Bildungssystem und Professionalisierung in internationalen Vergleichen*. Stuttgart: Klett-Cotta.

DOUGLAS, M. (1986). *How Institutions Think*. Syracuse, NY: Syracuse University Press.

EISENSTADT, S. N. (1987). *Kulturen der Achsenzeit*. Frankfurt: Suhrkamp.

—— and GIESEN, B. (1995). 'The Construction of Collective Identity'. *European Journal of Sociology*, 36: 72–102.

GENNEP, A. (1960). *The Rites of Passage*. London: Routledge & Paul.

GIESEN, B. (1993). 'Intellektuelle, Politiker und Experten: Problem der Konstruktion einer europäischen Identität', in B. Schäfers (ed.), *Lebensverhältnisse und Konflikte im neuen Europa: Verhandlungen des 26. Deutschen Soziologentages in Düsseldorf*. Frankfurt: Campus, 492–504.

GREENFELD, L. (1992). *Nationalism: Five Roads to Modernity*. Cambridge, Mass.: Harvard University Press.

HAFERKORN, H. J. (1974). 'Zur Entstehung der bürgerlich-literarischen Intelligenz des Schriftstellers in Deutschland zwischen 1750 und 1800', in B. Lutz (ed.), *Deutsches Bürgertum und literarische Intelligenz*. Stuttgart: Metzler, 113–275.

KOSELLECK, R. (1973). *Kritik und Krise: Eine Studie zur Pathogenese der bürgerlichen Welt*. Frankfurt: Suhrkamp.

NORA, P. (1992). *Lieux de mémoire*. Paris: Gallimard.

SHILS, E. (1981). *Tradition*. Chicago: University of Chicago Press.

TURNER, V. (1969). *The Ritual Process: Structure and Anti-Structure*. Ithaca, NY: Cornell University Press.

WUTHNOW, R. (1989). *Communities of Discourse: Ideology and Social Structure in the Reformation, Enlightenment, and European Socialism*. Cambridge, Mass.: Harvard University Press.

PART II

Projects for Full Citizenship in the Euro-Polity

4

Citizenship and the European Union

Klaus von Beyme

This contribution will examine the relationship of citizenship and the European Union in two ways:

(1) by analysing the different *national traditions of citizenship* in Europe which have to converge in order to develop a minimal consensus about European citizenship;

(2) by analysing the *first steps to developing European citizenship* in the documents of the European Union and confronting them with contradictions and restrictions emerging from the process of integration.

Incompatible National Traditions of Citizenship in Europe

The Four Pillars of Legitimation

The internal conflicts regarding the ratification of the Maastricht Treaty showed the difference of traditions in the perception of citizenship: some countries followed their doctrine of parliamentary sovereignty and had the treaty ratified by a parliamentary majority. Britain, when it admitted a referendum on the question of adherence to the European Community, deviated from its basic constitutional principles. Some Scandinavian parliamentary systems followed the British example. But even when a country voted 'no'—as Norway has already done twice—the West European constitutional mystique was sufficiently generalized to respect such a decision. In some countries the tiny majority in favour of further European integration caused misgivings, such as in France or Denmark.

Only Germany seemed to be the deviant case, which attracted much criticism for its special way of accepting Maastricht. The majority in the Bundestag was comfortable. But the second round of legitimation of this decision in the Federal Constitutional Court aroused suspicion about a new German *Sonderweg* (special path). No other country has developed such far-reaching consequences of *judicial review* as Germany, though some countries—such as Austria or Italy—also have a fairly well developed constitutional court. The German Constitutional Court—deliberately not accepting *a doctrine of political question* which would certainly be applied by the Supreme Court of the USA—showed, however, its normal sense of *judicial restraint* in matters of foreign policy. But as in many other foreign policy decisions—such as the basic treaty with the GDR (1973)—its message was 'Thus far—and no further'. The Maastricht judgment and certain statements made by judges, such as those of Paul Kirchhof (1992), caused a wave of polemical analysis. The judgment did no harm, but its underlying argument uncovered a deep-rooted deviance in the German perception of citizenship.

The critics have admitted (Weiler et al. 1995: 13) that the Court launched a *soft version* of the perception that there is *no European demos*. The *hard version* of nationalists would go much further and declare: there will never be a 'European'. Both statements are largely accepted by the critics: the 'not yet version' is hardly contested and the 'there will never be a European demos version' is only a likely truth in the future. But it applies only to a demos in the German statal and intellectual tradition: the demos which is identified with the *ethnos* (*Volk*) and *state*.

In European history the dissolution of the old *societas civilis* was prepared by the absolute rule of monarchs and completed by the overthrow of absolutism after the French Revolution. Up to the period of roughly 1750–1850 (called by Koselleck the '*Sattelzeit*' in which decisive developments towards the modern world took place), the nations of Europe still had many beliefs in common. But the era of the French Revolution did not only cause internal fragmentation of parties but also differentiations of national developments concerning the perception of citizens. In spite of these differences, four waves of the substitution of religious and monarchical legitimation were universal in Europe. Only the timing of these processes and the legitimation mixture in the predominant constitutional culture diverged. Bourgeois self-consciousness, which substituted step by step the traditional collective feelings of identity, built on religion and a hierarchy of estates (Eder 1985: 299), was not strong in various European countries. Only in this decisive era was a 'German *Sonderweg*' constituted.

The 'four waves' of modern legitimation were the development of:

(1) the legal state;
(2) the national state;
(3) the democratic state; and
(4) the welfare state.

This fourfold typology, deviating from Marshall's 'holy trinity' of *civil, political,* and *social* perceptions of citizenship, showed already the happier British development. Nation in the sense of '*Volk*' was not included. The islanders—though not always tolerant towards ethnic diversity—were sufficiently united in their 'natural' insular qualities in order to avoid continental debates of national identity. Postmodernists were dissatisfied with the missing link of *cultural citizenship* (Turner 1994: 159) and criticized the concentration on the economic and social citizen in Marshall's concept. Only some postmodern theorists in the development of anti-racist and anti-chauvinist concepts of citizenship (Vogel and Moran 1991) tried to do justice to the so far discriminated notion of *ethnos* which had been abused by the Fascist regimes. Most postmodern thinkers cultivate rather a postnational mood. Only in some cases there was a latent danger that under the cover of a new postmodern terminology the old organicist notions such as '*ethnos*' or '*Volk*' would return into professional debates. Thinkers upholding the flag of classic modernism— who went through a Marxist stage in their life—such as Férenc Feher and Agnes Heller (1994; Heller and Puntscher Riekmann 1996) remained worried by the postmodern tendency to bring back organicist notions such as 'body', 'race', '*Volk*', or, 'nature' into the centre of political philosophy.

Generally, however, thinking in terms of a postmodern 'patchwork of minorities' revived interest in *ethnos* only in the case of the lost nations which demanded *recognition* and not only *redistribution* as they did in the period of an unbroken optimism of modernism. Compared with the lusty colour of *multiculturalism*, the theory of citizenship has the *historical merit* of offering a differentiated analysis of the aspects of citizenship and the lasting tensions between *inclusion and exclusion* of groups of citizens on various levels (Meehan 1993: 21). Some postmodern thinkers, close to postnationalism, show the possibilities of a transnationalization of certain citizens' rights which have so far been stagnating in the cage of national legal traditions (Roche 1992: 192 f.).

It was, however, hardly this sophisticated debate on subnational and transnational developments which dominated the debate of the political elite about the Maastricht Treaty. The German Constitutional Court was guided by a reified version of an ethnic demos which rather belonged to the thinking of early modernism. A 'from Carl Schmitt to Paul Kirchhof thesis' was developed to denounce the German special way to Europe (Weiler 1995: 12). The remnants of a traditionalist court which may one day be overruled by European law would have less worried the European partners if it had not been combined with a German rigidity in manœuvring the unified new European superpower into the role of a watchdog of the criteria for the admission of countries to monetary union by 1999. The German emphasis of '*Volk*' is explosive only in its combination with an emphasis on economic and social citizens which is alien to some of Germany's neighbours. It is not by chance that Germany was blamed for the hardships of the French government during the strikes of December 1995.

No country has oscillated between the four pillars of legitimation so frequently as Germany. Every German system in history has had a different pattern of combination of the four elements of citizenship (matrix). Nevertheless there is—if we exclude the two German dictatorships—a certain constant pattern of deviance from the French or the British model of citizenship. This deviant model was not based on any particular undemocratic character of the Germans. The various forms of schemes of German history, in the style 'from Luther to Hitler' or at least 'from Schelling to Hitler' (Georg Lukàcs), have unduly underestimated the democratic traditions, especially in the German cities and even in the history of ideas, so that the counter-hypothesis was developed in summaries such as 'from Cusanus' or 'from Althusius to Kant'. Even this version of an inappropriate simplification indicated, however, already the *German Sonderweg*. Why was there no later exponent of democratic and liberal thought than Kant who could be compared with the liberal tradition of other countries?

The Particularity of Germany

The 'liquidization' of modern social relations, differentiation, and mobility was hampered by various factors of German history (Giesen 1993: 155) such as the following:

1. The incapability to found a *national state* before it was accomplished by blood and iron. This development, which had long been achieved by Germany's neighbours, led to a romantic exaggeration of the cultural element, increasingly interpreted in terms of organic objective factors. It was even felt under the two post-war German regimes. Chancellor Schmidt stated in one of his governmental declarations that the Germans had no possibility of escaping the identity of the German *Kulturnation*, even if they wanted. Honecker in East Germany echoed this hidden objectivism and reification by varying the topic of the *class nation* which history will show to be the inescapable fate of the Germans.

Citizenship in the nineteenth century was predominantly defined in narrow *legal terms*: citizens are members of certain states. The Germans, with an unhappy history of successive exclusions of German-speaking parts of the former Empire, seemed to be forced to accept the blood principle in order to mitigate the hardships of exclusion, after 1866 and 1871. Even when Germany tried to be democratic, after 1918, and when it became democratic in its western parts after 1949, the integration of 'former citizens of the German Empire' was inevitable. Only after reunification is it time to abandon the *ius sanguinis* and to normalize as a nation among others in accepting the mere principle of *civil citizenship*. This would greatly facilitate the overcoming of the traditionalist views of the Constitutional Court by legal faits accomplis and prove the internal Europeanization of German political culture.

2. Since Germany did not overcome the remnants of late absolutist rule,

modernizing it under the so-called *monarchical principle*, neither the national state nor the democratic state were able to develop. Germany emphasized the *legally constitutionalized* state. The 'bourgeois' were still deprived of many possibilities of participation which other countries offered, but they were compensated for their economic activities by greater legal security than in other less authoritarian regimes.

3. German citizenship stabilized the *bourgeois* in compensation for what was lacking in terms of the *droits de l'homme* and the rights of the *citoyen*. Even when all these rights were added to the constitutional concept of citizenship in 1919 and in 1949, German legal-mindedness—in compensation for its unparticipatory attitude—was a topos of all political culture studies, until Germany unexpectedly in the early 1980s became the 'Mecca of unconventional behaviour' due to the rise of the alternative and Green movements. The strong position of the Constitutional Court and the extreme aversion of the political elites to any plebiscitarian forms of participation is a characteristic legal feature of present German citizenship. The French perception of a nation as a '*plébiscite de tous les jours*' (Renan) had in many periods of French history a much less exclusive regulation of citizenship. Although the declarations of the more liberal Constitution Girondine of 1793 (Art. 1) and the more radical 'acte constitutionnel' of June 1793 (Art. 4) agreed—which would have hardly been possible in Germany—that '*tout homme né et domicilié en France*' at the age of 20 is allowed to exercise the '*droit des citoyens Français*'. *Double citizenship* of two states was, however, excluded (Art. 5). The 'acte constitutionnel' differentiated the social conditions relating to the acquisition of French citizenship. Those who worked, purchased property in France, married a French woman, adopted a child, or supported an old citizen were entitled to French citizenship (Duguit et al. 1952: 65). France did not actually implement these extremely liberal principles. But it was important that the concept of citizenship was linked to participation in the political and social sphere. The change from constitutional government to revolutionary government was accompanied by a stronger emphasis on the goal of society, '*l'utilité commune*', not quite correctly translated as 'common happiness', which appeared in Art. 1 of the Declaration of the Rights of Man. When Robespierre and Saint Just achieved defining power of the constitutional principles, the idea of the *pursuit of happiness* went into a coercive direction (Ionescu 1984: 79). These principles developed an important impact only after the rise of the welfare state, if we exclude the intermezzo of the '*comité de salut public*'. Liberal interpretations, however, have always denounced the mobilizing aspects of the radical democratic concept of citizenship as a kind of terror.

4. The *welfare state* was—not by chance—first developed in rather traditional societies such as Germany and Italy to compensate for the deficiencies of other spheres of citizenship. But liberal democracies which were increasingly demanding of their citizens, in terms of taxes raised and sacrifices

imposed in world wars, were also forced to develop the welfare state as the fourth pillar of legitimation.

A functioning democracy has to *balance the four principles* of legitimation in its concept of citizenship. For a minimal consensus on the appropriate balance of the elements of citizenship in Europe, Germany represents, so far, the main problem.

The anxieties of other European nations that Germany might turn to nationalism after its reunification were unjustified. On the contrary, Germany was eager to push self-limitation and self-integration in Europe. The old device of the German allies in the time of the Cold War, that the Western security and integration system served two purposes: 'to keep the Soviets out, and to keep the Germans down' was transformed into 'keep the Germans in'. The German population is no longer more EU-oriented than other people. But it is hardly more nationalistic on the whole. Empirical surveys on the European level—especially in the Eurobarometers—show that Germany is a low-scorer when its citizens are asked: 'are you patriotic' or even 'very patriotic'? Germany ranks even below Belgium where intellectuals sometimes ask whether the country is still one nation. More sophisticated measures are necessary. A Mannheim project showed that a minority in West Germany (43.6 per cent, East Germany 51.2 per cent) belong to the category of *traditional nationalism*. But this does not mean that even the traditionalists all believe in a *pre-political ethnic foundation* of the nation. Quite a few conceive the nation to be *transpolitical* and *cultural* (Lepsius 1990). A second type of 'reflected patriotism', which is roughly identical with '*constitutional patriotism*', was represented by 32 per west in West Germany and 30.3 per cent in the former GDR territories. *Postnationalism*, as a third category, was found only among a quarter of the population in the West (24.4 per cent) and 18.5 per cent in East Germany (Westle 1994: 64). As expected, East Germany is slightly less modern or postmodern in its outlook on the national question, but it constitutes only one-fifth of the German population. In spite—or because—of this traditional patriotism East Germany normally casts even fewer votes for nationalist right-wing extremist groups than West Germany.

These figures support two conclusions:

(1) a majority of the Germans in category 2 and 3, strengthened by a proportion of transnational cultural patriots in category 1, are open to a non-ethnic concept of nation;

(2) the concept of the elites—still strong in the Basic Law and in the legal provisions for German citizenship—expressing itself in the rather traditional judgment of the Constitutional Court on the Maastricht Treaty, is less modern or postmodern than the perception of the majority of the citizens. Unfortunately, the more sophisticated typology of patriotism has not yet been applied to all the European Community members. If this

were done, Germany would probably figure among the more enlightened nations.

But surveys do not determine the public debate on future European citizenship, but rather the more influential statements of official bodies, such as the Constitutional Court.

The Commonalities in Europe

If we compare the possibilities for a proper balance of the four elements of citizenship in Europe, we find a number of processes which make the concepts of citizenship in Europe less divergent than they used to be.

1. The *Rechtsstaat* and the legal protection of citizens and human rights was expended. The German concept of *judicial review* had an even stronger impact than the competing concepts of the American Supreme Court, especially in the budding new democracies in Eastern Europe. There remain, however, differences in the perception of how the law should be created, determined by different legal cultures (common law or Roman law tradition). There are differences of the influence of the democratic concept of *plebiscitarian rule-setting* or sticking to the *representative rule-making* procedure, and the impact of courts on the development of legal norms and constitutions.

2. The search for *national and cultural identity* is unbroken in the European systems. It was strengthened by globalization and Europeanization, on the one hand, and the rise of subnational claims from ethnic or regional groups, on the other—not only in Eastern Europe. Most West Europeans continue to have their favourite enemy, as transnational surveys have uncovered (France, the North Africans 42 per cent, Spain, the gypsies 50 per cent; Germany, the Poles 49 per cent and the Turks 46 per cent; Russia, the Caucasians 46 per cent; and Britain, the Irish 21 per cent (Times Mirror 1991: Qu. 64: 73–9).

The everyday culture reveals that many cosmopolitan attitudes turn into forgotten pretentions as soon as the national soccer team loses an important game. A humoristic definition of nation reads: 'nations are territories which form a national soccer team supported by fan clubs'. According to this criterion, Scotland is a nation, Bavaria is not. There are no soccer wars in Europe, but vandalism of migrating fan clubs became a serious problem of transnational police coordination. Oddly enough, postmodernism has postulated that *culture* is the primordial functional subsystem of a social system. But culture is no longer elitist. The new cultural trends are proud of a *levelling of high and low culture* from pop art to soccer. The cultures and subcultures of a system developed few integrating capacities. This is probably one reason why patriotic outbursts at certain cultural events seem to be the only national bond shared by a majority. Soccer is certainly a sphere where intellectuals and the normal citizen can agree in the most unproblematic way.

Enlightened *constitutional patriotism* seems to be poor on the emotional side of citizenship and this is one of the reasons why cultural identity, language, and pride in one's historical past tend to remain latent buttresses of the sense of legal citizenship. Even the foes of the 'no European demos hypothesis' are convinced that there will never be a European demos in terms of linguistic and cultural homogeneity. Part of the constitutional provisions—tuned with protection of minorities, and recognition rather than redistribution—support the existence of these emotional divergences. They only correctly demand a decoupling of citizenship and cultural or national identity feelings.

3. The *democratic concept of citizenship* has become more convergent. Most of the systems in Europe are varieties of parliamentary government. The renewal of an old-fashioned debate on parliamentary and presidential systems found the hybrid of a semi-presidential system (France, Finland, less open in Austria or Portugal, spreading over most East European countries, except Czechia and Hungary) an appropriate way out of an institutional crisis. But most of these discussions blur the fact that even semi-presidential systems—with popular election of the president and generally more opportunities for the people to participate via referenda—are but one branch of the parliamentary system. They do not leave the parliamentary majority without influence over the destiny of the president's government, and do not leave a president without the possibility of a dissolution of the legislature as do fully presidential systems.

The European tradition was characterized by two variations of concepts of citizenship, long before the systems turned to democracy:

(1) the *liberal tradition* developing out of a concept of natural rights which considered the institution for participation of citizenship in a rather individualistic and instrumental way, based on organization and the legal status of citizens;

(2) this concept competed with the other, traced back to Aristotelian tradition, which conceived citizenship as *ethical and cultural community*. Its emphasis was rather on '*moeurs politiques*' and political culture than on institutions.

It is not by chance that during a crisis of the formalistic concept of citizenship in some European countries the communitarians rediscovered the old *holistic concept of citizenship* (Taylor 1989; Habermas 1992: 640 f.). Constitutional patriotism was liberated from its narrow connotations with the *Rechtsstaat*, which were dominant in the German tradition, and was linked to a new democratic participatory ethos. The gap in the liberal–communitarian debate was smaller than assumed. Michael Walzer and other communitarians were liberal enough to recognize that communitarian waves normally serve the purpose of counterbalancing the exaggerations of liberal individualism.

Communitarianism in Europe was largely an import, and its influence on the intellectuals was strongest where there was least institutional crisis, such as in Germany. But crisis solution—without reference to republican communitarian ideals—in the 1990s sometimes followed rather the communitarian concepts of citizenship. When institutions face a crisis they take resort to plebiscitarian measures and rediscover the demos. It happened even in German parties but with the odd contradiction that the Social Democrats got a leader elected by the majority of members, and when he seemed to fail, organized the coup by an amendment to the party statutes so that the party convention was able to revert the popular decision. This was rather German in its legal-representative thinking, connected with a profound undercurrent of anti-plebiscitarian anxieties. But these events effected only subsystems of the political system. The variety of citizenship strategies of the member states of the European Community could be demonstrated by comparing how Italy and Germany tried to solve a crisis. Italy in a crisis of its political class and institutions turned to referenda for a change of the electoral system to a variation of a majority system. Even the most sophisticated political scientists, such as Sartori (1994), turned to instrumental *constitutional engineering* for a partial regime shift in order to facilitate the introduction of their favoured electoral system with two ballots according to the Gaullist tradition. The Italian demos, so far, failed to go far enough and the result was a system '*maggioritario ma non troppo*' (Bartolini and D'Alimonte 1995). Germany, on the other hand, facing the crisis of the reintegration of the dilapidated east, resisted all temptations to leave the path of a liberal representative democracy. Parliamentary sovereignty remained dominant. Even the constitutional amendments—though they were far from being revolutionary or even innovative—were not allowed to be endorsed by popular referendum. Though West Germany had to impose considerable sacrifices on its population to finance reunification, this was mostly done in barely transparent ways (via the parafisci of the social security system). Germany, nevertheless, got away with the hidden concept: taxation with representation, but no plebiscitarian participation.

The Italian example of a search for a way out of the institutional crisis via referenda has so far failed and this will hardly encourage the more republican concepts of citizenship in Europe. Italy was the representative parliamentary system which used most frequently—and with considerable wisdom on the whole—the popular instruments of the democratic state. Nevertheless the country got into a crisis much deeper than the representation-minded systems in Europe. Communitarians might argue: constitutional engineering does not lead to authentic virtue orientations and it is an illusion that either representative democracy or plebiscitarian democracy are appropriate means against *tangentopoli* and a corrupted political class. In spite of some deviant cases in the temporary balance between elements of democratic citizenship, the European countries expose few fundamental divergences on the development of a consensus. They can agree on a variety of *proportional electoral laws* (except Britain) and on a predominantly representative concept of *parliamentary government*. They increasingly accept *judicial review* as a mediating power, though it contradicts both variations of citizenship, the communitarian as well as the liberal-parliamentary concept.

4. The *welfare dimension of citizenship*—so strongly emphasized by Marshall—oddly enough today is least diverging in Europe. The genesis was different. Those countries, such as Germany and Italy, where democratic participation was underdeveloped and the national state was not 'naturally' accepted as in Britain or France, were the first to develop the social dimension in order to prevent political disintegration. This was done by *conservative* forces. The *socialist groups*—who claimed to be the torchbearers of welfare state ideas, unless they were revolutionary and followed Lenin's device 'the worse, the better' (for us)—only after 1918 became the main actors in creating social policies. In the second half of the twentieth century *all political forces* with some slight differences promote social policies. The old historical divergences wither away. Some forerunners of the welfare state, such as Germany, are no longer on top of the achievements.

But in spite of different profiles of benefits, the importance of the welfare dimension is high in most of the countries. European integration is determined much more by hopes (the poor countries) and anxieties (the paying countries) than by national resentments or the non-acceptance of the institutions of democracy which can be observed in the rest of the European world. Citizens are no comparative political scientists. But envy about divergent levels of welfare creates comparativist attitudes even among those citizens who have little information about neighbouring countries.

All the European countries are on the road to deregulation and cuts in social benefits. Social traditions, labour relations, the regulations of a labour law determine how resistant individual countries are to the decrease of former social benefits. Britain—after Thatcher's victory over King Arthur—apparently has a wider margin of tolerance in this respect than Germany or France. The fourth pillar of citizenship in Europe is predominant, because most of the citizens' rights so far are located in the sphere of freedom to work, to move, and to own property wherever citizens want within the Community.

The European Concept of Citizenship *in Nuce*

The enormous divergence of the national mixes of the four elements of citizenship invites compromises by formulas and hidden contradictions of the definitions of citizenship. This is certainly not worse than in the case of diverging key principles such as *subsidiarity*. Britain and Germany could not agree on the principles of federalism. They rather accepted a term which was completely alien to the British intellectual tradition and close only to the Catholic part of the Christian Democrats in Germany. Concrete legal concepts, such as citizen rights, cannot be manipulated in the way that cloudy guiding ideas can be handled.

The *legal nature* of the Union is interpreted according to the variations of legal cultures and intellectual schools. The Union avoids its self-definition. Whereas the national states in their constitutions define the nature of the systems such as 'federal', 'social', '*Rechtsstaat*', or 'Republic' and sometimes protect these definitions by 'eternity clauses' which invite the overthrow of the constitution for those who wish innovations, the Union only hints at its functions 'shall have its task, by establishing'. Lindberg and Scheingold's 'Would-Be Polity' (1970) seems to have survived. '*Sit venia verbo*'—the character of the Union is a draft for the future. Biblical connotations come to mind as well when Art. 8.1 creates the citizenship of the Union '*ex nihilo*' (Jesserun d'Oliveira 1994). The nature of the Union is unclear. The German notion of a *Staatenverbund* is misleading because it is hardly translatable. The *Verbund* will be translated as *federation* or *confederation*, according to the political preferences of the translator. Most German constitutional lawyers are excellent in Latin but poor in English or French. But the nature of citizenship is not a draft for the future: 'Citizenship of the Union is hereby established.' The more uncertain the social roots of this European citizenship seem to be, the more the European legislator turned back to absolutist phrasing: '*car tel est notre plaisir*'.

Maastricht is more than a treaty and less than a constitution. Some observers think of the treaty as a constitution *in nuce*. The *in nuce* version is close to our recent constitutional experience. The American founding fathers wanted a constitution to be '*short and obscure*'. The development of the legal state and democracy turned to the target that a constitution should be '*long and clear*'. Constitutions after recent transformations (1970s in Southern Europe, 1990s in Eastern Europe) tended to bring about constitutions which were '*long and obscure*' (Beyme 1994).

The dramatic statement that European citizenship 'is hereby established' is less clear than many national constitutions. Is this wording sufficient to implement the rights and duties given to European citizens? Art. 8a provides possibilities to 'facilitate the exercise of the rights referred to in paragraph 1'. Increasingly national legislators distrust the implementing powers and ask for reports on satisfactory progress. Art. 8e of the Maastricht Treaty is no exception: 'The Commission shall report to the European Parliament' and other Community institutions: 'every three years on the application of these provisions'. Supervising institutions have become common in national legislations:

the *Ombudsman* of Art. 8d and Art. 138e is empowered with functions of supervision.

The Four Concepts of Citizenship in the Maastricht Agreement

What is the balance of the four concepts of citizenship in the Maastricht agreement?

1. The *legal state* is the most efficient part of the concept of citizenship. An eminent binational scholar, such as Dahrendorf (1990: 823), with considerable experience as a former member of the Commission of the European Community, once stated that he felt to be a quite 'unreconstructed Kantian' who believed that true constitutional patriotism was possible only when a unified law could be enforceable throughout a larger supranational territory. The literature agrees on the fact that the European Court of Justice is quickly progressing in this direction—even in many policy areas which are still the domain of national legal systems. Legal protection of citizens' and human rights is, however, hardly without lacunae. The less developed the implementing powers of the Union are, the more institutions are entrusted with protecting these rights. Normally systems with a strong adherence to the principle of *judicial review* avoid an *ombudsman* in order to avoid countervailing powers in this touchy area (the German military ombudsman is an exception to this rule). The German Constitutional Court rejected the ECJ's claim to exclusive *judicial Kompetenz-Kompetenz* and claimed in 1993 that the limits to Community law-making power was as much a matter of German constitutional law as it was a matter of Community Law (BVerfGE 89: 155 ff., here: 188). This doctrine is probably only the tip of a transnational iceberg hidden under the surface of European national states. Other courts remained, however, more silent because the people decided on Maastricht.

In systems which did not develop judicial review of legislation by a Constitutional Court, such as Denmark, the government had to formulate its reservations and did so most explicitly on the concept of citizenship: 'Citizenship of the Union is a political and legal concept which is entirely different from the concept of citizenship within the meaning of the Constitution of the Kingdom of Denmark and of the Danish legal system. Citizenship of the Union in no way in itself gives a national of another Member State the right to obtain Danish citizenship or any of the rights, duties, privileges, or advantages that are inherent in Danish citizenship.' This statement was blunt for a system not known for an illiberal policy of naturalization of citizens. The Edinburgh Summit tried to mitigate the conflict: 'The provisions of Part Two of the Treaty . . . do not in any way take the place of national citizenship.' The definition is, however, not watertight (Jesserun d'Oliveira 1994: 135). A number of rights are granted in order to take part in the public and political life of the member states.

This is especially true of the treaty's attempt to promote the *right to vote* and the right to stand as a candidate at *municipal elections* in the member state in which one resides (Art. 8b1). In the *European elections*, the non-citizens of member states shall be equalized with the native citizens (Art. 8b2). It is not by chance that the necessary regulations for implementing these provisions have not been agreed upon in due time.

In matters of European foreign policy, the treaty (Art. 8c) regarding the protection of rights of Community citizens is more explicit than regarding the implementation of internal rights in a case of conflict between the various layers of jurisdiction.

But even the fundamental human rights, though mentioned in many EEC and EU documents, are open to disagreement. Art. F2 of the Union Treaty states: 'The Union shall respect fundamental rights, as guaranteed by the European Conventions for the Protection of Human Rights and Fundamental Freedoms.' The additional clause reads: 'and as they result from the constitutional traditions common to the Member States, as general principles of Community Law'. It has correctly been noted (Jesserun d'Oliveira 1994: 133) that this Article would have merited a separate lettering. The casual mentioning causes misgivings and the traditions of the member states are divergent on this matter. Germany has a very restricted catalogue and hardly any social rights. Environmental values are emphasized, but included into the lower status of a '*Staatszielbestimmung*' (declaration on the goals of the state), a notion which might cause metaphysical horrors in an Anglo-Saxon tradition. Non-citizens of member states are granted the same rights—a correct application of the universalistic concept of human rights. But again, in the national legal systems this problem of wider inclusion is regulated in different ways and may cause conflict if applied.

Since the member states of the Community normally respect the fundamental rights—though Amnesty International denounces every year exceptions to this rule—only the primordial basic right of European citizens can be the cause of conflict: the right in Art. 8a to 'move and reside freely within the territory of the Member States'. The widespread abuse of mentioning restrictions in national constitutions is prolonged in the treaty: 'subject to the limitations and conditions laid down in this Treaty and by the measures adopted to give it effect'. But what is the right to move in Europe without the right to work? The treaty grants the 'Freedom of movement for workers shall be secured within the Community by the end of the transitional period at latest' (Art. 48). Not a right to work but a right to work in other countries is granted by this provision. But again, what is a right to move to work if there is no right to work? The different perceptions of social citizens' right will cause additional conflicts. Some countries included a right to work in their constitutions, such as Italy. Others, like Germany, found it more honest not to include it, well knowing that the state in a market society has little possibilities to enforce such a right. But again, the different national concepts of civil and social right are open to disputes among member states.

The legal aspects of citizenship are closely related to the national and ethnic dimensions of citizenship. *Recognition* in the sense of Nancy Fraser (1995) should not too schematically be opposed to *redistribution*. Every move towards *affirmative action* needs redistributive measures in support of legal 'recognition' of a claim. But recognition comes first. To what extent is the Union tolerant towards the minorities? The traditions again vary. Radicals who praise the republican notion of citizenship of the French Revolution tend to forget that this tradition is still responsible for banning any rather superficial deviation from the symbols of the '*nation une et indivisible*' in public schools. Most Germans, trained in a less democratic tradition, are more liberal than the French citizens and resent to a lesser extent the symbols of Muslim fundamentalism in school. To what extent can the legal system tolerate certain customs from countries in the Third World? Political philosophy drew the line somewhere in between 'circumcision of female children' and 'mitigating circumstances for grievous bodily harm' when kids from Africa are maltreated by their parents with scars as a tribal symbol (Parekh 1991: 201). We know, however, that all these borderlines are voluntaristic decisions.

Many optimists think that Europe promotes *multiculturalism*. In some respect, the internal migration is slight. The Union looks more similar to a *cartel of national states defending their ethnic homogeneity*. There is the danger that Union law does not promote multiculturalism and ethnic tolerance but at best promotes selective tolerance for those who belong to the club. The European *Rechtsstaat* is developing, but more by regulation and judicial review than by the creation of a consistent 'constitutional' framework. Some writers insist on the necessities of a constitution, as an orienting point for the attachment to a European legal state (Weidenfeld 1991), others urgently warn us to avoid a European constitution which raises expectations without being able to fulfil them (Grimm 1995: 51). Legal specialists are trained to disagree. But within the national states they would certainly agree that a constitution is essential for 'nation-building'.

2. The aspect of *national identity* is regulated more clearly in the provisions of Maastricht. German elites may dislike it, but Maastricht clearly decouples citizenship from *ethnos* or *Volk*. There is no European demos envisaged in terms of cultural and national homogeneity. Citizenship in Europe is set on the road of *constitutional patriotism*. The European Community requires a decoupling of the 'European peoplehood' from natural, organic, ontological categories such as *Volk*, nation, and even the state—so dear to many German lawyers.

There are no hints in the treaty that fears for the disappearance of *national demoi* are justified. Europe provides that citizens of national states are European citizens, not the other way around. This Swiss concept—in the relation of Cantons and the 'Confederation Helvétique'—is, however, inconsistent. It leaves the member states *to define the conditions of inclusion* of citizens. The German deviance from the liberal tradition of enlightenment with its *ius sanguinis* thereby is protected from change. Europe can only hope for the long-run effects of juridification tendencies inherent in the process of integration of modernization. *Multiple citizenship* seems to be a way out of the dilemma in the long run. The question of *loyalty* does no longer arise because a war between European countries is no longer conceivable (except between Greece and Turkey, but the latter will not be member of the EU very soon). Germany has a great aversion to multiple citizenship which is the consequence of its ontological concept of ethnic citizenship (Weiler et al. 1995: 22). Even without double citizenship the modern concept can only be *'critical citizenship'*. The ethnic foundation of citizenship, stemming from a rather paternalistic attitude of the rulers, was also meant to create uncritical emotionally bound citizens. This type of citizen cannot develop in Europe. As someone has noted ironically, 'one cannot love a market'. In spite of the citizenship rhetoric Europe remains predominantly a market. The Maastricht Treaty is full of provisions for a market. Only in this field it is clear and without major contradictions.

The corollary of inclusion is exclusion. Immigrés are excluded in many respects, except in matters of human rights. The immigration policies and the procedures of naturalization are still quite different in Europe, but since the Schengen agreement they converge in many European countries. Germany with its declaration of the *right to asylum*—partly undermined by recent constitutional amendments—is still formally unique. But Germany had to compensate for its constitutional goodwill declaration as a consequence of a dark historical past by cumbersome restrictive measures in the details of immigration policies. Most European countries see the necessity of creating an immigration law but remain reluctant to admit that they are immigration countries. Turning to immigration policies and undiscriminating quota systems according to the model of the USA, Australia, or Canada is debated as a way out of the predicament. Political elites discover that such provisions allow for a more controlled influx of immigrés who have to pass literacy tests than those countries which are criticized for their history of a *voelkisch* assimilation of minorities and immigrés (Weiler et al. 1995: 18). We should not overlook that criteria of cultural assimilation play a role in most immigration countries. *Multiculturalism* is rather the result of legal and illegal immigration than the goal of deliberate immigration policies. All European countries are far from the inclusionist view of the French revolutionary constitution (Art. 4) which stated that only one year of residence is necessary for acquiring citizenship. Marriage helps in many countries, to support elderly people helps in none. Adoption leads to citizenship for Third World kids, but normally below the age for the exercise of political citizen's rights.

The most important differences in the sectors of cultural and national identity lie in the provisions for acquiring political citizenship in various countries. For the first time in its history since the French Revolution, Germany is in the position to give up its *ius sanguinis* and to turn to more civil definitions of citizenship. Oddly enough, Israel has inherited from Germany the problem of abstract definitions of who is a Jew, accepting—so far—everybody born by a Jewish mother, even if he or she does not adhere to the Jewish religion and does not (yet) speak the Hebrew language.

European countries—without major influence from regulations in Brussels—came to a '*negative integration*' of citizens from EEC countries. Italians are no longer 'guest workers', as the German euphemism dubbed them. They belong to the lower bourgeoisie of the host country and they keep their ties to the home country, where they normally return after retirement. Citizens from Spain or Portugal are no longer considered as 'servant's nations' in France. There is hardly a problem with foreigners within the EU. There are only problems with migrants from the Maghreb countries and Turkey. Recent waves of migrations were caused by the erosion of Communism and by poverty in the Third World. These had little to do with the Community. But they strengthened exclusionist tendencies in all the European countries. Migration caused or reinforced the labelling approach towards the 'outs'.

The inclusion of foreigners into political—not social or cultural—citizenship tends to be easier in countries which were founded by émigrés. European countries continue to be governed by 'native' majorities to a much greater extent than the United States, Canada, or Australia. Prospects for an 'Americanization' of civic attitudes in Europe are dim (Walzer 1992: 237). Some writers (Münch 1993: 95) even speculate that the exclusion of foreigners will be an important instrument for building up a real sense of community in Europe. The enthusiasts for European citizenship should bear in mind that Europeans in the process of building up their citizenship might lose in cosmopolitism what they gained in Europeanhood.

3. The aspects of *democratic citizenship* show the most criticized shortcomings in the legitimation of the Union. The character of an international agreement and the division of powers which gives the Council of Ministers a strong veto position prevents full democracy. Many national states which tried to avoid full democracy with universal suffrage—among them the most liberal ones, such as Britain—lived through a long period of *parliamentarization*. Full democracy in many cases was not added before World War I. In the case of the European Union further parliamentarization would not even lead to parliamentary government, because the strongest institution cannot be ousted from office by a vote of no confidence in the European Parliament.

The European Union has democracy in the sense of its minimal condition: universal suffrage. But it is *segmented democracy*. As in the determination of European citizenship, each member state so far determines according to which electoral law this European right is implemented. The British Liberals long for a unified electoral law in Europe. But time has not yet come to make this possible without alienating the two major political forces in the country. The '*segmented integration*' of Europe is sometimes thought to be inevitable as long as no integrated parties and interest groups are developed (Lepsius 1993b). The integration of parliamentary groups in the European Parliament works. But the parties are so far without grass roots. As long as there is no unified electoral law, there are few incentives to change this. Interest groups can afford to work in a more segmented way. *Consociational* or *corporatist* *strategies* can overcome the deficiencies of integrated organizations.

The *right to petition* is certainly a political right of citizens (Arts. 8d, 1, 138d), but nobody will be able to sell this as a democratic right. The most autocratic monarchies knew the right to petition as the only right citizens had. The Russian word '*otkladyvat' v dolgiy ashchik*' (deposit into the long box in the wall of the Kremlin—figurative sense: to postpone without possible results) even today is a remainder of the language of Aesopus under conditions of autocracy.

The treaty is, however, more participatory than that. A new aspect of democratic rights in many post-war constitutions (Italy, Germany, France) was the insertion of the collective right to *mobilize in parties*. No country went as far as Germany. The democratic citizens' rights of participation in the German étatist tradition was conceived of as a more collective and state-oriented right. Germany thus paved the road for the development of publicly financed organizations which loosen their ties with society and become more and more part of the state apparatus. Only in Italy has this development of *partitocrazia* led to a major crisis. Nevertheless, the other European countries accepted the German hobby horse to praise the functions of parties (Art. 138 ff.).

Will this increase democratic citizenship throughout Europe? Confronting constitutional poetry with social reality shows that the European parties are in a predicament: the most likely scenario is the continuation of the *transnational* party systems. In Denmark the model of a *split-level party system* was visible, the desired result of a *truly European party system* is not likely to develop, unless a unified electoral system is created. But it is not sure that this will have the required result. Some analysts (Andeweg 1995: 69) anticipate the American split of Federalists and Antifederalists with the consequence that the *states' rights parties* might be stronger in Europe than in the early periods of the USA.

Whether the Union develops into a federation, a confederation, or something in between which the Germans dubbed '*Staatenverbund*': full democratization is hardly possible. All confederations in history have passed through a stage where *amicabilis compositio* of elites dominated. In certain areas *conso-ciational strategies* may be completed by *corporatist strategies*, based on the alliance of national governments and transnational interest groups. But this would hardly be less elitist.

Federalism contains certain limitations to democracy. In the nineteenth century it was a commonplace that democracy and even parliamentary government is not compatible with federalism. Unequal representation gives privileges to Luxembourg and disadvantages to Germany. Germany renounced additional representation after its reunification—for good reasons. But will this wisdom continue to exist in forthcoming generations?

The *subnational opposition of regions* is pressing for unholy alliances with the institutions of the EU. The Committee of the Regions presses for develop-ment into a Third Chamber. This new line of representation may increase grass-roots democracy, but will complicate the national decision-making process concerning Europe (Hooghe 1995).

Judicial review is another limit to the majoritarian concept of democratic citizenship inevitable in a confederation. The European Union was meant to develop according to the rules of *American dual federalism*. Experience shows that it rather developed in the direction of the *German model: intergovern-mental policy making* and strengthening the executives at all levels (Scharpf 1994: 152). *Over-coordination* in some policy areas does not exclude *under-coordination* in others and will certainly call for more *juridification* in the representative bodies.

The democratic deficits may diminish. But under normal evolutionary conditions they can never disappear quickly enough to meet rising expecta-tions. This gap between the institutional possibilities of democratic citizen-ship and the rising expectations of democratic citizens is probably the strongest argument against the premature introduction of a European consti-tution (Grimm 1995: 51).

The radical concept of democratic citizenship with a high degree of mobil-ization sometimes expects further progress in democratic integration from *plebiscitarian instruments* of decision making. The prospects for such a scenario are dim. The national experiences—especially in Italy (cf. above) do not show convincingly that a system's change is secured by referenda. The referenda of the Maastricht Treaty in various European countries fostered the fear of the political elites that they might wreck the whole European project (Franklin 1995: 115). Maastricht was accepted by a narrow margin, even in France. The more people feel affected by the decisions in Brussels and the more unpopular governments take resort to European integration in order to solve unsolvable domestic problems, the more citizens of the national states are unsatisfied with a Community which gives them still less influence than in their respective national systems.

4. The reading of the Maastricht Treaty leaves the impression that it is

aimed at creating a new form of a *welfare state*. In the long run this is important. New members such as Sweden, Finland, or Austria tried to lure their citizens into the Union by promising at least diminishing prices for consumer
goods, since most citizens are not interested in the freedom of movement for
labour, capital, transport, and services.

The European citizen, however, is predominantly constituted by elements
which have no importance for the life of the large majority of European
people: right to move and to reside in other countries. The social rights of citizens are formulated in a rather conditional way: 'In order to improve employment opportunities for workers in the internal market and to contribute
thereby to raising the standard of living, a *European Social Fund* is hereby
established' (Art. 123). It will be administered by the Commission, with the
assistance of the Economic and Social Committee, the accord of which is
required (Art. 125). In hardly any other field is the gap between promises and
benefits so great as in the sphere of the expectations of social citizens.

The Community is fostering *equality* in many fields. But there is no such
clause, as in the German federation, which speaks of requirements of protecting 'the *homogeneity of the conditions of life* exceeding the territory of one
Land' (Art. 72.2), a clause listed among the provisions for the concurring
competences of the Länder in legislation. The Union has hardly the competences (Majone 1990) neither exclusive nor concurring, to create the homogeneity of life conditions throughout Europe. But terminological
compromises aim in this direction: as 'federalism' was impossible as a catch-
word and was substituted by 'subsidiarity'—immediately interpreted by the
European Parliament as a first step towards federalism—'homogeneity' of life
conditions was smoothed down to 'make possible . . . (the) *harmonization . . .
of the standard of living*' (Art. 117).

The Maastricht Treaty does not contain an exhaustive list of social rights
which would not have got the agreement of Germany and Britain. The Latin
countries are less opposed to exuberant social promises according to their
constitutional traditions. Spain pushed the specification of European citizenship when the Rome Meeting—in preparation of the Maastricht summit—
was being prepared. The result is a catalogue of rights derived from citizenship
scattered throughout the treaty without any formal coherence and frequently
under the *clausula rebus 'non' sic stantibus*, because it was conceived as a
dynamic concept. It was linked with hopes that the dynamics of integration
would soon overcome the fragmented integration of the *status quo*. Most of
the rights derived from the concept of citizenship are truisms and reformulate
existing laws. Others are granted under the provision that integration rapidly
progresses which is by no means the only alternative of history. The document
is—and how could it have been otherwise—a compromise of sweet sounding
formulas. Each country smuggled certain formulas into the text. A coherence
from this lobbying method of drafting something similar to a constitution

was hardly to be expected. The rights of social citizens are considerable—but they have to be confronted with the social realities. For decades, the leftists polemicized against the capitalist 'SuperMarket' of the multinational corporations. Only in the era of Maastricht did the politics of fusions of enterprises on the European level become true in a larger scale. There are social rights— but they meet with insufficient possibilities of control from the Union. There will be no unified wages policy and collective bargaining in the foreseeable future (Joerges 1991: 283). This will probably lead to the unsatisfactory result that some rights of social citizens in Europe to move (capital, technologies, commodities) will be privileged at the expense of others (work). First signs of social unrest are visible in countries such as Italy and France. The easiest way out is to blame the Federal Bank in Frankfurt for domestic economic problems. But these ideological strategies may comfort citizens of some national states. It will not strengthen the sense of Europeanhood.

Conclusion

Citizenship became a battle-cry. Sometimes it was the flag under which the opposition against neo-liberal restrictions of local democracy, functional democracy, and co-determination, and the dismantling of the welfare state gathered (Held 1991: 19). Citizenship suffers from its popularity. Lawyers remind us that the new fashion tends to blur the limits of 'man', 'citizen', 'bourgeois', or 'worker' and confuses the binding force of various clauses subsumed under the general notion of citizenship (Ferrajoli 1993). The Maastricht Treaty promotes this confusion in an almost irresponsible way, because it raises expectations which the Union can hardly fulfil within the limits of its competences.

What is worse is that most of the scattered codified rights are neither new nor are they citizen's rights. Most of them apply to citizens of countries outside the Community as well. The bulk of the social rights which are a privilege of European citizens are no rights proper. They are *good will declarations* of the Union to act in this direction within the limits of its funds and competences. In German terminology and hierarchy of norms: they are a gigantic enumeration of *Staatsziele* (goals of the state) without the existence of a state.

The Union is still predominantly a market and most of its freedoms to move are of interest only for property and commodity owners. Property rights, however, are not as fundamental as other human rights—in spite of the Lockean tradition. After the collapse of Communism, however, the Maastricht countries may think of property rights as primordial because most of the clauses in the treaty deal with the conditions of free movement of the factors of production (capital, work, human capital, technological innovation).

Lawyers do not have the last word. But their efforts to clarify the nature of various citizens' rights is essential for their transformation into social reality. But a meaningful concept of citizenship cannot be satisfied with an enumeration of four pillars of citizenship in modern society.

Citizenship in modern society is directed towards equality: legally, everybody can cooperate with everybody else. This cooperation—even in a Common Market which pretends to be a political union—is not strictly determined by economic considerations or differences in political power. Citizenship shares with markets and political communities the *medium of discourse*. Some analysts (Meehan 1993: 152) hope for an appeal of the right of citizenship, at least for the British migrating middle-class worker who will 'enjoy a sense of Europeanness because infrastructures, amenities, and education are treated more seriously on the continent as a component of citizenship'. But this includes the precaution that a sense of Europeanness and loyalty is hardly the automatic product of social rights and amenities. The radical republican tradition of political citizenship has always emphasized the *civil religion*. It did not exist, but it had to be created by education (Heater 1990: 203).

Radical communitarians advocate the new sense of civic engagement and virtue. Even this much ridiculed notion—allowed at best to political philosophers, such as Hannah Arendt, in the perception of the behavioural and analytical mainstream of political science—made its way back into the discussion. But the history of the French Revolution taught us that propaganda for *virtues* is always in danger of overshadowing the rights involved in the notion of *citizenship*.

There is a more serious objection to the dreams of the 'after virtue school'. It insists on the fact that the process of individualization leads to the spread of different *senses of identity*—though there is not yet a substitute for the national state (Horseman and Marshall 1994: 263 f.). But when global communication transcends the limits of states (van Steenbergen 1994: 156), there is little hope that it will stop at some borders which do not even encompass the whole of Europe. The Union even in the first decade of the third millennium will be restricted from the Atlantic to the Bug—or from 'Brest to Brest'.

More convincing than historical analogies are theoretical discussions about the impossibility of spreading one civic virtue in a differentiated society. This is probably the only point on which all shades of system's theory agree—from the Parsonians to Luhmann. The autopoietic school would consider the propagation of virtue as an old European non-sense, without any steering function because of the undercomplexity of its concepts. The Parsonians would agree that *systemic integration* by any subsystem, political, moral, or religious, is impossible. But citizenship has the function of *social integration* which Parsons opposed to the outdated systemic integration (Münch 1994: 384).

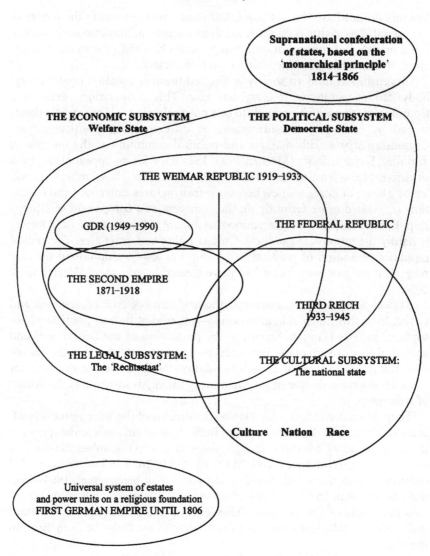

Fig. 4.1. Typology of the aspects of citizenship

Citizenship is a kind of *symbolic uniting of various roles* citizens perform in the different functional subsystems of society. Even in European politics we should not differentiate too schematically *symbolic politics* from *efficient policy making*. Both are always combined in any political decision in various mixes of the elements. But European citizenship is still very close to the pole of symbolic politics. It needs further elaboration to become a flag around which the integrationists in Europe can gather.

REFERENCES

ANDEWEG, R. (1995). 'The Reshaping of National Party Systems'. *West European Politics*, 3: 58–78.

ANDREWS, G. (ed.) (1991). *Citizenship*. London: Lawrence & Wishart.

BARTOLINI, S., and D'ALIMONTE, R. (1995). *Maggioritario ma non troppo*. Bologna: Il Mulino.

BEYME, K. (1994). 'Die Renaissance der Integrationstheorie: Zentripetale Kräfte und funktionale Sachzwänge in der Maastricht-Runde der Europäischen Einigung', in V. Eichener and H. Voelzkow (eds.), *Europäische Integration und verbandliche Interessenvermittlung*. Marburg: Metropolis, 27–44.

BOGDANDY, A. (1993). *Die Europäische Option*. Baden-Baden: Nomos.

DAHRENDORF, R. (1990). 'Die Sache mit der Nation'. *Merkur*, 44: 823–34.

DEHOUSSE, R. (ed.) (1994). *Europe after Maastricht: An Ever Closer Union?* Munich: Law Books in Europe.

DUGUIT, L., et al. (1952). *Les Constitutions et les principales lois politiques de la France depuis 1789*. Paris: Pichon.

EDER, K. (1985). *Geschichte als Lernprozeß? Zur Pathogenese politischer Modernität in Deutschland*. Frankfurt: Suhrkamp.

FEHER, F., and HELLER, A. (1994). *Biopolitics*. Aldershot: Avebury.

FERRAJOLI, L. (1993). 'Cittadenanza e diritti fondamentali'. *Teoria e politica*, 9: 63–76.

FRANKLIN, M. N., et al. (1995). 'Referendum Outcomes and Trust in Government: Public Support for Europe in the Wake of Maastricht'. *West European Politics*, 31: 101–17.

FRASER, N. (1995). 'From Redistribution to Recognition? Dilemmas of Justice in a Post-Socialist Age'. *New Left Review*, 212: 68–93.

GIESEN, B. (1993). *Die Intellektuellen und die Nation: Eine deutsche Achsenzeit*. Frankfurt: Suhrkamp.

GRIMM, D. (1995). 'Braucht Europa eine Verfassung?' *Vortrag gehalten in der Carl-Friedrich-von-Siemens-Stiftung am 19. Januar 1994*. Munich: Carl-Friedrich-von-Siemens-Stiftung.

HABERMAS, J. (1992). *Faktizität und Geltung: Beiträge zur Diskurstheorie des Rechts und des demokratischen Rechtsstaats*. Frankfurt: Suhrkamp.

HEATER, D. (1990). *Citizenship: The Civic Ideal in World History, Politics and Education*. London: Longman.

HELD, D. (1991). 'Between State and Civil Society: Citizenship', in G. Andrews (ed.), *Citizenship*. London: Lawrence & Wishart, 19–25.

HELLER, A., and PUNTSCHER RIEKMANN, S. (eds.) (1996). *Biopolitics: The Politics of Body, Race and Nature*. Aldershot: Avebury.

HOOGHE, L. (1995). 'Subnational Mobilisation in the European Union'. *West European Politics*, 3: 175–98.

HORSEMAN, M., and MARSHALL, A. (1994). *After the Nation State: Citizens, Tribalism and the New World Disorder*. New York: Harper Collins.

HRADIL, S., and IMMERFALL, S. (eds.) (1997). *Die westeuropäischen Gesellschaften im Vergleich*. Opladen: Leske + Budrich.

IONESCU, G. (1984). *Politics and the Pursuit of Happiness*. London: Longman.

JESSERUN D'OLIVEIRA, H. U. (1994). 'European Citizenship: Its Meaning, its Potential', in R. Dehousse (ed.), *Europe after Maastricht: An Ever Closer Union?* Munich: Law Books in Europe, 126–48.

JOERGES, C. (1991). 'Markt ohne Staat? Die Wirtschaftsverfassung der Gemeinschaft und die regulative Politik', in R. Wildenmann (ed.), *Staatswerdung Europas?* Baden-Baden: Nomos, 225–83.

KIRCHHOF, P. (1992). 'Der deutsche Staat im Prozeß der europäischen Integration', in J. Isensee and P. Kirchhof (eds.), *Handbuch des Staatsrechts der Bundesrepublik Deutschland*, Bd.VII. Heidelberg: Springer, 855–87.

LEPSIUS, M. R. (1990). 'Nation und Nationalismus in Deutschland', in M. R. Lepsius (ed.), *Interessen, Ideen und Institutionen*. Opladen: Westdeutscher Verlag, 232–46.

—— (1993*a*). 'Die Europäische Gemeinschaft und die Zukunft des Nationalstaates', in M. Lepsius (ed.), *Demokratie in Deutschland*. Göttingen: Vandenhoeck & Ruprecht, 249–64.

—— (1993*b*). 'Nationalstaat oder Nationalitätenstaat als Modell für die Weiterentwicklung der Europäischen Gemeinschaft', in M. Rainer Lepsius (ed.), *Demokratie in Deutschland*. Göttingen: Vandenhoeck & Ruprecht, 265–88.

LINDBERG, L. W., and SCHEINGOLD, S. A. (1970). *Europe's Would-Be Polity: Patterns of Change in the European Community*. Englewood Cliffs, NJ: Prentice Hall.

MAJONE, G. (1990). 'Preservation of Cultural Diversity in a Federal System: The Role of the Regions', in M. Tushnet (ed.), *Comparative Constitutional Federalism*. New York: Greenwood, 67–76.

MARSHALL, T. H. (1976). 'Citizenship and Social Class', in T. H. Marshall, *Class, Citizenship and Social Development*. Westport, Conn.: Greenwood, 67–122.

MEEHAN, E. (1993). *Citizenship and the European Community*. London: Sage.

MÜNCH, R. (1993). *Das Projekt Europa: Zwischen Nationalstaat, regionaler Autonomie und Weltgesellschaft*. Frankfurt: Suhrkamp.

—— (1994). 'Politik und Nichtpolitik: Politische Steuerung als schöpferischer Prozeß'. *Kölner Zeitschrift für Soziologie und Sozialpsychologie*, 46: 381–405.

PAREKH, B. (1991). 'British Citizenship and Cultural Difference', in G. Andrews (ed.), *Citizenship*. London: Lawrence & Wishart, 183–204.

ROCHE, M. (1992). *Rethinking Citizenship: Welfare, Ideology and Change in Modern Society*. Cambridge: Polity.

SARTORI, G. (1994). *Comparative Constitutional Engineering*. London: Macmillan.

SCHARPF, F. W. (1994). *Optionen des Föderalismus in Deutschland und Europa*. Frankfurt: Campus.

STEENBERGEN, B. VAN (ed.) (1994). *The Condition of Citizenship*. London: Sage.

TAYLOR, C. (1989). 'Cross-Purposes: The Liberal Communitarian Debate', in Nancy L. Rosenblum (ed.), *Liberalism and the Moral Life*. Cambridge, Mass.: Harvard University Press, 159–68.

Times Mirror (1991). *The Pulse of Europe: A Survey of Political and Social Values*. Washington, DC: Times Mirror for the People and the Press.

TURNER, B. S. (1994). 'Postmodern Culture, Modern Citizens', in B. Steenbergen (ed.), *The Condition of Citizenship*. London: Sage, 153–68.

VOGEL, U., and MORAN, M. (eds.) (1991). *The Frontiers of Citizenship*. London: MacMillan.

WALZER, M. (1992). 'Vereinigte Staaten von Europa?', in M. Walzer (ed.), *Zivile Gesellschaft und amerikanische Demokratie*. Berlin: Rotbuch, 237–40.

WEIDENFELD, W. (ed.) (1991). *Wie Europa verfaßt sein soll*. Gütersloh: Bertelsmann Stiftung.

WEILER, J., et al. (1995). 'European Democracy and its Critique'. *West European Politics*, 3: 5–39.

WESTLE, B. (1994). 'Traditionalismus, Verfassungspatriotismus und Postnationalismus im vereinigten Deutschland', in O. Niedermayer and K. Beyme (eds.), *Politische Kultur in Ost- und Westdeutschland*. Berlin: Akademie Verlag, 43–76.

5

The Scope of Citizenship in a Democratized European Union

From Ecomonic to Political to Social and Cultural?

Philippe C. Schmitter

Citizenship has recently become a much discussed, if still unresolved, concept. It seems to begin with the acquisition of a status or condition, protected by law, that grants to a select group—usually native born (*ius soli*) or genetically correct (*ius sanguinis*) adults—a general equality of opportunity and treatment with respect to a (varied) bundle of rights and obligations. It becomes a practice or process whereby those who have that status make use of it—politically, legally, administratively, economically, and socially—to reduce their uncertainties and satisfy their interests. Presumably, it terminates in a result or product which is, legitimacy, i.e. the integration of citizens in conformity to the norms and practices of the polity that granted them the status in the first place.

Needless to say, in the real world, there are lots of potential disjunctures in this scenario. The distribution of the status may be too narrow or the content of the rights too restricted to protect citizens from arbitrary treatment, social discrimination, or economic exploitation. The beneficiaries of the process may exploit their favoured status to increase the uncertainty of others and/or to satisfy their interests at the expense of the resident aliens ('denizens') who are excluded. The outcome of the process may not always be to generate a single sense of loyalty or community, but might even convince some citizens that another regime or polity could offer them greater security and satisfaction. For it is important to stress that the granting of citizenship logically involves a complex set of choices about inclusion and exclusion, and was closely linked historically to the development of national consciousness and the emergence of the nation state as the dominant form of political organization in Europe.

In a justly famous essay, T. H. Marshall (1950) suggested that the content of citizenship has evolved over time. As he reconstructed the process for Great Britain, initial concessions by authorities provided a lever that could be wielded to demand others and these, in turn, lead to further claims for equal treatment. It began in the eighteenth century with the struggle for equal rights and obligations before the law, expanded in the nineteenth century to cover equal formal participation in political life, especially through universal suffrage, and in the twentieth century shifted its attention to equal opportunity to share in the country's material and cultural heritage, especially through state provision of welfare.[1] Marshall's sequential account is logically satisfying, but it is certainly not historically generalizable or functionally imperative. Both France and Germany took rather different routes to reach, more-or-less, the same bundle of rights and obligations in the end.

It is also not clear from Marshall's analysis whether the process of citizenship has terminated with the attainment of the contemporary welfare state, or whether that merely places new levers in the hands of more actors demanding further extensions of equal rights (and, to a lesser extent, equal obligations). Ralf Dahrendorf, for one, sees a serious danger in pushing its principles into new domains:

the extension of citizenship has reached in recent years, the apparently insurmountable walls of ascribed status. Men and women are not merely to be given the suffrage and equal wages for equal work, but they are supposed to be treated as equals in all respects; society is to be arranged in such a way that the differences can be ignored (1974: 683)

From his account, it is not clear whether he regards such an eventuality as a social impossibility or rejects it because of the state intervention it would require. But what if the next Marshallian extension did not involve empowering those who are already national citizens with new rights and obligations in existing polities, but transposing some of those that they already have and creating some new ones at a different, more encompassing level of aggregation, i.e. what if the next stage involved the status/condition, process/practice, and eventual result/product of European citizenship?

Facing the 'Spectre' of Euro-Citizenship

The Treaty of European Union already does this formally in its Arts. 8, 8a, 8b, 8c, 8d, and 8e, which outline an initial set of rights.[2] The last of these even invites the Council of Ministers 'acting unanimously' and only on a proposal from the Commission and only after consultation with the European Parliament to strengthen or to add to this list in the future. But what could the EU do to further empower its citizens that is not already better and more securely provided by its respective member states? In order to do this, we first have to look a bit more closely at the concept of citizenship itself.

Rogers Brubaker (1989) has recently laid out for us the six 'membership norms' that he claims define the ideal-typical conception of citizenship. According to this model, membership should be:

(1) unitary, i.e. all holders of the status should have full rights and obligations;

(2) sacred, i.e. citizens must be willing to make sacrifices for the state community that grants them the status;

(3) national, i.e. membership must be based on a community that is simultaneously political and cultural;

(4) democratic, i.e. citizens should be entitled to participate significantly in the business of rule and access to citizenship should be open to all residents so that, in the long run, residence in the community and citizenship in it will coincide;

(5) unique, i.e. each citizen should belong to one and only one political community;

(6) consequential, i.e. citizenship must entail important social and political privileges that distinguish its holders from non-citizens.

These six normative criteria could be applied, *mutatis mutandis,* to any efforts at 'citizenizing' the Euro-polity. Even so, the potential reformer should tread cautiously, since, as Brubaker himself notes, 'this model of citizenship is largely vestigial. That it survives is due less to its own normative force that to the lack of a coherent and persuasive alternative. It is, moreover, significantly out of phase with the contemporary realities of state-membership' (Brubaker 1989: 5). Moreover, I propose to add a seventh criteria which I presume to have been implicit in Brubaker's list, but which deserves to be discussed (and questioned) explicitly:

(7) individual, i.e. citizenship is an attribute that can only be possessed and exercised by individual human beings, although adult parents may be considered to be acting in lieu of their children and, hence, for the family as a collective unit.

With these seven criteria and Brubaker's warning in mind, let us then evaluate what might be involved in developing European citizenship.

Unitary

Here, the ideal normative imperative is that the status of 'citizen of the European Union' should be general, as well as equal. In principle, no adult person (or, as we shall see, no recognized organization) should be subject to only some of its rights and obligations and none should enjoy special treatment. In practice, this would mean retaining in the strictest sense, the acquis communautaire such that all member states and all citizens of those states would have identical rights and obligations.

Now this is precisely what is not likely to happen if either a consortial or a condominial fate awaits the EU (Schmitter 1996). In both cases (with different degrees of freedom), members will be enabled to choose from different packages of rights and obligations—and the impact of this will extend *a fortiori* to their citizens. For example, freedom of movement and establishment could vary over time and perhaps across professions or issue arenas; the right of individuals or firms to transfer funds or to open anonymous bank accounts may not be the same for everyone; some member states might even grant all citizens of other EU countries resident in their territories full voting rights, others might restrict it to the present objective of voting only in local elections; a self-selected 'social democratic' subset of countries could move towards full equivalence in their social security and health insurance systems—even establishing common pension funds and budgetary arrangements—while another 'neo-liberal' subset could even be dismantling their social safety nets and privatizing their health care systems—*et ainsi de suite.* All would depend on the pattern of future treaty adhesions, as it does now for Euro-citizens depending on whether their respective states have signed such documents as the Schengen agreement or demanded derogations from such specific obligations as the Monetary Union or the Social Charter.

Sacred

This principle has already been considerably attenuated for individuals at the national level. Not only has citizenship been somewhat 'secularized', at least in the western part of Europe, by the decline in militant nationalism and rigidly ethnic definitions of collective identity, but the 'heavy' and 'mystical' obligations historically linked to it have also declined. With the abolition of military conscription and militia-type armies in several countries, individuals are no longer required to die for their nation or state.[3] The various symbolic allegiances expected of citizens, e.g. flag saluting and anthem singing, have become increasingly ritualistic[4], and one hears less that classic slogan of unreflective national allegiance: 'My country, right or wrong!'

All this bodes well for an even less sacred (and, hence, more attenuated) conception of Euro-citizenship. Individuals and organizations would have a common obligation to obey the law, especially the supremacy of EU law as interpreted by the European Court of Justice. They would agree to transfer a (small) proportion of their taxes to EU institutions, although their net contributions might differ considerably depending on the bundle of functions chosen or the effect of *juste retour*. They should be willing to help others in time of emergency, treat fellow Europeans with respect and tolerance in their increasingly frequent exchanges, and to be prepared to redistribute some benefits or make concessions in the name of solidarity and the eventual social cohesion of Europe as a whole. That last item is, of course, the most difficult because the territorial and functional parameters of that unit are not yet known and the internal variation within these parameters in terms of development levels, language use, cultural norms, and political tendencies is vastly greater than the variation contained within any of its member states.

What is still far from clear is the role that the EU (or any 'affiliated' regional organization) will eventually play with regard to collective security and defence policy. Historically, the obligation to serve in the defense of one's country and the common experiences which have ensued from this (at least, for males) have been extremely important in the development of a sense of common fate and shared sacrifice which, in turn, contributed to cementing the tie between state membership and national identity. Should the EU move in this direction, not only would it have to acquire far more 'statelike' properties than it currently has in order to coordinate and finance such a collective effort, but also it would be very likely to generate a more sacred (and perhaps controversial) relationship with 'its' citizens. This would be the case even if, as has been happening in the member states, recruitment to the armed forces involved would be purely voluntary, selective, and professional. There is nothing like the experience—direct or vicarious—of combating a common enemy to feed the flames of sacredness.[5]

National

Nowhere have the strict principles of citizenship diminished more than on this item. It is no longer so preposterous to describe oneself as 'a citizen of the world' or, at least, of something beyond the nation state. Admittedly, the Eurobarometer data on public opinion do not show any monotonic tendency towards an increasing sense of 'feeling European' or of being 'a citizen of Europe'—indeed, this personal identification has decreased rather than increased in the aftermath of the Single European Act and the Treaty of European Union.[6] Nevertheless, the sentiment is much more prevalent among younger people and could pick up and even accumulate across generations in the future.

More to the point, the act of acquiring citizenship used to imply the joining of a coherent, well-defined national community with its own homogeneous culture—and, of course, of only being allowed to join one such community. In many countries, this involved a lengthy and demanding 'apprenticeship' in national laws and mores.[7] First, foreigners were made into natives and then—and only then—were they granted citizen status. Indeed, naturalized second-generation immigrants were often said to behave 'more like Americans than the Americans'. Nowadays, those becoming citizens can insist that they be allowed to retain their culture of origin and not be thrown into the 'melting pot'. They may even legitimately demand that the state of which they have become a citizen should subsidize and protect their subcultures from discrimination and attenuation. In short, citizenship for individuals is no longer an assurance of membership in a correspondingly unique national culture.[8]

But how far can this go? Is it possible to draw enough personal satisfaction out of belonging to a 'community' that does not have a common ethnic, language, religion, mores, or lifestyle? Would this not be so attenuated a sense of membership that appeals for sacrifice or solidarity would fail to invoke any response—much less one that would allow the 'supra-nation' to respond as a unit to an external crisis or redistribute benefits consensually within its internal borders?[9]

Inversely, why should individuals (and, for that matter, organizations) in the Euro-polity have to be 'nationals' in some sense in order to act like citizens? Why could they not be loyal to a common set of institutions and political/legal principles rather than to some mystical charismatic founder or set of mythologized ancestors? Why could Renan's *plébiscite de tous les jours* not be about rights and procedures in the present, rather than sacrifices and glories of the past?[10]

That, it seems to me, is the major issue. Not whether the eventual Euro-polity will be able to reproduce on an enlarged scale the same intensity of collective sentiment that was once characteristic of its member nation states, but whether it can produce an encompassing system of stable and peaceful political relations without such a passionately shared identity or community of fate. Admittedly, this places a heavy burden on interest calculation and instrumental reason at a time when it is more fashionable to presume the rising importance of collective enthusiasms and consummatory values. And admittedly, there are several cases out there of pluri-national polities that have recently broken up or are currently being threatened with secession, seemingly in defiance of rational interest and confirmation of passionate belief. If, as some believe, the post-industrial, postmodern condition necessarily entails precisely such a shift from the rational to the emotional, then, the very notion of citizenship in a non-nation would be oxymoronic. If, as I am inclined to believe, this condition is not so constraining, then, non-national citizenship may not be such a far-fetched possibility. Indeed, it may become a commonplace in the future.

Democratic

This is the most crucial principle from the perspective of this essay. For the EU to succeed in regaining its momentum and re-establishing its legitimacy, its member states will have to agree upon reforms that not only make its institutions function more effectively, but also make its rulers more accountable to its citizenry. In the traditional conception of citizenship, the way of doing this is to increase the political participation of adult individuals—by granting them the right to vote in contested elections, to present themselves as candidates for representative positions, to form and join associations, to speak out publicly and petition authorities for redress, to consult and be consulted on matters of policy and even—in direct democracies—to be physically present and decide on all issues binding on the community. A secondary concern is openness or transparency, i.e. rendering the conditions under which binding public choices are made accessible to more actors and, most particularly, to those who had been previously excluded or discriminated against.

This is not the place for a disquisition on the increased impoverishment of individual participation in the democracies of EU member states. In almost all of them, voter abstention has increased. Trade unions have lost members. Traditional parties have lost militants and core voters. Individuals identify less and less with a particular party. And the reputation of politicians is at an all-time low. Nor is there space for a discussion of the increased opaqueness of national public policy making under the influence of the sheer complexity of the problems they are required to deal with and the consequent role that technocratic expertise plays in their resolution. The German term, *Öffentlichkeit*, as developed by Jürgen Habermas (1990), captures a good deal of the dilemma. Under ideal conditions, democracies should arrive at their decisions through a process of transparent disclosure and deliberation in which citizens—collective as well as individual—restrict their actions and positions to those that are publicly visible and defensible. In actual practice, organized subgroups of citizens use their privileged resources to hire specialists to represent their particular interests and these professional representatives, in turn, collude with rulers to arrive in less than public ways at arrangements which are subsequently proclaimed to be 'in the public interest'. It should be noted that some theories of democratic citizenship would go a good deal further than merely ensuring the opportunity for participation and openness. These would insist that individuals and the organizations they form be themselves 'internally democratic'. The former should be respectful of authority, other-regarding, tolerant, and willing to compromise, i.e. individuals should have a 'civic culture'. Their parties, associations, and movements should be not only all of the above but also conduct competitive elections for their leaders, guarantee the rights of minority factions in their midst, and faithfully keep their commitments with members and authorities! Needless to say, national polities have, by and large, given up on insisting on internal democracy. The capacity for indoctrinating their citizens with a singular conception of civic values and for monitoring the internal politics of their representative organizations is simply too limited—and the effort to do either would conflict with other democratic rights and practices.

What forms of participation and *Öffentlichkeit* can the EU possibly offer its citizens that would not compete with or displace those that already exist in the member states? Recognizing that national citizens have been reducing their levels of participation and that most national polities have become more secretive and less transparent, is it at all likely that the emerging Euro-polity could do anything to reverse such anti-democratic trends? Of course, the EU has already attempted to do some things for individuals. Direct elections for the European Parliament since 1979 was supposed to produce more parti-cipation—and has had very little effect other than revealing that citizens are much more preoccupied with exploiting them to send 'messages of disgruntlement' to their national politicians.[11] Moreover, these elections are even losing their appeal for this purpose: voter abstention in them has grown monotonically in almost all member countries (Reif 1985). The TEU broke new ground by enfranchising residents of other EU member states to vote and run as candidates in local elections—which could be the first step in extend-ing the right to all Euro-citizens to vote in all elections in the constituencies where they permanently reside, regardless of their national citizenship.

This very same treaty reaffirmed the rights of individuals to petition the European Parliament and created an Ombudsman office at the EU level.[12] This person has finally been chosen after a lengthy squabble and it remains to be seen whether he will be successful in opening up a new conduit for indi-vidual access. This same treaty also pledged to make the proceedings of vari-ous EU institutions more 'transparent'. If initial reaction to a timid effort during the (Belgian?) presidency to publicize the discussions and voting behaviour in the Council of Ministers is any portent, it seems doubtful that much will be accomplished at this level in the future (Lodge 1994). The Commission, par contre, has made greater progress along these lines, although some of its initial public relations efforts have been widely ridiculed (Lodge 1994, 1995).

Of course, since its very foundation the Euro-polity has distinctively privi-leged the participation of functional interest associations—especially those organized by business interests at a European level—in its deliberations. It has even encouraged the formation and subsidized the activities of many such organizations—without, however, much success in creating the stable Euro-corporatist arrangements they desired (Schmitter and Streeck 1991; Traxler and Schmitter 1994, 1995). The informal system of representation that has emerged is much more pluralist (multiple, non-hierarchic, overlapping, and voluntaristic) in nature and manifestly skewed to favour the interests of busi-ness. The formal Economic and Social Council with its officially nominated members representing business, labour, and 'other' interests has proven to be utterly ineffectual since its founding in the Treaty of Rome.

More recently, both the Commission and the Parliament have gotten around to registering and regulating the associations and movements that lobby them, although they insist that, in so doing, they have no intention of creating a privileged—much less a monopolistic—set of organizational citizens or of imposing strict criteria of representativeness upon them. The register will be open to all and access will be, at least formally, equal. No effort will even be made to favour those which are distinctively European in scope, as opposed to those which represent local, provincial, or national interests and passions (McLaughlin and Greenwood 1995).

Which brings up the issue of participation by and openness to yet another set of democratic constituencies: the territorial subunits of national member polities. By its very nature as the product of an international treaty, the EU was created exclusively by existing sovereign states. Their Länder, regioni, provinces, estados autonómicos, municipalities, etc. enjoyed no special status. If they were interested in participating, the only channel that seemed to be open to them was to pass through their respective national governments. Nevertheless (and, in some cases, despite considerable resistance by these governments), these subnational regions and cities gradually established their own structures of representation—to the extent that almost fifty of them currently have quasi-embassies in Brussels (Marks et al. 1996). Again, the TEU took a modest step in a more democratic direction when it created a consultative Comité des Régions, leaving it however to the national governments to establish the criteria for which units would be represented and how they would be chosen.

All this does indicate some effort to address the twin issues of participation and openness, even if the channels that have been created so far either lead to relatively powerless institutions or remain highly skewed in terms of the citizens that have effective access to them. Certainly, none seems to have seized the imagination of the public or to have dramatically changed the accountability of EU authorities. Future increases in the political role of the European Parliament and possible changes in the system for electing MEPs might improve the situation, but are unlikely to transform it substantially.

Unique

This is a quality that presently seems almost anachronistic at the individual level and would definitely have to be abrogated in the development of Euro-citizenship for both individuals and organizations. Many persons now have dual national citizenships without this causing great confusion or corruption. Even resident foreigners (denizens) who formerly were denied the right to organize and petition—often on the alleged grounds that this would interfere in the internal affairs of their country of origin—now have virtually the same political rights as national citizens. Once the tight link between citizenship and national culture had been loosened, this sort of an evolution came an obvious adjustment to an increasingly interdependent and physically mobile world. Individual firms and persons, regardless of their formal national status, have been allowed (*de facto* if not *de jure*) to join and contribute to as many national and international associations or movements as they wish, in as many countries as they live or operate. And these associations or movements are allowed to operate in more than one political jurisdiction—beneath or beyond the nation state—provided they obey the same laws as those operating only at the national level.

The only issue that may be unique to Euro-citizenship is that of the number of potential levels. In all federal systems, individuals and organizations have at least dual citizenship. They 'belong' both to the subnational and the national states.[13] With the development of an intermediate 'regional' level of political authority and policy competence in so many member states and its gradual assertion at the level of the EU, it becomes at least feasible to think of 'four-layered' citizenship becoming possible for many Europeans. Each of these layers, the local, the regional, the national, and the supranational, could have its (admittedly overlapping) set of rights and obligations, regulated in a general way by the principle of subsidiarity (see Berten 1992).

Consequential

There is no doubt that the acquisition of national citizenship by individuals no longer carries with it the serious consequences in terms of rights and obligations that it once did. In contemporary Western democracies, resident aliens are protected from most of the dangers of arbitrary and discriminatory treatment by the 'state of law', and they are usually eligible for the benefits of the 'state of welfare'—once they have lived there for a sufficient period and/or if they can demonstrate that they entered legally. They can usually exercise some participatory rights, such as forming associations and petitioning authorities, although they are often denied the right to vote in elections, the right to certain forms of state employment, the obligation to serve in the armed forces (where there is still conscription), and, in the United States, the obligation to serve on juries. One indirect proof of this growing inconsequentiality would be the increasing proportion of those who are eligible to become citizens of the country in which they reside who do not even bother to attempt to do so.[14]

The consequentialness of developing European citizenship is much more problematic. The symbolic trappings are almost all there: a capital city, a flag, an anthem, a symphony orchestra, a passport and, eventually, a driving licence—but they do not bear the same meaning (and, in the last two cases, one has to pass through a national government to acquire them). Most of the TEU provisions concerning Euro-citizenship were not novel. They had already been 'acquired' without much fanfare via the internal regulations of the EP or ECJ, or included in various treaties sponsored by the Council of Europe. Many of them are not even exclusive to EU membership, but apply to legally resident aliens and firms as well. Even if one were to assemble a list of all the rights that Euro-citizens have acquired since the EEC's founding in 1958—regardless of their source or substance—it might be difficult to convince most individuals that they had gained much that their respective national governments was not already providing.

For example, the much publicized 'Four (better, Five) Freedoms' of the Single European Market: (1) freedom for the exchange of goods; (2) freedom for the movement of persons; (3) freedom of professional establishment; (4) freedom for the provision of services; and (5) freedom for the circulation of money and credit are also, by and large, available to outsiders—thanks to GATT and other multi- or bilateral arrangements. Some of the more recent 'Euro-goodies' have been more selectively provided, namely, the grants and subsidies that are being distributed under such acronyms as BRITE, JESSI, ERASMUS, LINGUA, COMMETT, etc. However, consequential these may be for the individual or firm that is privileged to receive them, they do not amount to very much in the aggregate. Ironically, agricultural subsidies which are the most lucrative and broadly distributed EEC/EC/EU pay-off directly to its citizens have only succeeded in creating a deeply resentful group that seems to feel no special affection for its supranational benefactor!

What is certainly more important in the long run are the procedural/legal guarantees that Euro-citizens enjoy concerning equal treatment of women and part-time workers, better consumer and environmental protection, emergency medical care and legal help when traveling within the Union, fair competitive practices between firms, uniform conditions for company formation, minimal health and safety standards, and protection against foreign (read, American) subversion of their cultures. No matter how extensive these rights and protections are or how much they accumulate in the directives approved by the Council, the regulations of the Commission and the decisions of the ECJ, these aspects of 'market membership' have only an indirect impact upon the quality of 'political citizenship'.

Individual

Democratic theory seems unequivocal on this issue: citizens must be individual human beings. Only an adult person capable of ethical reasoning and independent action can be expected to fulfil his or her rights and obligations. This theoretical presumption clashes with the obvious empirical fact that the relation between individual citizens and public authorities has become increasingly organized and intermediated. Participation may be individual, but effective access to decision makers depends on organizations. Communication among citizens passes increasingly through the parties, associations, and movements of which they are members or followers. Moreover, these organizations are not (and cannot be) democratically constituted. They invariably introduce interests of their own, significant distortions of citizen preference, into the political process and they can pursue their objectives in multiple sites and over long time periods. It does not seem an exaggeration to suggest that these intermediaries have tended to displace (if not supplant) the efforts of individuals and traditional collectivities. In short, organizations have become the predominant and effective citizens of national democratic polities.[15]

Moreover, these associations and movements have already acquired 'quasi-citizenship' rights at the national level. Actually, it would be more accurate to say that they have taken certain liberties with the political process because, instead of commonly defined and equally accessible rights, they have succeeded in influencing authorities on a piecemeal basis—class by class, sector by sector, profession by profession. Many have been formally recognized by national policy makers, sometimes as monopolistic organizations, and accorded regular access to their deliberations with a presumptive right to be consulted on all issues in their respective domains before binding decisions are taken.[16] Some have even received the equivalent of welfare entitlements: to financial subsidies, goods in kind, state-mandated obligatory dues, offloaded public services, etc. All that is missing from this tale of gradual and uneven accumulation of organizationally privileged access is a general and systematic practice of equalizing access to these rights and obligations for all organized interests.

To the extent that size and complexity are key factors in enhancing the relative importance of organizational over individual citizens, there is every reason to expect that they will be even more influential at the level of the emerging Euro-polity. The Commission seems to have recognized this from the very beginning when it deliberately encouraged and financed the formation of European-level associations.[17] It also established a procedure for recognizing their special Euro-status which implied privileged access to its deliberations, even if recognition was not always limited to only one organization per category. Each of its Directorates-General soon surrounded itself with a vast number of standing, advisory, and management committees, most of which were based on functional rather than territorial principles of representation.[18] Apparently, in the early stages, the Commission attempted to confine lobbying to interactions with certified Euro-level associations, but this practice was subsequently relaxed to permit an increasing volume of direct contacts with national interest representatives (Sidjanski and Ayerbeck 1987; Caporaso 1974: 23–52).

This structure of advisory committees and expert groups has mushroomed over the subsequent years. The Commission itself has never employed very many officials, and has depended heavily on comitologie, i.e. consultation with interest representatives, national government employees, and experts for both drafting its directives and monitoring compliance with them.[19] Interest representatives are well remunerated for attending these meetings and these payments could even be interpreted as a conscious subsidy for the development of an 'appropriately structured' system of interest intermediation.

Despite these consistent efforts at promoting Euro-associations, the officials in Brussels have not been successful in establishing viable Euro-corporatist arrangements, except on a less visible and consequential sectoral ('meso-corporatist') basis (Schmitter and Streeck 1991; Traxler and Schmitter 1994, 1995). As one well-informed observer has put it: 'Bruxelles is getting closer to Washington than to Bonn, Paris or London' (Grant 1990). If so, the implications for the future of the Euro-polity and its legitimacy could be quite substantial. At least on the continent, it has long been recognized that formally organized and officially recognized interest intermediaries played a key role in screening and diverting group preferences into broader class and sectoral channels and in subsequently governing the behaviour of their members. These organizations permitted, even encouraged, a mode of economic production and a distribution of social benefits that was distinctive. 'Organized Capitalism' was the label sometimes affixed to the more extreme national versions of this, and there was every expectation that something like it would become the hallmark of supranational integration. Instead, there is growing evidence of 'disorganized capitalism' at the Community level without the elements of official recognition, assured access, hierarchy, and monopoly (Lash and Urry 1987). In such a disjointed and competitive setting, Euro-associations are not necessarily privileged interlocutors, and higher-order peak associations may not be preferred over more specialized ones. They must compete for influence with a wide variety of other units: national states, para-state corporations, subnational governments, large private firms, and even lobbyists and lawyers intervening on behalf of individual clients. The policy outcomes become less predictable; majorities become more difficult to mobilize. The power of public coercion is blunted, but so is the capacity of the state to overcome private exploitation. The most accurate appellation for this system of interest intermediation is pluralism.

Moreover, in the emerging Euro-polity, this trend towards supranational pluralism in both the structures of authority and the associations of interest has advanced unchecked by powerful mechanisms of territorial representation and electoral accountability—as they were previously at the national level. Whether this 'Americanized' form of collective citizenship and influence-wielding will be regarded as legitimate—except by the British—is a matter for serious conjecture.

Making Some Modest Proposals for Reform

As we have noted above, the Treaty of Maastricht and the Intergovernmental Conference leading up to the Treaty of Amsterdam invited actors to propose reforms in the form and substance of Euro-citizenship and eventually (contingent upon the support of the Commission) to present them for the (unanimous) approval of the member states. In the light of this invitation, and with the assumption that democratizing the EU by expanding the role of Euro-citizens in its deliberations and decisions is a desirable goal, I would like to advance some 'modest proposals' that might not only be feasible in the immediate future but also produce some consequential changes.

Modest Democratic Proposal No. 1

There is one potential measure which would be relatively easy to implement (and perhaps even be acceptable to member national governments under present conditions) that might have a rapid and dramatic impact: the insertion of direct (but non-binding) referenda into the existing Euro-elections. What if either the European Parliament by absolute majority or any group of European citizens over a certain size and distributed across a certain number of member states could place on the ballot, along with the usual lists for electing MEPs, two or three items for popular approval?[20] The number would have to be limited for practical purposes and some mechanism would have to be set up to decide which items to favour at a given moment (the most democratic solution would be selection by lot). Even if the results of these referenda were not binding, they would almost assuredly have a considerable influence on policy makers at both the national and supranational levels.[21] Most importantly, competition for 'yes' and 'no' votes would definitely increase public attention with regard to European issues in general and improve the *Öffentlichkeit* with which specific measures would be discussed and defended. The very fact that Euro-elections do not, by and large, coincide with national elections and that they presently involve only a rather simple choice of party candidates by closed national list (except in Great Britain) has created a potentially attractive 'political space' that could be utilized at very little additional cost. And, who knows, inserting referenda items on significant issues might even invert the present tendency towards declining participation.[22]

Modest Democratic Proposal No. 2

A second innovation might also contribute to differentiating Euro-elections from their national counterparts and serve to forge a more personal and enduring link between the Euro-voter and his or her representative to the EP.

Beyond the obvious need to reform nomination procedures and the constituencies within which votes are solicited and tallied (a matter I will address in an accompanying essay), one could imagine a dual system in which each Euro-citizen would be entitled to vote twice: once, for his or her preferred candidate (on a party list) and, again, for that candidate's term of office—say, one or two terms. Not only would this allow for a novel opportunity to express individual intensities of preference, but could even promote the formation of a more stable and dedicated corps of Euro-deputies by making the position more attractive and allowing for the accumulation of expertise. Presumably, the longer serving MEPs would be explicitly legitimated by the electorate for this purpose and their greater professionalism would free them of the usual dependence on national party apparatuses and political careers.

Modest Democratic Proposal No. 3

Following this line of trying to make participation in Euro-elections more distinct from national elections, it would seem desirable that Euro-citizens should vote over a lengthier period of time and cast their ballots by mail or, better, by electronic means. What if Euro-citizens were given an entire week (during which polls or other projections of outcome would be prohibited) to contemplate the candidacies and the referenda items and eventually to register their preferences at their leisure—either by mailing in their votes via the traditional method for absentee balloting or by using their home computers or minitels.[23] Information could be made available through these same instruments; fraud could be kept in check through the use of national personal identification numbers (which already exist). Traditional democratic theorists, with their fondness for the agora, will object that this eliminates the crucial element of face-to-face interaction and collective deliberation (some of which might be vicariously replaced by the development of 'virtual groups' making imaginative use of e-mail—although admittedly these are not likely to form a random sample of the citizenry). Feminists might argue that voting in the home could result in male domination or appropriation of the choice process (although this probably ignores, in my opinion, the changing role of women in the workplace and underestimates the capacity of housewives for independent action). What such a reform would definitely accomplish would be to place the EU very visibly and resolutely in the forefront of technological change—something that the Commission has been trying to do since the 1980s.

Modest Democratic Proposal No. 4

If, as argued above, what is needed for the future legitimation of EC/EU decision making is more of an effort at distinguishing 'market membership' from 'political citizenship', then, some more explicit and dramatic political commitment will have to be made—if only to remind Europeans that do enjoy distinctive rights and obligations as a result of their respective national polity's membership in the EU. One response has already been suggested: the EU should subscribe to the European Convention for the Protection of Human Rights and Fundamental Freedoms and, thereby, make it unequivocally enforceable through the European Court of Justice. In point of fact, the ECJ has already 'appropriated' these rights in its jurisprudence, but the member states have so far been reluctant to place them explicitly within the *acquis communautaire*.[24]

What is likely to be much more controversial would be to succumb to the tendency to go beyond the existing Convention and to include some of the so-called 'Third' or 'Fourth' generation of human rights. The most obvious candidate for inclusion might be 'environmental rights', since there exist relatively high expectations that the EU should exercise greater authority in this policy arena where manifest cross-border externalities are so frequent. Other possible candidates could be 'women's rights', 'sexual rights', 'children's rights', and even 'animal rights'. Needless to say, any such attempt to load up the list of items initially to be placed above and beyond the democratic process will be hotly contested and could endanger the whole effort.

Of course, in the 'big bang' federalist scenario, this European Bill of Rights should be appended to a definitive constitutionalization of the entire integration process. Recognizing that nothing remotely so ambitious is likely to emerge from the 1996 IGC or in the near future, it might still be significant just to make a minimal symbolic gesture, especially if it were to be combined with an explicit codification of the economic and social rights that have already been acknowledged in previous EEC/EC/EU treaties and directives.

Modest Democratic Proposal No. 5

Another, admittedly more controversial, proposal would be to 'endow' the EU with a special responsibility for defining and protecting the status of permanent residents in the member states who are neither national citizens of these states nor of any other member state of the EU. Let us call this the creation of a special status for Euro-denizens.[25] It would entitle those who acquired it to a uniformity of treatment within the EU with regard to the economic freedoms of trade, capital movement, personal travel, and professional establishment and whatever social entitlements and protections are negotiated between the member states, but would not necessarily ensure that they would have equal political rights.[26]

Until now, the status of Euro-citizens has been clearly contingent upon the prior acquisition of citizenship in one of the member states—and various protocols have insisted that only national authorities have the capacity to define how this status is granted or acquired. The status of Euro-denizens has been much more ambiguous—and subject to considerable variation on a country-by-country basis. Depending on the possibilities for obtaining 'legal entry', 'permanent residence', and eventual 'naturalization', all member states have within their borders large numbers of 'non-EU persons'—legally or illegally residing.[27] Moreover, there is every indication that their numbers (presently estimated at 15 millions) are growing rapidly and posing ever more acute social and political problems. Given such pressures on the ill-defended and often ill-defined borders of the EU, combined with the unrestricted freedom of movement among the so-called Schengen countries, it is certainly conceivable that some member country will create a market in denizens—provided that its clients could be counted upon to move on and establish themselves elsewhere. One could even imagine a country's selling its citizenship to foreigners who wish to live elsewhere in the European Union.[28] The major advantage of an explicit status of Euro-denizenship would be to standardize these conditions of entry and residence and, thereby, preclude opportunistic practices by individual countries. It could also combine rather nicely with the embryonic efforts under Title VI of the Treaty on European Union to develop a more uniform policy on visa requirements, political asylum, and other immigration issues. I rather agree with Castro Oliveira (1996) that, in the present political climate, it is highly likely that the result would be 'a restrictive immigration policy accompanied by some improvements in the rights of third country nationals', but it would represent a significant extension of EU competences in an area of growing policy concern. Moreover, there is every indication that the creation of such a status would eventually generate spillover effects in other policy realms through the mechanisms of declarative statements and judicial interpretation.[29]

Modest Democratic Proposal No. 6

The European Union could, with relatively little effort and not much immediate effect, become the first polity in the world to practice genuinely universal citizenship, i.e. grant full rights of membership in the Community from the moment of birth to all persons born within its territory or to one of its citizens living abroad, as well as to those children who are subsequently naturalized. Recognizing the manifest incapacity of children to exercise the formal political rights directly and independently, this reform further proposes that the parents of each child be empowered to exercise the right to vote until such time as the child reaches the age of maturity established by national law. To the best of my knowledge, the EU would be the first polity to accord multiple votes to adult child-raising citizens.

In line with the general objectives of making the exercise of Euro-citizenship distinctive from that of national citizenship and of ensuring that Euro-citizenship supplements and not supplants national citizenship, universal citizenship—even if vicariously exercised until maturity—would seem to have a number of political advantages:

(1) It should make the emerging Euro-democracy more 'future-oriented'. Not only would allowing children the vote constitute a symbolic recognition that the Euro-polity has a responsibility for future generations, but it would also provide a real incentive for these youngsters to develop an early interest in politics and to do so through an awareness of the importance of the European level of aggregation.

(2) Precisely because of this incentive, it is to be expected that children—once they become aware of the right that their parents are exercising in their name in elections to the European Parliament—will increasingly hold their parents accountable for the way in which they distribute their electoral preferences which, in turn, might make the parents more aware of the importance of these elections.

(3) Which also suggests that the measure should increase various forms of inter-generational discussion about political issues and partisan orientations in general—strengthening channels of political socialization and improving elements of citizen training within the family that seem to have considerably diminished in recent decades. It may even compensate for the prodigious decline in sense of party identification at the national level and improve that at the supranational level.

(4) Enfranchising children and youths will contribute to a greater equilibrium of the political process over the life cycle. With increasing lifespans and a stable age of retirement, older persons have become a larger and larger component of the total citizenry and they have both the time and financial resources to participate disproportionately in the policy process—with the result that an increasing proportion of public funds are being spent for the health and welfare of the aged and a decreasing sum on the education and training of youth. In the longer run, this is bound to be a self-defeating process as a smaller and less productive set of active workers must pay for a larger and larger set of retired workers.

(5) Although I personally doubt the effect will be great, the reform might have some positive impact upon the birth rate. It would even more assuredly provide a major signal of support for the integrity of the family and for 'family values'. Providing child-bearing families with multiple votes should provide a significant incentive for politicians to pay more attention to such issues.

Injecting Some Less Modest Proposals for Reform

So far, all of the reform measures I have proposed focus exclusively on the form of eventual Euro-citizenship. Each represents an effort to make the exercise of this newly acquired political status different from the one that citizens have long experienced at the national level. Now, it is time to consider the desirability and possibility of reforming the substance of citizenship, i.e. of introducing new elements of social and cultural equality at the level of Europe as a whole.

Compared to the resounding (if rather vacuous) commitment in the Treaty of Maastricht to political citizenship, the EU has made only fitful and erratic progress in defining its social citizenship. As I have argued elsewhere, no one should be surprised that there is so little 'Social Europe' (Schmitter 1997). If anything, the absence of any substantial commitment by the members of the European Union (EU) to harmonize, or even to coordinate, their social policies is overdetermined. So many objective features of what Europe is not—at least, not yet—combine with several subjective aspects of the conjuncture in which Europeans are presently living that it is highly unlikely that much progress will be made in this domain for the foreseeable future.

First, the member states are at different levels of economic development. Their factors of production operate at systematically different levels of efficiency and relative scarcity and, hence, command different levels of income and return on investment.

Second, the member states have acquired over the past 100 or more years quite diverse 'packets' of social policies and ways of financing them; moreover, their mass publics seem relatively firmly committed to their respective national status quo.

Third, the interest associations that have grown up around (and also within) national social policy regimes, as well as the general systems of industrial relations, vary considerably among member states and are notoriously resilient to change.

Fourth, the influence of neo-liberal ideology with its hostility to state intervention in general and preference for privatized insurance schemes in particular has spread unevenly across member states and remains a salient issue of dispute within them.

Fifth, even if the above items could be overcome, the EU itself is not close to becoming a sovereign state with its own legitimate powers of enforcement and taxation and, hence, it is limited both by its dependence upon member states for the implementation of whatever social policies would be decided and by the reluctance of these polities to provide it with the funds necessary for any positive effort at redistribution or compensation.

Finally, the system of representation that has emerged *pari passu* with the integration process has provided privileged access and accountability to business interests and ineffectual incentives for the organization of 'policy takers', making it more difficult for workers, pensioners, consumers, patients, students, and the impoverished to articulate their demands at the supranational level. The European Parliament, where such demands might predictably be expected to focus, has only a limited power of budgetary review and virtually no capacity to determine the policy agenda. As long as there is no 'balance of class forces' and no 'effective party system' surrounding the definition of social citizenship at the European level, and as long as capitalists are convinced that such a commitment is not in their interests, there is virtually no chance that major substantive policies will be enacted.

If all this were not enough, monetary unification and the impending prospect of Eastern enlargement will only make the situation worse by introducing new elements of social inequality into this embryonic polity!

The fact that so little has been accomplished so far does not mean that nothing can be accomplished in the near future. It just means that, strategically, one should proceed *à petits pas* (as Jean Monnet would have put it) and that, tactically, one should take advantage of emerging 'opportunity structures' (as Sid Tarrow would say). The latter is provided by the impending disruptions of monetary unification and Eastern enlargement; the former could be fulfilled by what I shall call 'a Euro-stipendium'.

Less Modest Democratic Proposal No. 1

An Euro-stipendium would consist of the monthly payment of a stipulated amount of Euros to all citizens or permanent residents living within the EU whose total earnings correspond to less than one-third of the average income of everyone living within the EU.[30] By standard convention, those falling in this category are classified as 'in extreme poverty'.[31] Initially, the total sum of expenditures for this purpose could be set at a figure corresponding to the present combined value of all EU agricultural subsidies and regional/structural funds and the amount of the individual stipendium adjusted accordingly. In other words, provided it were possible to shift the basis of EU 'welfare' from payments to agricultural enterprises for producing (or not producing) specific crops and from grants to the governments of designed subnational regions for coming up with plausible development projects to simple money transfers to individuals, the aggregate cost would be zero![32]

Needless to say, this is not likely to be politically feasible—either because the group interests affected have sufficient clout to prevent a negative redistribution of the EU funds to which they have become 'entitled', or because the national and subnational governments involved would receive significantly less of the *juste retour* than they have become 'accustomed' to receive from the EU. It should be possible to 'fine-tune' the initiative during an intermediate period so that farmers could become eligible at a lower threshold (say, at one-half rather than one-third of the EU average income) and that (allegedly) underdeveloped regions and countries might be compensated for not having enough people living in extreme poverty. Nothing should be done, however, to sustain the substantial welfare benefits that presently go to wealthy and productive agricultural entreprises and to consultants and other intermediaries involved in inventing reasons for spending regional/structural funds. And, it is important for symbolic reasons that the amount of the Euro-stipendium be the same throughout the EU and that it be based not on national income distributions, but on the distribution of income at the level of EU member countries as a whole.

Not only would such a policy be much easier and less costly to administer than the existing ones, but it would also distribute benefits directly to targeted individuals—who, incidentally, have a high propensity for immediate consumption of relatively labour-intensive goods and services and, hence, who would generate lots of aggregate demand and additional employment.

Needless to say, as is the case with any social policy, its creation provides actors with incentives for 'gaming'. Member governments might reduce or even eliminate programmes aimed at the extremely poor in order to qualify more of their citizens for the Euro-stipendium; individuals at the bottom income fringes might lower their (reported) income or refuse to take jobs at marginal wages; national accounting systems might be 'adjusted' to exclude new sources of unreported income. None of these possibilities militate against trying the experiment as such, but they do suggest the necessity of reviewing the policy after it had produced its intended and unintended consequences. Moreover, if the Euro-stipendium is successful in eliminating (or, at least, alleviating) extreme poverty at a cost acceptable to the European population as a whole, it could easily be extended upward—simply by revising the coefficient of average income at which a citizen or legal permanent resident becomes eligible. It is not even too far-fetched to imagine that this 'means-tested' welfare policy could eventually be converted into a universalistic one that would provide a minimal basic income to everyone, regardless of his or her earned income (Van Parijs 1992, 1997; Atkinson 1995). The political context that makes this 'immodest' proposal especially appealing at this moment is formed, first, by monetary unification and, subsequently, by Eastern enlargement. One predictable effect of a single European currency and interest rate will be increasing regional disparities within member countries. The present policy of structural/regional funds is much too rigid to cope with such an eventuality—especially if the increased inequalities at the margin are not concentrated in areas already designed for such funds. The Euro-stipendium would both ensure that all those dramatically and negatively affected would be protected and it is not tied to any fixed territorial criterion. Those who slipped into extreme poverty as an indirect and unintended consequence of monetary unification would be protected no matter where they lived and no matter whether others in their vicinity were similarly affected. Moreover, the compensation would be automatic and not necessitate the (time-consuming, costly, and politically contingent) intervention of price-setting committees or project designers.

But the major appeal stems from the anticipated impact of Eastern enlargement. Everyone recognizes that the existing EU welfare policies of agricultural subsidies and regional grants cannot simply be extended eastwards—without very substantial and politically discriminatory modifications. The sheer fact that all of the immediate candidates have per capita incomes lower than that of the lowest existing member state (Greece) cannot be ignored. Average income in Euros is bound to decline with their entry which, of course, would be automatically reflected in the calculation of the Euro-stipendium. By eliminating (or sharply redefining) the existing programmes before Eastern enlargement and by defining *ex ante* a total sum to be used to alleviate poverty within the EU as a whole, one could set the initial levels of the stipendium at an acceptable aggregate cost—and, then, extend it in the future *au fur et à mesure* as the necessity arises, as experience with the programme accumulates, and as dispositions for solidarity within the EU change.

Less Modest Democratic Reform No. 2

Claus Offe has recently advanced a proposal that nicely parallels the one outlined above and that could relatively easily be transposed from the national to the supranational level (Offe n.d.).[33] In my terminology, it would involve a 'Euro-sabbatical'. All citizens and permanent residents of the EU would be entitled during their lifetime to the payment of a fixed and equal salary for varying periods of time during which they would voluntarily forego their usual paid employment. Similar to university professors and other privileged professionals, they would become eligible for six months to one year of pay (although not at their previous level of pay) for each ten to twelve years during which they had been employed (whether regularly or not). The decision on what use to make of one's sabbatical would be entirely in the hands of the individual— subject to certain constraints. For example, it might be thought desirable not to make it available until the citizen/denizen was at least 30 years old in order to encourage her or him to seek an initial active insertion into the labour market. The length of the sabbatical might then be timed to encourage its use for shorter periods early in life—say, one six-month period from 30 to 40, one year from 40 to 50, one and a half years beyond 50—but the overall term of eligibility would be the same for everyone and some degree of discretion should be left to the individual for special circumstances: sickness, childcare, home-building, voluntary service, etc. While it would be hoped that the sabbatical would be predominately used to upgrade one's skills in the labour market (especially by lower income earners), this should not be a require-ment.

The amount of the Euro-sabbatical could be set equal to that of the Euro-stipendium, for which most citizens/denizens would also be simultaneously eligible—unless they were receiving unearned income that exceeded the 'extreme poverty' level. They presumably would also be eligible for differing additional benefits from their respective national welfare systems. It is obvi-ously important that the net income provided by the Euro-sabbatical be higher than that of normal social assistance or unemployment benefits—otherwise, the freedom it provides for 'opting out' of the labor market would be illusory for most and only attractive to the very lowest level of wage-earn-ers. Moreover, those who make this choice should be given some assurance of what Offe calls 'preferential re-hiring'—otherwise, the risk incurred might seem excessive.

In Offe's presentation of this policy initiative, the primary intended purpose is to help the labour market adjust to a situation in which 'gainful' employment at a socially acceptable wage is not possible for everyone. The 'sabbatical account' would not only free up additional places in the labour market (while upgrading the skills and eventual productivity of those who occupy them), but it could also serve to transform public attitudes to work itself. Instead of a singular fixation on 'full-time, remunerated employment' as the standard of self-worth, individuals would learn through their own experi-ence and that of their fellow citizens/denizens that self-provision, voluntary service, and unpaid labour are also socially valuable (and personally reward-ing) activities.

Seen from the European perspective, one might wish to emphasize the contribution that such a reform might make to 'cultural' as opposed to 'social' or 'economic' citizenship—especially if the enjoyment of one's sabbatical could be tied to incentives to use it for study or residence in another European country than one's own. While there are good reasons (hinted at above and detailed more in Offe's essay) why individuals should control access to their sabbatical account as much as possible, it does not seem too far-fetched to require that, for at least one half of the time one receives a Euro-sabbatical, it should be spent in another member state of the EU or in some project of the EU sited elsewhere. Admittedly, this might skew the geographical distribution of such funds towards those parts of the continent that have better climates, more attractive cultural assets, and/or lower costs of living, but (appropriately and fortunately) these are precisely the regions of Europe most in need of assistance in catching up to those that developed earlier and faster.

As for financing, one could envisage various options—all of which would have to involve finding a new source. And this would have to be derived from the 'own resources' of the EU. As was the case with Euro-stipendium, a strong case could be made (on grounds of subsidiarity) for leaving the member states in charge of existing social programmes and their funding. What they wish to do above and beyond the Euro-stipendium and the Euro-sabbatical should be their own affair—and no requirement should be placed upon them to transfer either national obligations or funds to the EU. Only if the sabbatical account is exclusive to the EU and funded through it is it likely to have the desired effect in promoting a sense of supranational citizenship.

Both of these 'immodest' proposals are designed to respect the principle of subsidiarity. They would leave the vast bulk of spending and regulating the labour market to member states. These are the policy-making agencies that are closer to the needs of citizens/denizens; these are the units most capable of applying rules and distributing funds in ways that respect national (and subnational) peculiarities. A priori, there is nothing that would preclude applying the notions of a stipendium or a sabbatical at this level, although the country or region that did so first would suffer some initial competitive disadvantage. Moreover, in the case of the Euro-stipendium, it is intended precisely to respond to the anticipated externalities generated by the uneven impact of EU policies—first, monetary unification and, later, Eastern enlargement. Admittedly, should it be extended in the future to cover a wider range of the 'disfortuned' population and, especially, if it were to be converted into a basic citizen/denizen wage for all those who live in the EU, then, it might well replace substantial chunks of national welfare policy—but that would represent a very deliberate (and presumably consensual) policy of shifting sovereignty to the supranational level. The Euro-sabbatical is much less obviously connected to EU-generated externalities—the underlying employment problem is by no means limited to its member states, nor is it especially exacerbated by its policies—and it is only by attaching a cross-national obligation to it that one can justify its implementation across all member states.

Drawing Some Conclusions about the Potential for Euro-Citizenship

Europeans seems to have rapidly grown accustomed to the elements of economic citizenship that the EU has provided for them. Those freedoms to buy and sell goods, to invest and exchange currency, to receive and deliver services, to move personally, and to exercise one's profession across national borders are positively appreciated (and largely taken for granted), but they certainly have not generated a high level of political identification with the institutions that produced them.[34] Now, the question is whether the EU can graft on to these economic freedoms a new set of explicitly political rights and obligations that Europeans will find sufficiently appealing and consequential that they will finally (if not exclusively or definitively) come to identify with the supranational polity that protects them. Most of the proposals suggested above for the development of Euro-citizenship are deliberately modest. They recognize the impossibility of founding or re-founding Europe *ex novo* and of simply replacing the extremely rich and complex set of symbols, identities, expectations, and affective ties that bind national citizens to their respective polities. At best, Euro-citizenship is condemned for the foreseeable future to be 'supplementary'—which does not mean that its development cannot contribute the legitimization of the integration process as a whole. A great deal hinges, in my opinion, on the symbolic novelty of these new rights and obligations, as well as upon the net material advantages they generate for those who enjoy them.

But, by making Euro-elections as different as possible from national ones and by recognizing the emergence of new forms of collective and generational citizenship, the promoters of an increasingly politicized integration process would be taking a calculated risk. Putative Euro-citizens/denizens will not only have to evaluate their newly acquired freedoms as consequential enough so that it is worth their time and effort to exercise them, but they must also recognize them as democratic, i.e. as capable of rendering the rulers of the Euro-polity more accountable.

The previous gamble upon direct elections to the European Parliament seems, so far, to have failed on both counts. Another such failure could diminish not strengthen the legitimacy of the Euro-polity as a whole. Which is another way of saying that modest reforms in the form and substance of citizenship introduced in an isolated fashion (and, especially, if they are 'granted' without any prior mobilization and struggle) are not likely to make much of a positive contribution to democratization; moreover, not all of those proposed are likely to be approved and implemented. Upon deliberation, some are bound to seem more acceptable than others. And those that are found most acceptable are likely to prove least consequential—at least, in the short run.

So, we must not expect too much from Euro-citizenship. Alone, it is definitely not the panacea that will resolve the EU's rising problems with legitimacy. Even if all of the above advocated reform measures were approved and implemented, their effect would only be gradual and marginal. What is required if the process of European integration is to shift from a logic of functional interdependencies to one of politicized exchanges is a broader package of reforms—however modest the individual elements—not just in the scope of citizenship, but also in its forms of representation and its rules of decision making.

APPENDIX I. SIMULATING THE DISTRIBUTIVE EFFECT OF EURO-STIPENDIA

Simulating the probable distributive effect of a Euro-stipendia policy is not difficult—providing one had adequate data. Unfortunately, the only data I have (so far) been able to acquire on income distribution in the member states is expressed in national terms, i.e. in relation to the national average earned income (corrected for size of family, etc.). Since it is precisely the purpose of a Euro-stipendium to base eligibility for it on the Europe-wide distribution of income, this is a serious (but not insuperable) limitation. In the text and tables that follow I will make use of this national data, although the reader should take into account that the proportion of the, say, Danish population that earns one-third of the Danish average income (2.8) and, hence, would be eligible for a Euro-stipendium would definitely diminish when shifting to a European basis. In other words, being poor in Denmark is not the same as being poor in Spain. In the former, the extremely poor earn an average of 5,783 Euros; in the latter, they only earn 3,863 Euros.[35]

My second assumption is that the total amount of Euros potentially available to finance the scheme is equal to the sum total of funds for the guarantee of agricultural prices plus those presently allocated for structural/regional policies. That produces a 'pot' of ca. 63,139,000,000 Euros.

On this basis, there are 8,323,000 'extremely poor' persons in the present fifteen-member European Union. If the money putatively available for this purpose were to be distributed equally to each and every one of them—regardless of where he or she lives within the EU—each would receive 7,586 Euros!

This is much too much. It would more than double their present average income (which is 5,051 Euros)—and, therefore, amount to a very socially undesirable 'premium' for being extremely poor!

Faced with this result, there would seem to be two options:

(1) distribute this same sum over a larger population base, i.e. give the Euro-stipendium to all those in the EU who are poor (earning less than one-half the average income in the respective country). This would increase those eligible to 27,104,000 and result in a stipendium for each of 2,329.5 Euros;
(2) fix the amount of the Euro-stipendium at a 'reasonable' sum—I suggest 1,000 Euros (which would mean a supplement of ca. 20 to an average income of 5,051 Euros)—and distribute it only to the extremely poor. The (sizeable) remaining sum could be used to support existing programmes in agriculture and/or regional assistance, although hopefully some way can be found to avoid perpetuating some of the perverse income effects of these policies.

Needless to say, the second option is likely to be easier to implement politically. The first one would have a much more immediate and direct effect upon aggregate demand and job creation through income transfers to a larger number of eager consumers, but might at the upper fringe threaten the 'relativities' to which the middle class is so noto-

TABLE 5.1. *Simulated distribution of Euro-stipendia to 'extremely poor'*

Countries	Total population in extreme poverty	Average per capita income (GDP in current Purchasing Power Parities) (in Euros) in 1996	Average per capita income of the poorest people (those having less than one-third of the median income) (in Euros)	Countries' receipts from the EU budget for CAP guarantee and structural policies in 1996		Countries' receipts from the EU budget for a 'Euro-stipendium'[a]	
				ECUS		ECUS	Percentage
Austria[b]	128,000	17,040	5,680	1,450,100	2.29	971,008	1.53
Belgium	90,000	17,052	5,684	1,480,500	2.34	682,740	1.08
Denmark	140,000	17,351	5,783	1,463,000	2.31	1,062,040	1.68
Finland	80,000	13,863	4,621	784,500	1.20	606,880	0.96
France	1,370,000	16,237	5,412	11,510,900	18.23	10,392,820	16.46
Germania	1,320,000	16,571	5,523	9,485,800	15.02	10,013,520	15.85
Greece[c]	344,000	9,547	3,182	4,924,600	7.79	2,609,584	4.13
Ireland	102,000	14,348	4,782	2,906,500	4.60	773,772	1.22
Italy	960,000	15,610	5,203	7,247,500	11.47	7,282,560	11.53
Luxembourg	2,000	25,316	8,436	34,600	0.05	15,172	0.02
Netherlands	370,000	15,713	5,237	1,804,900	2.85	2,806,820	4.44
Portugal[d]	337,000	11,067	3,689	3,607,500	5.71	2,556,482	4.04
Spain	1,320,000	11,590	3,863	10,288,700	16.29	10,013,520	15.85
Sweden	290,000	14,810	4,936	718,700	1.13	2,199,940	3.48
United Kingdom	1,470,000	14,974	4,991	5,431,200	8.60	11,151,420	17.66
EU COUNTRIES	8,323,000	15,155	5,051	63,139,000	99.88	63,138,178	99.93

[a] If the EU expenditures on agriculture guarantee and structural policies were used to finance it. On the basis of the year 1996 when such expenditures were 63,139 million ECUS, each extremely poor person in the EU would receive an average of 63,139 mECU/8,323,000 = 7,586 ECUS
[b] On the basis of Germany's percentages.
[c] On the basis of Spain's percentages.
[d] On the basis of Spain's percentages.

TABLE 5.2. *Simulated distribution of Euro-stipendia to 'extremely poor' + 'poor'*

Countries	Total poor population (those in extreme poverty and in poverty)	Average per capita income (GDP in current Purchasing Power Parities) (in Euros) in 1995 (and 1996)	Average per capita income of the poorest people (those having less than one-third of the median income) (in Euros)	Average per capita income of the poor people (those having one-third to less than half of the median income) (in Euros)	Countries' receipts from the EU budget for CAP guarantee and structural policies in 1996		Countries' receipts from the EU budget for a 'Euro-stipendium'[a]	
					ECUS		ECUS	Percentage
Austria[b]	491,000	17,040	5,680	8,520	1,450,100	2.29	1,143,784	1.81
Belgium	520,000	17,052	5,684	8,526	1,480,500	2.34	1,211,340	1.91
Denmark	410,000	17,351	5,783	8,675.5	1,463,000	2.31	955,095	1.51
Finland	340,000	13,863	4,621	6,931.5	784,500	1.20	792,030	1.25
France	3,890,000	16,237	5,412	8,118.5	11,510,900	18.23	9,061,755	14.35
Germania	5,050,000	16,571	5,523	8,285.5	9,485,800	15.02	11,763,975	18.63
Greece[c]	1,044,000	9,547	3,182	4,773.5	4,924,600	7.79	2,431,998	3.85
Ireland	410,000	14,348	4,782	7,174	2,906,500	4.60	955,095	1.51
Italy	3,790,000	15,610	5,203	7,805	7,247,500	11.47	8,828,805	13.98
Luxembourg	18,000	25,316	8,436	12,658	34,600	0.05	41,931	0.06
Netherlands	950,000	15,713	5,237	7,856.5	1,804,900	2.85	2,213,025	3.50
Portugal[c]	1,031,000	11,067	3,689	5,533.5	3,607,500	5.71	2,401,714	3.80
Spain	4,030,000	11,590	3,863	5,795	10,288,700	16.29	9,387,885	14.86
Sweden	430,000	14,810	4,936	7,405	718,700	1.13	1,001,685	1.58
United Kingdom	4,700,000	14,974	4,991	7,487	5,431,200	8.60	10,948,650	17.34
EU COUNTRIES	27,104,000	15,155	5,051	7,577.5	63,139,000	99.88	63,138,768	99.94

a If the EU expenditures on agriculture guarantee and structural policies were used to finance it. On the basis of the year 1996 when such expenditures have been of 63,139 million ECUS each extremely poor and poor person in the EU would receive an average amount of 63,139 mECU/27,104,000 = 2,329.5 ECUS

b On the basis of Germany's percentages.

c On the basis of Spain's percentages.

d On the basis of Spain's percentages.

riously sensitive. It is one thing to justify normatively a policy designed to benefit the manifestly destitute (who are often socially and spatially removed from the bulk of middle-class citizens); it is another to shift 'unearned' income to a category that is just adjacent to such a well-organized and politically mobilized segment of the population!

Also note that one very appealing 'evolutionary option' would be to revise the policy upward after an evaluation of its initial (hopefully favourable) impact while gradually phasing out the agricultural subsidies and regional funds that some groups have gotten so accustomed to receiving.

In Tables 5.1 and 5.2, I have simulated the distributive impact of two alternative uses of the entire sum of present EU funds across the fifteen member states and compared these figures with what these same countries are presently receiving as a proportion of agricultural + regional funds. For example, from Table 5.1 where all the extremely poor are given an income supplement of 7,586 Euros each, the net winners are quite clear. The United Kingdom would leap from 8.60 to 17.66 (or from 5,431,200,000 to 11,151,420,000 Euros) as a reflection of its neo-liberal policies that have helped it to produce the most unequal distribution of income in the EU.[36] Rather surprisingly, Sweden with its much more equal income distribution is also a net winner, but presumably this reflects its modest benefits from agricultural subsidies and regional funds. From present receipts of 718,700,000 Euros, its take would increase to 2,199,940,000 Euros. Germany, Italy, and the Netherlands also do relatively better.

The biggest proportional losers are Austria, Denmark, Belgium, Ireland, Luxembourg, Greece, and Portugal. The former five's decline in receipts seems 'deserved'; whereas, the latter two may be an artefact of my having used Spanish income distribution data to estimate their respective number of extremely impoverished citizens/denizens. In any case, once the basis of calculus was switched from the national to the supranational, Greece and Portugal would certainly become 'more deserving'.

Several countries would break approximately even: Finland, France, and Spain. Again, based on Europe-wide statistics, I suspect that Spain and, perhaps, France would benefit relatively. In Table 5.2, I simulate the more 'utopian' prospect of awarding a Euro-stipendium to all of the poor living in the EU—at the rate of 2,329 Euros to all those whose total earned income was less than one-half of the national average. My general impression of the distributions is that they fall closer to the existing one established by agricultural and regional funds, but there are some interesting exceptions. The United Kingdom is an even greater net gainer, as are Germany and Sweden. France does much worse. Portugal and Greece also do worse—but that may be due to a calculation error.

There seems no sense in simulating the relative impact across the fifteen of what seems to me to be the most desirable initial policy, namely, to give each of the extremely poor a Euro-stipendium of 1,000 Euros and to work out an interim formula for distributing a smaller (and, perhaps, declining) amount of agricultural and regional funds. Presumably, the outcome would tend to reproduce the existing payout—although everyone seems to understand that this cannot be sustained without substantial changes when Eastern enlargement occurs.

Finally, one should take account of the timing of this proposal. Its immediate implementation would provide a much needed 'insurance policy' against the risks that monetary unification generates for those least likely to be able to take advantage of the expanded opportunities it offers. This, incidentally, also applies to the extremely poor in the four EU countries that have not accepted the obligations of Monetary Union. But its real 'timeliness' is in relation to the incorporation of four to five new members whose per capita income is markedly lower than that of existing member states. Fortunately, the post-Communist candidates have a more even distribution of income. There is no question that, if the Euro-stipendium is instituted and the total sum of EU transfers remains roughly the same, there will be a very considerable shift eastward in their distribution—and this is what should happen. The average EU income will go down and more people in these countries (as well as Cyprus) will be earning less than one-third of it. Note, however, that under this policy it will be relatively easy to retain a cap on total spending (simply, by manipulating the total amount of the stipendium or the criterion of eligibility); whereas, agricultural subsidies are notoriously difficult to cap without very elaborate monitoring and bureaucratic controls.

NOTES

1. Or, as Marshall put it, 'the right to share to the full in the social heritage and to live the life of a civilized being according to the standards prevailing in the society' (1950: 11).
2. Significantly, the TEU only mentions rights and protections. It offers not a word or hint about obligations or duties.
3. Although as Michael Walzer (1970: 77–98) notes, citizens may still be compelled 'to live for the state', since national laws typically prohibit and punish suicide. To which I would add that the current evolution of American legal doctrine and public policy seems to be aimed at compelling its citizens 'to procreate for the state' by outlawing abortion.
4. Although the recent controversy in the United States over the burning of the flag suggests that the issue is far from over—at least in that most patriotic of advanced industrial societies.
5. Which raises the delicate issue of whether there is a functional substitute for mass mobilization and actual combat. The Cold War certainly enhanced the sacred image of the 'Western world' for several post-war generations. In its absence, ideologues have tried to replace it with an alleged 'clash of civilizations' and, more specifically, with the 'Green Menace' of Islamic fundamentalism. So far, this has not proven very credible. For example, any attempt to get the EU or the WEU to espouse the French policy of unconditional support for the Algerian military dictatorship against its Fundamentalist enemies would seem more likely to divide than unify contemporary Europe.
6. I am indebted to several conversations with and the reading of several unpublished papers by Karl-Heinz Reif, head of the Commission's Survey Research Unit in Brussels, for this (and many other) observations. For a very comprehensive and path-breaking analysis of popular attitudes in Europe towards the EU, see

Niedermayer and Sinnott (1995). For a more recent analysis of the downward trend, see Sinnott and Winston (1996).

7. Anyone who doubts this or believes that it has completely disappeared should watch the hilarious movie, *Die Schweizermacher.*

8. Which is not to say that there are not those who have considered such a trend alarming. In the United States, the struggle against 'multiculturalism' and in favour of imposing English as the legally exclusive language of the country are clear signs of a reaction against the 'de-nationalization' of membership in the American polity.

9. And, it should be pointed out that despite all the talk of Euro-citizenship, in order to enjoy its benefits one must first be a national citizen of one of its member countries—and these countries are (so far) exclusively responsible for setting the criteria under which this status can be acquired by foreigners. Needless to say, the national rules concerning naturalization remain very diverse. The TEU is very clear that no independent European citizenship is being created or even contemplated. Its Art. F(1) strongly commits the EU to respecting the national identities of its member states. For the benefit of the doubting Danes, the European Council meeting in Birmingham repeated that the rights and protections of citizenship in the EU do not in any way take the place of national citizenship. *Bulletin EC* 10–1992, pt. I.8, p. 9. Nevertheless, Gerard-René de Groot (1996) has shown that in analogous historical situations (the German Empire, Switzerland, and the United States), it eventually became imperative that the central authority establish some common rules and degree of control.

10. This seems close to what Jürgen Habermas has called *Verfassungspatriotismus.* For a more complete discussion of his views on the possibility of non-ethnic, non-national citizenship, see Habermas (1995). Jean-Marc Ferry and Paul Thibaud (1992) have engaged in a fascinating inter-generational debate in which the latter takes the traditional (one is tempted to say, French) position that nationality and citizenship cannot be severed from each other and the former defends this possibility. See also Ferry (1992).

11. See e.g. Lakeman (1990) where the EP elections are treated as mere extensions of national elections. Hence, the notion developed by Karl-Heinz Neunreiter (1994) that these elections are condemned to be 'secondary'. Also Lodge and Herman (1982).

12. The right of individuals to address the European Parliament or to bring cases before the European Court of Justice was already written into their respective internal regulations—and is not restricted to nationals of EC/EU member states. It seems that the right to petition the new Ombudsman is also open to third country nationals who reside in member states.

13. And, in the extreme case of Switzerland, they are also deeply engaged in membership at the communal as well as the cantonal and federal levels. So layered is the process that voting turnout tends to be higher in communal elections than in cantonal ones, and in cantonal than federal ones. In fact, in that country, naturalization first involves one's becoming a member of a commune and canton before acquiring the status of a Swiss national.

14. I know of no hard and firm data on this subject, time-series or cross-sectional, and would appreciate anyone's calling my attention to where I could find them.

My impression, based on the places I have lived in recent years, is that the proportion of denizens has tended to increase, but I would be the first to admit that this is hardly a representative sample. NB: a rival explanation for this (unproven) fact might be that more and more of the foreigners resident in advanced industrial societies believe that they will eventually return (or be allowed to return) to their country of origin.

15. The only person so far courageous enough to suggest such an eventuality and to place it in a published title has been, appropriately, a Scandinavian: Olsen (1983).

16. *Vernehmlassungsverfahren* is the untranslatable Swiss term for this.

17. For example, Sicco Mansholt seems to have played a major role in the founding of the peak association of European farmers, COPA. Lindberg and Scheingold (1970: 173). Other Commission officials helped found BEUC for consumers, according to Sidjanski and Ayerberk (1987: 180). In the extreme case of EUROFER, the EC deliberately sponsored the creation of a regional cartel.

18. Although it should be stressed that access to these committees is not restricted to functional interest representatives. Many involve designated 'experts' in the processes of decision making and implementation, although these may often be difficult to distinguish from interest spokespersons. For a description of 46 of these consultative bodies, see Economic and Social Committee of the European Communities (1980).

19. Current estimates suggest approximately 17,000 which include a very large number of interpreters and other staff personnel. Exercising policy functions, there is probably no more than 1,500 Eurocrats, although it should be observed that they are supplemented by an even larger number of national civil servants and interest association functionaries who are seconded for various periods of time to Brussels. Also, the Commission contracts out for much of its research.

20. The most obvious place to start would be to convoke a referendum on whatever reforms are proposed by the Inter-Governmental Conference of 1996. The only problem with that suggestion is that these proposals may turn out to be so modest and to be so much more oriented towards 'efficiency' than 'democracy' that Euro-citizens may not bother to turn out to either approve or disapprove them!

21. Which has been the experience of all the so-called consultative referenda held at the national level on the issue of membership. Indeed, the frequency with which this democratic device has been used for this purpose—even in countries without a tradition of referenda—establishes a worthy precedent for its extension to the EC/EU level.

22. For a more ambitious proposal along these lines, see Gross (1994).

23. A recent experiment with mailed ballots in the US state of Oregon resulted in a very significant increase in the rate of turnout.

24. For a concise description of how the ECJ managed to 'appropriate' the theme of protection of human rights, see Mancini (1991). A recent decision of the European Court of Justice (2/94 of 28 Mar. 1996) has declared that the EU cannot simply accede to the European Convention for the Protection of Human Rights and Fundamental Freedoms, but would have to do so *via* an amendment to the TEU. *Financial Times*, 16 Apr. 1996: 12.

25. My thoughts on this subject have been triggered by reading Castro Oliveira (1996).

26. According to Castro Oliveira, denizens already enjoy certain social and educational rights under EU legislation and their survivors are guaranteed benefits from national social security systems. They do not, however, enjoy freedom of movement or establishment in any country other than the one that has granted them permanent residence. As for political rights, there are some polities, e.g. Sweden and the canton of Neuchatel, that already permit resident aliens to vote in local elections, and there is even an evolving set of national court decisions and resolutions of the Council of Europe that have sought to extend this as a basic human/civic right.

27. In the Italian press, these persons are often referred to as 'extracomunitari', a sort of euphemism for undesirables and alleged criminals from Albania and Africa.

28. Something approaching this situation presently exists in the relation between Portugal and Macao. Large numbers of Hong Kong residents, denied citizenship by the United Kingdom, are buying property in Macao and thereby acquiring Portuguese nationality which they presumably can use in the future to enter, reside, and work in the United Kingdom. Analogous loopholes also permit descendents of Spanish, Portuguese, Italian, and Irish emigrants to 'recuperate' the nationality of their ancestors—and live wherever they please in the EU.

29. For instance, a joint Declaration Against Racism and Xenophobia adopted in 1986 by the European Parliament, the Council of Ministers, and the Commission affirms their resolve 'to protect the individuality and dignity of every member of society and to reject any form of segregation of foreigners'. If this sort of 'cheap talk' were eventually to be taken seriously by either politicians or judges, it could have far-reaching—if unintended—implications.

30. For calculation purposes, the actual unit would be the 'foyer fiscal'—the family considered in terms of taxation—with the assumption that the total revenue earned is divided evenly among family members.

31. Source in Luxembourg study. NB: eligibility could also be calculated in terms of one's position with regard to the standard deviation in average European income.

32. See Appendix I for a very approximate calculation of what such a programme would cost in EU-15 and how it would be distributed among the member countries.

33. I am grateful to Claus for sharing this paper and related ideas with me during a recent visit to the European University Institute.

34. As was expected by Ernst B. Haas, when he defined political integration as 'the process whereby political actors in several distinct national settings are persuaded to shift their loyalties, expectations and political activities toward a new centre, whose institutions possess or demand jurisdiction over the pre-existing states' (1958: 16).

35. Due to data limitations, I have had to estimate the number of extremely poor in three countries. For Austria, I have assumed that the national distribution of income is identical to that of Germany (for which there are data). The corresponding figures for Portugal and Greece are based on the 'guesstimate' that their distribution is identical to that of Spain. Greek relative poverty is certainly overestimated, since it seems to be well known that its distribution of national income is more equal than that of Spain or Portugal, due largely to a very dispersed pattern of land ownership.

36. Incidentally, this 'windfall' could be used to argued in favour of eliminating the UK's abherent 'give-back' in EU funds.

REFERENCES

ATKINSON, A. B. (1995). *Public Economies in Action: The Basic Income/Flat Tax Proposal*. Oxford: Oxford University Press.

BERTEN, A. (1992). 'Identité européenne, une ou multiple? Réflexion sur les processus de formation de l'identité', in J. Lenoble and N. Dewandre (eds.), *L'Europe au soir du siècle: Identité et démocratie*. Paris: Editions Esprit, 81–97.

BRUBAKER, W. R. (1989). 'Traditions of Nationhood and Politics of Citizenship'. *States and Social Structures Newsletter*, 9: 4–8.

BUTT, P. A. (1985). 'Pressure Groups in the European Community'. *UACES Occasional Papers 2*.

CAPORASO, J. A. (1974). *The Structure and Function of European Integration*. Pacific Palisades, Calif.: Goodyear Pub.

—— (1997). *Challenges and Dilemmas of the European Union*. Boulder, Colo.: Westview Press.

CASTRO OLIVEIRA, A. (1996). 'Resident Third Country Nationals: Is it too Early to Grant Them Union Citizenship?' Paper presented at the EUI European Forum Conference on, 'European Citizenship: An Institutional Challenge', Florence, 13–15 June.

DAHRENDORF, R. (1974). 'Citizenship and Beyond: The Social Dynamics of an Idea'. *Social Research*, 41: 673–701.

DE GROOT, G.-R. (1996). 'The Relationship between the Nationality of Member-States of the European Union and the 'European Citizenship'. Paper presented at the EUI European Forum Conference on, European Citizenship: An Institutional Challenge'; Florence, 13–15 June.

Economic and Social Committee of the European Communities (1980). *Community Advisory Committees for the Representation of Socio-Economic Interests*. Farnborough: Saxon.

FERRY, J.-M. (1992). 'Identité et citoyenneté européennes', in J. Lenoble and N. Dewandre (eds.), *L'Europe au soir du siècle: Identité et démocratie*. Paris: Esprit, 177–88.

—— and THIBAUD, P. (1992). *Discussions sur L'Europe*. Paris: Calmann-Lévy.

GRANT, W. (1990). Talk on 'Business Interests in a New Europe', Center for European Studies, Stanford University, 7 Feb.

GROSS, A. (1994). 'Zwölf Denkanstöße für ein (direkt-)demokratisch verfasstes Europa', in M. Wolters et al. (ed.), *Mehr als Demokratie für Europa: Ideen und Aufsätze*. Bonn: Stiftung Mitarbeit, 62–73.

HAAS, E. B. (1958). *The Uniting of Europe*. Stanford, Calif.: Stanford University Press.

HABERMAS, J. (1990 [1962]). *Strukturwandel der Öffentlichkeit: Untersuchungen zu einer Kategorie der bürgerlichen Gesellschaft*. Frankfurt: Suhrkamp.

—— (1995). 'Citizenship and National Identity: Some Reflections on the Future of Europe', in R. Beiner (ed.), *Theorizing Citizenship*. Albany, NY: SUNY Press, 255–82.

KARL, T., and SCHMITTER, P. C. (1991). 'What Democracy is and is not'. *Journal of Democracy*, 2 (3): 75–88.

LAKEMAN, E. (1990). 'Elections to the European Parliament, 1989'. *Parliamentary Affairs*, 43: 77–89.

LASH, S., and URRY, J. (1987). *The End of Organized Capitalism*. Cambridge: Polity: Press.

LINDBERG, L. W., and SCHEINGOLD, S. A. (1970). *Europe's Would-Be Polity. Patterns of Change in the European Community*. Englewood Cliffs, NJ: Prentice Hall.

LODGE, J. (1994). 'Transparency and Democratic Legitimacy'. *Journal of Common Market Studies*, 32: 343–68.

—— (1995). 'Democracy in the EU: The Interrelationship between Supranational, National and Subnational Levels of Government', in M. Telo (ed.), *Démocratie et construction européenne*. Brussels: Editions de l'Université de Bruxelles, 238–50.

—— and HERMAN, V. (1982). *Direct Elections to the European Parliament: A Supranational Perspective*. London: Macmillan.

MCLAUGHLIN, A. M., and GREENWOOD, J. (1995). 'The Management of Interest Representation in the European Union'. *Journal of Common Market Studies*, 33: 143–56.

MANCINI, G. F. (1991). 'The Making of a Constitution for Europe', in R. Keohane and S. Hoffmann (eds.), *The New European Community: Decisionmaking and Institutional Change*. Boulder, Colo.: Westview Press, 177–94.

MARKS, G., NIELSEN, F., RAY, L., and SALK, J. (1996). 'Competencies, Cracks and Conflicts: Regional Mobilization in the European Union', in G. Marks et al. (ed.), *Governance in the European Union*. London: Sage, 40–63.

MARSHALL, T. H. (1950). *Citizenship and Social Class*. Cambridge, Mass.: Cambridge University Press.

NEUNREITER, K.-H. (1994). 'The Democracy Deficit of the European Union: Towards a Closer Cooperation between the European Parliament and the National Parliaments'. *Government and Opposition*, 29: 299–314.

NIEDERMAYER, O., and SINNOTT, R. (eds.) (1995). *Public Opinion and Internationalized Governance*. Oxford: Oxford University Press.

OFFE, C. (n.d.). 'Precariousness and the Labor Market: A Medium Turn Review of Available Policy Responses'. Unpublished paper for the OECD.

OLSEN, J. P. (1983). *Organized Democracy*. Oslo: Universitetsforlaget.

REIF, K.-H. (1985). *Ten European Elections*. Aldershot: Gower.

SCHMITTER, P. C. (1996). 'Examining the Present Euro-Polity with the Help of Past Theories', in G. Marks et al. (ed.), *Governance in the European Union*. London: Sage, 1–14.

—— (1997). 'A Political Europe and a Social Europe'. Paper presented at the Seminar on a Social Europe, Gulbenkian Foundation, Lisbon, 5–7 May.

—— and STREECK, W. (1991). 'Organized Interests and the Europe of 1992', in N. J. Ornstein and M. Perlman (eds.), *Political Power and Social Change: The United States Faces the United Europe*. Washington, DC: AEI Press, 46–67.

SIDJANSKI, D., and AYERBERK, U. (1987). 'Le Nouveau Visage des groupes d'intérêt communautaires'. *Revue d'Intégration Européenne*, 10: 173–201.

SINNOTT, R., and WINSTON, N. (1996). 'Disintegrative Tendencies in EU Public Opinion'. Paper for the ECPR Joint Sessions, Oslo.

TRAXLER, F., and SCHMITTER, P. C. (1994). 'Perspektiven Europäischer Integration, verbandlicher Interessenmediation und Politikformulierung', in V. Eichener and H. Voelzkow (eds.), *Europäische Integration und verbandliche Interessenmediation.* Marburg: Metropolis Verlag, 45–71.

—— —— (1995). 'The Emerging Euro-Polity and Organized Interests'. *European Journal of Public Relations,* 1: 191–218.

VAN PARIJS, P. (1992). *Arguing for Basic Income: Ethical Foundations for a Radical Reform.* New York: Verso.

—— (1997). 'Basic Income and the Political Economy of a New Europe', in P. B. Lehning and A. Weale (eds.), *Citizenship, Democracy and Justice in the New Europe.* New York: Routledge, 161–4.

WALZER, M. (1970). *Obligations: Essays on Disobedience, War, and Citizenship.* Cambridge, Mass.: Harvard University Press.

6

Citizenship under Regime Competition

The Case of the 'European Works Councils'

Wolfgang Streeck

Regime Competition in Europe

As European integration progresses, expectations are waning that it will culminate in a supranational state replicating the post-war European nation state on a larger scale.[1] But as yet little attention has been devoted to the question of what this implies for integrated Europe, and what in particular it portends for the role of European nation states, and of statehood in Europe generally, *vis-à-vis* European societies and citizens. In part this may have ideological reasons. 'Euro-optimists', which include most students of European integration, tend to minimize the significance of the disappearance of the supranational state perspective. Rather than dwell on what is not happening, they prefer to deal with what is. For the rest, a tacit assumption has become widely accepted that the old neo-functionalist vision of a 'United States of Europe' was not meant to be taken literally in the first place, and that whatever emerges in its stead can be regarded without much questioning as its functional equivalent. It is here that the debate on European integration links up with contemporary discussions about the state. While empirical observations of a decline of state capacity in developed industrial societies are widely shared, they are often accompanied by assurances that this is not really a loss as other, non-state mechanisms of governance—and indeed normatively preferable ones—are waiting to fill the gap. Just like the mainstream of European integration theory, the rational choice liberalism that dominates social and political thought today prefers to downplay the significance or desirability of what is not or no longer. Its proposition, sometimes explicit and mostly implied, that 'soft' forms of order, constructed 'bottom-up' by rational individual actors and ranging from 'civil society' to 'international regimes', can do the same as states and better, must be highly congenial to integration theory in a post-federal Europe desiring to remain a harbinger of good news even without the prospect of a supranational state.[2]

But is it justified to be so sanguine, about both the state and Europe? Is there nothing that a federal Europe was expected to supply that cannot as well be supplied by a post-federal Europe devoid of an integrated state? And is a historical loss of state capacity, at national level where it existed as well as at supranational level where it has failed to emerge, really a loss of nothing else? If anything, it seems to be the issue of *citizenship* that offers itself as a site for exploring these important questions. European integration has vastly increased the opportunities for *cross-border mobility inside Europe*, in and out of formerly closed national societies, by obliging the latter in international law to open themselves up to a common 'internal market'. In this way integration has forcefully contributed to the rise of a *European civil society*. But since integration has not at the same time dissolved national polities, rights, and obligations of *citizenship in Europe* continue to reside in a plurality of heterogeneous and formally still sovereign national legal and political systems. While not absorbing national into supranational citizenship, and indeed as an alternative to doing so, European integration has enveloped national citizenship regimes in a transnational market and in the international institutional constructions that make up today's European Union. The result is a highly complex, multi-tier configuration of national and transnational institutions which has made national systems of citizenship increasingly accountable to international agreements and supranational law, by subjecting them to rules that limit what national governments can award or deny, not just to the citizens of other European countries but to their own citizens as well.[3]

The question is what exactly these changes imply—for the institution of citizenship, the role of the state in European society, and the 'nature of the beast' (Puchala 1972) of European integration. One influential and extremely well-argued position, that of Joseph Weiler (1991, 1995), takes the fact that national citizenship has become accountable to a supranational regime *that is clearly not a state*, as a sign of a highly desirable divorce of the principle and values of citizenship from the organizational form, not just of the nation state, *but of the state as such*. European integration, as I read what to me is the core of his argument,[4] may well have been primarily about the accommodation and promotion of cross-border mobility. But to accomplish this it had to make national systems of citizenship extend to foreigners from other European countries—but perhaps ultimately from everywhere—much the same rights that they have in the past come to extend to nationals. In this way, while leaving the national basis of citizenship in principle untouched, integration makes national citizenship less parochial and more universalistic than it used to and would otherwise still be. This it does because any discrimination on the basis of national origin, of people, or commodities, and of course also of people as commodities, obstructs the common internal market. States willing to build such a market—but also unwilling to dissolve into a common state—must therefore accept restrictions on their sovereign power to discriminate against foreigners, be they workers or traders, investors, and employers.

While citizenship may remain nationally based, and indeed in the absence of a supranational state *must* remain so, it must also cease to be nationalist, for which purpose it must be brought under supranational regulation through the organized collectivity of European states, the European Union.

Eliminating national parochialism from national citizenship can truly be regarded as civilizational progress. Weiler goes, however, several steps further. For him the fact that in the case of European integration such progress was not associated with the formation of a new super-state *is progress in itself* (Weiler 1991: 2478 f.). In particular, Weiler does not at all regard it as a deficiency that the European Union was not allowed by its member states to evolve into a supranational state capable of serving as a source of common European rights and obligations of citizenship. Nor does he consider the present, indirect method of making national citizenship regimes conform with universalistic rules of non-discrimination as a second-best solution, however fortuitously effective. Instead Weiler celebrates the European Union and its unique citizenship regime as evidence that a universalistic extension of citizenship beyond its traditional, nationalist limitations is not conditional on attendant growth of a bureaucratic-coercive state apparatus, with all the pathologies this has in the past clearly involved. Especially the way in which the European Court of Justice managed to make national systems of citizenship conform to universalistic principles of non-discrimination—essentially by a creative reading of human rights into market freedoms—indicates for Weiler that expanded rights of citizenship can be anchored in common values rooted in a common civil society, and can be had without expanded state capacity and power. The stark conclusion, with highly optimistic implications, is that growth of citizenship today can be decoupled from progress in state formation; that there is not just a non-national but also a non-statist basis for citizenship; and that obligations of citizenship can be institutionalized as obligations to a peaceful civil society integrated by common values, rather than to an exclusivist and potentially nationalist state kept together ultimately by coercion. In contrast to Weiler, this paper emphasizes the *limitations of citizenship separated from state power and state capacities*. As I will argue, such limitations apply also to a construction like the European Union that undertakes to reorganize national citizenship by *supranational regulation*,[5] as an alternative to vesting it in a supranational state. While citizenship may indeed often have been distorted by its association with the state, it is my view that it is also the case that crucial rights and obligations that are part of an advanced concept of citizenship are probably enforceable only in such association, and must become less enforceable if the latter is severed. As citizenship becomes grounded in stateless supranationalism, it may therefore very well become more value-based. But the values in which it will then be based are ones that can be enforced by a supranational non-state on national states, and *not* ones that would need to be enforced by a sovereign state on—some of—its subjects.

More specifically, I wish to argue that a supranational regime that requires national states to make their citizenship regimes allow for unimpeded mobility across national borders, is likely to weaken national powers of enforcement of *obligations* of citizenship without being able to replace them at supranational level. Intervention in national states by a supranational non-state aimed at making national citizenship more other-regarding may thus change the *content* of citizenship, tipping the balance between involuntarily accepted obligations and voluntarily accepted liberties in favour of the latter. In fact, as supranational regulation leaves the national basis of citizenship unchanged, it may at the end of the day not even make national systems much less parochial, as they will still be able to use their remaining sovereignty to defend their integrity. The result would then be an uncertain impasse between re-regulation and deregulation of national citizenship systems that can be expected to play itself out in a variety of complex and often paradoxical ways, depending on the issue at stake.

A perspective of this sort arises if the conceptual apparatus that informs an analysis like Weiler's is expanded to take into account that *the persistent plurality of national citizenship regimes in Europe is embedded in a common market economy*.

1. Supranational re-regulation of national citizenship may well increase mobility as much as supranational state formation would. Unlike the latter, however, and in its absence, the very same measures that are to make citizenship regimes more universalistic also expose them to *competition*. In the European Union as it has evolved, the national polities that continue to be the seat of citizenship exist side-by-side in an economy integrated, not least, through supranational obligations for nation states to allow for cross-border mobility, collectively imposed and enforced by national polities on themselves. Governance of the integrated economy then resides, not in an integrated state coterminous with it, but in a number of nation states coupled with each other through a complex variety of international and supranational arrangements, partly limiting and partly safeguarding their individual sovereignty. Unlike the European economy, that is to say, which is for all practical purposes integrated, state capacity and the rights and obligations of citizenship aligned with it remain *fragmented* the way European integration today proceeds. However effectively national systems of citizenship may therefore be coordinated by supranational obligations enhancing cross-national mobility, they continue to be embedded into and restrained by, not just a stateless supranational-intergovernmental institutional order, but also a free market much more encompassing than each of them.

In an *integrated market governed by fragmented sovereignty*, the wielders of that sovereignty compete with one another, in part for the respect of their citizens and those of other countries entitled to cross their borders, but most importantly for the allegiance of mobile production factors. National systems of citizenship, and of public power generally, that are part of a political-economic order of fragmented sovereignty lose their monopolistic status. What rights and obligations they extend to their citizens will depend, not just on internal considerations, for example their internal balance of power or their collective political will, and not only on whatever international obligations may apply, but also on the anticipated consequences for a country's competitive position in the common market. Such competition between states may well enhance citizenship by forcing state authority to become more responsive to citizen needs. But it is also possible that it will militate against those elements of citizenship that involve obligations, especially for fractions of the citizenry that are not only highly mobile but also in command of resources crucial to a country's competitive position in the common economy.[6]

States that have become embedded in a larger economy, and as a result lose their monopoly of governance, may find themselves constrained to respond to pressures from resourceful and potentially mobile citizens by changing the terms of citizenship in their favour. To protect themselves from this, all states located in a common market would without exception have to agree on an international regime binding them to common minimum standards, in addition to and above non-discrimination of foreigners, thereby exempting a floor of citizen rights and obligations from inter-state competition. Such a regime would clearly differ from one of national commitments to free movement across borders. Rather than unleashing competition, it would restrict it by building a cartel of sovereign states against market pressures, for the purpose of collectively restoring state capacity and authority. A regime like this, one of *positive as opposed to merely negative integration* (Streeck 1989, 1992; Scharpf 1994, 1996), would obviously be highly demanding to build and maintain; whether it would ever come about and on what subjects would seem a wide open question. It is important to note that complexities of this sort would be absent in a mode of integration that would replace fragmented national with unified supranational citizenship.

2. What is being integrated in Europe is not just a society but, primarily, an *economy*, and what moves across national borders are not just citizens but also *production factors*, especially labour and capital. As citizens, workers and employers may or may not adhere to identical values; as participants in economic exchange they also have *different interests*. As citizens, they have rights and obligations in relation to the state; as participants in production, they create rights and obligations *for each other*. And while as citizens they are equal, their position in the economy is *highly unequal*. Advanced forms of citizenship take account of differences in interest and capacity, as well as of asymmetrical ('class') relationships within civil society, by attaching *differential status rights and obligations*[7] to different economic positions—what

Marshall (1964) has called *industrial citizenship*—and adding them to the civil and political rights awarded to all citizens alike.

Rights and obligations of industrial citizenship are *reciprocal*. Rights of workers, for example, to collective bargaining, information, consultation, and co-decision-making, are reflected in corresponding duties of employers, such as to bargain in good faith, inform truthfully and in good time, listen open-mindedly, and refrain from acting on specific matters without the agreement of the workforce. They are also *asymmetric*, as they are designed to balance the underlying, pre-existing asymmetry in economic power between employer and employed. Moreover, protected by means of public authority, they are supposed to be *non-negotiable* between the labour market participants to which they apply, insulating them against the impact of differences in bargaining power. For example, just as workers cannot sell their right to bargain collectively, or agree to work for less than the minimum wage, employers are not allowed to buy themselves out of their obligation to consult.

With open borders and competing sovereignties, however, industrial citizenship is likely to become *increasingly contractual*, which in turn must shift its balance of obligations and rights to conform more closely to market conditions. If employers are free to choose between alternative industrial citizenship regimes that impose differently burdensome obligations on them, they will *ceteris paribus* migrate to the regime that they find least demanding. For jurisdictions competing for economic resources inside an international system of fragmented sovereignty, lowering employer obligations and, with them, worker rights may offer itself as an effective strategy for attracting migrant capital. In fact, for industrial citizenship to erode actual migration may not even be necessary. States, but also workers, that are faced with the possibility of employer exit may agree to reduce employer obligations, i.e. worker rights, to prevent such exit, or they will refrain from using rights or calling upon obligations even though these may—still—be on the books. Mobility and the attendant decline of state monopoly will thus encourage a *de facto* renegotiation of, supposedly, non-negotiable terms of industrial citizenship, in favour of employers as these are more mobile and command more indispensable resources. In the process the rights and obligations of industrial citizenship are bound to become *less public* in character and *more private, less status-like* and *more contractual*, and overall *less like institutions of citizenship* and *more like arrangements of the market*.

3. Rights of citizenship refer not just to equal treatment by the state; to free participation in market exchange; or to an equitable balance of rights and obligations in employment. They also include *social rights* to a minimum standard of living regardless of market condition and productive contribution. Rising cross-border mobility and declining state monopoly under fragmented sovereignty affect such rights as well. If generated by a national polity located within an international free market, social rights are also *costs* that may give rise

to competitive disadvantage and, to the extent that they require taxation of employers operating under international competition, may trigger migration of capital to less costly jurisdictions, or the threat of such migration.

In national states obliged under international rules to open their borders, the benefits of social rights must be extended to all workers, including foreigners deciding to migrate in, whereas the costs can be imposed only on employers that not only reside in the country but also decide not to migrate out, which in principle they easily could. Non-discrimination as a supranational regulatory norm governing national citizenship thus tends to add foreigners to those entitled to a social minimum, while allowing nationals unwilling to pay the bill to go elsewhere. This imbalance between a potentially rising number of beneficiaries and a potentially shrinking number of payers, and in fact already the anticipation of such imbalance, is bound to exert pressure on national systems to cut back or, at the very least, not to expand their provisions of social citizenship, in effect returning to the market the determination of a growing share of their citizens' income and welfare.[8]

The purpose of this paper is to show that there is little justification in Europe today for exalted hopes for a non-statist expansion of citizenship, provided citizenship is to be more than the civil right of individuals freely to enter into contractual relations.[9] To demonstrate this I will explore in some depth a prominent area of European Union social policy, the institutionalization of workplace participation rights, in particular through the 1994 Directive on European Works Councils.[10] The picture that will surface differs from Weiler's: it is one of *weak supranational rights weakening strong national rights of social and industrial citizenship*, and indeed facing considerable limitations even in what allegedly is the principal strength of the European quasi-constitution, the enforcement on national systems of equal treatment of foreigners. In the European Union's system of fragmented sovereignty, I argue, attempts to make national systems of citizenship more other-regarding often do not get beyond a very elementary stage, if at all, while in the process they call forth pressures for a reversal of the historical evolution from civil to industrial and social rights. Small gains in civil rights, smaller than one might expect, are likely to be paid for with considerable losses in social and industrial rights. While only marginally extending citizenship across national borders, European integration as we know it tends to weaken it within them.

The Case of the 'European Works Councils'

Industrial citizenship, as defined by Marshall, combines elements of civil, political, and social rights. Its origin was the recognition of the right to collective bargaining, which in turn was the result of the labour movement learning to use political rights to collective organization for economic purposes. Through the new *hybrid institution* of collective bargaining 'social progress was being sought by strengthening *civil rights*, not by creating *social rights*; through the use of contract in the open market, not through a minimum wage and social security' (Marshall 1964: 93; my emphasis). Freedom of contract, however, was exercised *not individually but collectively*, and was therefore 'not simply a natural extension of civil rights (but) represented the transfer of an important process from the political to the civil sphere' (Marshall 1964: 94). In this way, as Marshall puts it, the union movement created 'a secondary system of industrial citizenship, parallel with and supplementary to the system of political citizenship' (1964: 94).

Rights of industrial citizenship take different forms in different countries. But in most European welfare states, they have come to include rights to *collective participation of workforces at their place of employment*, through information, consultation, and co-decision-making, together with corresponding obligations of employers to respect such rights and enable their effective use.[11] Legally, such rights and obligations are inseparably attached to socio-economic status: the former come with being employed, the latter with being an employer. Moreover, just as workers cannot sell their rights, employers cannot buy themselves out of their obligations, even if they considered this to be in their best interest. This is because industrial citizenship constitutes part of the public machinery for the social regulation of labour markets and employment, as an institution of *public* rather than private governance. Created to balance the fundamental asymmetry of power involved in relations of employment, it would cease to be what it is if it were open to renegotiation in the shadow of this asymmetry.

To insulate industrial citizenship rights to workplace participation from market pressures, post-war European welfare states typically institutionalized them in statutory law, which in effect inserted them as compulsory elements in any individual employment contract regardless of the will of the contracting parties, and if necessary against their will. Technically workforce participation rights came to be written either in company law or in labour law. Rights based in company law ensure collective participation of workforces in a firm's economic decision making; as they touch upon the exercise of property rights, they represent a stronger version of industrial citizenship that is politically more demanding to institute. Rights based in labour law are more concerned with the workplace as such, or with the plant as distinguished from the enterprise. While company-law participation rights interfere with the rights of owners in the firm, labour-law participation rights modify managerial prerogative in the day-to-day governance of the employment relationship. The two kinds of participation rights are not always entirely separable, and some issues can in principle be addressed under either company or labour law. Indeed in a country like Germany where both modes coexist in strong versions, there is often considerable functional overlap between them.

Europeanizing Workplace Participation

Capital mobility across jurisdictional boundaries, as promoted by economic integration without political integration, affects nationally based industrial citizenship as it exposes it to competition. As rights of industrial citizenship exist in most European countries, although in different forms and different strength, economic integration raises the question of how to protect and where to locate such rights in the political economy of united Europe. From the beginning, and long before the emergence of the cross-nationally integrated production systems of today, the subject arose in the context of three different projects:[12]

1. *The project of a unified European industrial citizenship.* An important initial motive, linked to a European federal state-building agenda, was to eliminate differences in industrial citizenship between European countries, on the premiss that a united Europe had to provide for equal rights for all its citizens. This required a general European model of workplace participation to be installed in all member countries, resulting in 'harmonization' of national systems and taking industrial citizenship out of economic competition. In the political and economic environment of the early 1970s, with the various *autunni caldi* of the preceding decade still fresh on everybody's mind, harmonization was deemed possible only at the highest national level. Generally there was a widely shared presumption that a European model of industrial citizenship, and in particular of workforce participation, would have to be roughly like the German one.

2. *The project of a unified European company law.* From early on in the integration process, a unified European company law was seen as both beneficial for and required by economic integration. By enabling firms to incorporate in just one legal system for all their European operations, a common company law would offer them an opportunity to economize on the ('transaction') costs of incorporating in a multitude of national systems. At the time, a unified European company law without strong provisions for workforce participation was considered politically impossible. Institutionalization of industrial citizenship rights in corporate governance was regarded as the price European business had to pay for the economic benefits of company law harmonization. It was also regarded as the best way of protecting multinational companies from having to deal with a variety of different national participation regimes.

3. *The defence of the integrity of national legal systems and of an integrated free market.* With increasing numbers of multinational firms, more and more

plants, and workforces in Europe are managed by company headquarters located in foreign jurisdictions. To the extent that decisions affecting such firms' local industrial citizenship obligations are made centrally, the participation rights of local workforces are potentially threatened: with management extraterritorial to the legal system governing the local plant, subjecting it to legal sanctions is difficult in a regime of sovereign nation states (Eser 1994: 93). For example, a multinational firm might try to evade consultation obligations in a host country by claiming that decisions are made at headquarters, with local management neither involved nor informed. While local management could therefore not be held responsible, central company management would remain beyond the reach of the host country's law enforcement. The issue this raised was one of *equal rights* of workforces, albeit *not across national boundaries but within them*. It also could be construed as one of *fair competition*, in that foreign firms might be advantaged over domestic firms who had to play by local rules whereas the former had not.[13] Generally the rising importance of multinational firms put to a test the capacity of national governments to uphold their respective 'law of the land'. Countries could have dealt with the problem through a web of bilateral treaties. Alternatively they could have tried to write national legislation allocating statutory responsibility for compliance with local labour regimes to agents they could hold responsible in national law. But while the former would have been cumbersome at best, the latter would have raised difficult questions of extraterritorial enforcement of national law liable to trigger discord between sovereignty-conscious nation states. This suggested a collective, integrated response. However, legal integration for the collective defence of national sovereignty in an international economy requires instruments that are effective without requiring a supranational European state. As will be seen, the solution that was ultimately found for this was extremely complicated, precisely because it had to be compatible with continued fragmentation of sovereignty and citizenship.

While all three projects were pursued simultaneously by different agencies in Brussels, different member states and different social groups inside them, over time the emphasis moved from unified citizenship to the defence of national regime integrity in an international economy, and its compatibility with free competition in the 'internal market'. This coincided with, and found expression in, a change in the *approach to integration* which evolved in three stages, from attempted *harmonization* of national systems to their *incorporation* as building blocks in an internally diverse supranational system to, finally, their *coordination* through a supranational regime.

1. *Harmonization.* This phase began in the early 1970s, with ambitious projects promoting the rise, and ultimately dependent on the emergence, of a European *supranational welfare state*. The leading objective was harmonization of industrial citizenship arrangements, by means of statutory intervention

superseding or homogenizing national systems and proceeding primarily in the realm of company law.

2. *Incorporation.* In response to lasting lack of success, a modified strategy emerged that tried to incorporate the diverse national systems as building blocks in a common European system. Policies continued to pursue common European industrial citizenship, but in a variety of—presumably equivalent— institutional forms reflecting and arising out of national traditions. Increasingly attention shifted *from company to labour law.* Moreover, proposed European legislation began to offer *menus of alternative solutions* for actors to choose from, as a substitute for politically unrealistic uniform solutions, indicating a movement from mandatory towards more voluntaristic approaches.

3. *Coordination.* In the third phase policies began to be aimed at *supranational regulation of national systems,* as in Weiler's model of national citizenships coordinated under a common European regime. Form and extent of nationally constituted industrial citizenship rights were no longer questioned. The leading objectives of European policies were to ensure that fragmented citizenship did not interfere with the integrated market, and to protect the integrity of national systems against some of the externalities arising from economic integration. Company law as a tool for instituting workplace participation was sidelined, and European-level policy became *entirely confined to labour law.* Also, as much as possible policy gave *precedence to voluntary agreement* and refrained from statutory prescription.

Movement through the three phases was caused by powerful opposition against positive integration and supranational state formation from both national and business interests. The path of withdrawal from the 1970s project of integrated European industrial citizenship was continuous and linear. As time passed, the issue came to be seen as an international problem of *external effects undermining the governability of national industrial relations systems,* and its solution was sought as a condition of the effective functioning of the *internal market,* and in particular of *diversity of national institutions coexisting with cross-border mobility of capital and,* increasingly, *diversity of corporate cultures.* In the process, workplace participation was relegated from the domain of company law to that of *labour law,* and the design and implementation of industrial citizenship was increasingly turned over from public authority to the *voluntarism,* first of national governments, and later of multinational firms.[14]

Phase One: Harmonization

The first initiatives for a European system of industrial citizenship[15] aimed at Europeanization of the German model, with a combination of parity co-determination at company level and of legal rights of works councils or unions to information, consultation, and co-decision-making at plant level.[16] Two paths were simultaneously pursued.

1. In the early 1970s the Community regarded differences in national systems of company law as 'restrictive conditions on the freedom of establishment within the Community' (Art. 54 of the Treaty of Rome), deriving from this a mandate to pursue 'approximation and harmonization' of such systems. For this purpose, the Commission drafted a number of directives on company law. One of these—the *'Fifth Directive'*, first issued in 1972—dealt with the governance structure of public limited liability companies. Its passage would have meant that all member countries would have had to rewrite their company law in accordance with it. Responding among other things to the then social-liberal German government, it proposed a two-tier board system with an obligatory supervisory board that would include employee representatives.

2. Parallel to its efforts at harmonizing national company laws, the Commission also proposed a *European Company Statute*. Firms based in at least two member countries would be given the option to incorporate under that statute, as an alternative to incorporation in national law. A firm incorporated as a 'European Company', or *Societas Europea*, would have the advantage of being *ipso facto* considered incorporated in all Community countries, making it unnecessary to seek incorporation in different national systems. The first drafts of the Statute were presented in 1970 and 1975 and required European companies to have a supervisory board that included employee representatives with full rights to information and co-decision-making, as well as a European Works Council. This combination of company- and workplace-level co-determination was the closest the Community came to a wholesale adoption of the 'German model'.

Harmonization of national systems, if it goes far enough, makes a separate European company law as dispensable as special legislation on participation in multinational firms. It also eliminates regime competition. The latter does not necessarily hold if a new layer of European company law is added to national laws. Not only would competition between national legal systems continue. Without strong elements of industrial citizenship, a European company law may cause *legal exit* from national company law that includes such elements. At the same time, if European law did include strong citizenship rights, firms from countries where industrial citizenship is weak might hesitate incorporating in it, jeopardizing the objective to accelerate economic integration. Whether or not a European Company Statute with strong workplace participation rights would be accepted by firms would ultimately depend on how they value the economic benefits of incorporation in a common legal system. Unlike Fifth Directive-style harmonization, a European

Company Law approach to industrial citizenship depends to an important extent on voluntarism.

Neither the Fifth Directive nor the European Company Statute ever came close to adoption. The main reason for this was their linkage to the issue of industrial citizenship. For national governments, the political costs of changing their national systems of corporate governance in a German direction loomed ever larger the more time had passed since the labour revolts of the late 1960s. Employers, for their part, had always been opposed to any Community social policy that went beyond non-binding general principles. European legislation on German-style workforce participation in particular was rejected as 'inflexible' and destructive of 'the variety of information and consultation procedures evolved by companies to suit their particular circumstances' (Hall 1992: 9). Objecting to industrial citizenship being anchored in company law were not just employers unfamiliar with co-determination, but also the German employers—who preferred the pressure of regime competition on their national system over a statutory 'leveling of the playing field'. With time employers also seem to have concluded that multinational firms could if necessary live with different national company laws. In any case, the costs of this came to be regarded as lower than those of Europeanized industrial citizenship on the German model, and pressures from European business for company-law harmonization subsided.

As to European Unions, Community legislation on workforce participation in company law threatened to force them to decide between nationally and ideologically sacrosanct principles such as union-based and union-independent forms of industrial democracy; legal co-determination and voluntary collective bargaining; and bargaining at company and sectoral level. Such decisions were and continue to be beyond the political capacities of European union confederations. Also, a unified European system of industrial citizenship would have required most unions, except those on whose national system it was modelled, to change their mode of operation, resulting in possible advantages of unions from some countries over unions from others. Fears of this kind gave rise to *institutional nationalism* even among unions that were otherwise far from happy with their national institutions.[17] While the conflicting preferences of European unions were not always visible—especially when legislation seemed unlikely to be actually passed—employers and governments successfully used them to argue that strongly normative proposals like the first drafts of the Fifth Directive and the European Company Statute were 'unrealistic' and did not have undivided support even from the union side.

Phase Two: Incorporation

To break the deadlock, the Commission in subsequent years offered a series of concessions to nation state concerns over sovereignty; to union institutional nationalism; and to employer pressures for protection of property rights and more 'flexibility'. The action shifted to labour law, although some rearguard battles continued to take place on company law. Legislative proposals, while still envisaging a unified European system of industrial citizenship, attempted to institutionalize it in different forms in different countries, in anticipation of the later discovery of 'subsidiarity'. Attempts were made to ensure that different national versions of European workplace participation were equivalent; where this was not possible, equivalence was heroically assumed. Although the concessions offered approached a point where the objective of a common European system, of company law as well as of workplace participation, seemed in danger, they did not go far enough for legislative progress.

It was only after the initiatives on company law had come to nothing that workforce participation came to be dealt with as a matter of labour law. In 1980 the then Commissioner for Social Affairs, Henk Vredeling, issued a broadly written draft directive on information and consultation rights for workforces, which came to be known as the *'Vredeling directive'*. The initiative tried to utilize the momentum of the Community's Social Action Programme of 1972, which had resulted in passage of a number of social policy directives. Two of these, the Collective Redundancies Directive of 1977 and the Transfer of Undertakings Directive of 1979, provided for workforce information and consultation in connection with the specific events they addressed. The Vredeling draft was an attempt to generalize the information and consultation rights member countries had accepted for firms undergoing economic restructuring, bypassing the issue of corporate governance by bringing workforce participation within the ambit of Community labour law.

The 1980 Vredeling draft was largely agnostic on structure. While it specified in great detail a wide range of *information* on financial, economic, and employment issues to which workforces were to be regularly entitled, and in addition established legal *consultation* rights on decisions likely to have 'serious consequences' for employees, it assigned the exercise of the new rights to 'existing employee representatives by law or practice'. Another defining feature of the draft was that it focused on *companies with subsidiaries*, and on access of workforces in branch plants to information held by management at headquarters. Two aspects of the draft were particularly notable:

1. The draft addressed two different situations at the same time: where headquarters and subsidiary are located in the same and where they are based in different Community countries.[18] While the first condition can in principle be handled by national legislation, the directive would have mandated a common floor for all national systems and would to this extent have harmonized them. The second condition suggests itself as a classical case for supranational regulation of transnational externalities that undermine the governability of national systems.

2. In case a multinational company failed to enable its local management at a foreign subsidiary to comply with its information and consultation obligations under the directive, the Vredeling draft gave workers the right to deal directly with the central management, ultimately by taking it to the local courts of the host country (Danis and Hoffman 1995: 185). More than anything else, it was this 'bypass' provision of the draft that incited the opposition of business. It can be assumed, however, that it also appeared less than reassuring to sovereignty-conscious member states.

The draft Vredeling directive met with unprecedented hostility from business, European and extra-European (DeVos 1989). Although the Commission in 1983 watered it down significantly—by confining its jurisdiction to firms with at least 1,000 employees and reducing the range and frequency of the information to which workforces would be entitled—it was unable to save it. A last-minute offer to limit the directive to multinational firms, dropping its harmonization component,[19] failed to turn the tide. Under heavy fire from business and with a British veto certain, the Council in 1986 formally suspended discussion of the directive.

After its defeat on Vredeling, the Commission returned to company law. Already in 1983 it had presented a new version of the Fifth Directive, offering both countries and companies a choice between *four alternative models* of workforce participation: the two-tier board system of the first draft, with between one-third and one-half of supervisory board members coming from among the workforce; a single board with the same proportion of employee representatives as non-executive members; a company-level representative body of employees only (something akin to a works council without, however, being so called); and any other participation structure provided it was agreed between employer and workforce and conformed to specified minimum standards. To prevent regime shopping by firms, the draft tried to ensure that access to information and rights to consultation and co-determination were equivalent in all models. In addition, national legislators were given the possibility to limit the choice of firms based in their country, in the extreme case to just one of the four models. When progress on the Fifth Directive failed to materialize, the Commission in 1989 issued a revised version of the European Company Statute, which was further amended in 1991. Unlike earlier drafts, which responded primarily to German concerns about German firms escaping from co-determination by emigrating into European law, the new proposals seemed to be more concerned with fears in other countries and by employers of being forced into a 'German model'. To this end, they offered the same menu of alternatives for board participation as the 1983 draft of the Fifth Directive. Provisions on a works council were no longer included, separating company law from labour law. Foreshadowing subsequent developments, discussion of works councils was referred to the 'social dialogue' between unions and employers (Zügel 1994: 139). Moreover, whereas the initial drafts had emphasized co-management and co-determination, the 1989 version stressed information and consultation, moving closer to the revised Fifth Directive as well as to Vredeling, and worker participation was described as an instrument of stable labour relations contributing to the success of the firm (Eser 1994).

Not surprisingly, a central issue in the debate became the choice of alternatives the new draft proposed to allow. While the Commission insisted that its different models were equivalent, this seemed more than doubtful to many observers, especially German ones (Addison and Siebert 1991: 622). Moreover, given the great diversity of the models, it seemed questionable whether the original objective of a unified European company law was still being served (Eser 1994). In any case, to reassure national legislators, the drafts, just as the 1983 version of the Fifth Directive, granted them the power to limit the range of models from which national firms could choose. Where firms were given a choice by national law, they had to consult with their workforce; the final decision, however, was to rest with management as otherwise it was considered unlikely that a firm would be willing to incorporate in European law.

Another significant change was that the Commission divided the original draft into two, one on the statute of the European company and another on worker participation in it (Eser 1994). According to the Commission, this was not to sever the link between the two issues and enable passage of European company law without European rules on worker participation. Arguing that it was unacceptably cumbersome for multinational companies to be subject to different participation regimes in different countries, the Commission insisted that the two proposals be passed at the same time. The reason for dividing the draft was to facilitate legislation by changing its treaty base: instead of drawing on Art. 235, which would have required unanimity, the Commission now drew on Art. 100a for the European Company statute and on Art. 54(3)(g) for worker participation,[20] *under both of which decisions could be taken by qualified majority* (Eser 1994). This was widely seen as an attempt to make it impossible for Britain to veto the insertion of worker participation rights in the European Company statute. What was less noticed was that it also ruled out a future German veto of European Company law without worker participation equivalent to German co-determination. Still, for the next half decade the European Company statute failed to make legislative progress.

Phase Three: Coordination

The European Works Councils Directive, which after long agony was passed in 1994, is widely regarded as a classic example of the Union's post-Maastricht 'policy innovations' of the 1990s. Indeed in the euphemistic language that has spread from the Commission to large parts of the community of students of European integration (see Hall 1992), the directive is depicted as a model of the new European Union virtues of decentralization, subsidiarity, respect for national and cultural differences, and an intelligent use of legal patchworking techniques for creating a diverse, pluralistic, non-statist, and even post-Hobbesian social order. On this background, it is useful to remember that compared to its hapless predecessors, the directive is extremely modest in its ambitions (McGlynn 1995). All it does is create an obligation in international law that member states make it obligatory in national law for nationally based firms with significant employment in other European Union countries to negotiate, with a body representing their entire European workforce, on a European-wide workforce information arrangement. If no agreement is reached, firms must set up a 'European works council' with representatives from all their European plants, and member states must endow such councils with a common minimum of legal rights. In line with Weiler's model of national citizenship regimes bound by international law to extend rights to non-citizens, the directive thus indeed requires national systems to include non-nationals. But apart from this it does very little.[21]

1. Like Vredeling, the directive stays away from company law and remains strictly in the realm of labour law, avoiding any suspicion that the industrial rights it undertakes to create might interfere with civil rights of property.

2. Moreover, unlike Vredeling, the directive relates exclusively to multinational firms. Workplace participation in firms with no foreign plants remains fully controlled by national systems. The latter the directive does not touch, not even in multinational firms. All it does is graft an international on the national representation arrangement at a multinational company's headquarters, relying for the recruitment of representatives on the national systems of its various plants. In this way, the directive not only avoids harmonization, but also sidesteps any judgement on the equivalence or non-equivalence of participation rights in different countries; it merely *coordinates* these within a select number of firms.

3. Participation rights under the directive amount to no more than the provision of *information* on a yearly basis and in exceptional emergencies. There is no obligation for management to consult, if the concept means that management can act only after workforce representatives had an opportunity to present a considered opinion.[22] There are also no rights to co-determination, under which works council consent would be a condition of management going ahead with a decision.

4. Finally, the directive goes to great lengths to preserve a wide space for *contractual voluntarism*, leaving it almost entirely to negotiations between management and labour in individual firms to determine the structure and

rights of their European works council. Although the Directive does provide for a compulsory fall-back solution, great care is taken to ensure that it never applies.[23] First, management and labour remain free to agree not to have any workplace participation arrangement at all. They can also decide to set up an 'information procedure' for existing national workforce representatives, instead of a European body entitled to receive information. Furthermore, agreed-upon rights of workers under the procedure, or the rights of a European works council if one is set up, may remain below the fall-back option, difficult as that may seem. Agreements that are negotiated before the directive takes effect—which it does only after its transposition in national law by all countries concerned, which is expected in early 1997—are considered valid, even if the body that negotiated them on behalf of the workforce was not representative.[24] Finally, the obligatory solution comes in force only after three years of negotiations, from the day of the directive taking effect. Workers that want to have a European works council before the end of the century may as a consequence have to agree to rights that are inferior even to the statutory minimum.

If nationally fragmented citizenship is to be *coordinated rather than integrated*, critical questions of institutional design must arise. If the objective is *equal treatment* of workforces in non-domestic subsidiary plants, the standards of either the host or the home country of the employing firm could be applied. In the first case, the rights of subsidiary workforces would equal those of workers of other employers in their country; in the second, subsidiary work-forces would be given the same rights as workers in the firm's country. However, host country equality would fragment industrial citizenship rights within multinational firms, affording different national segments of a company's workforce different rights to participation at its supranational headquarters. Being impracticable and inimical to economic integration, this solution was never pursued. Equality in terms of the company's home coun-try standards, on the other hand, would fragment industrial citizenship in host countries, as the rights of a potentially growing share of national work-forces would be determined by a multitude of foreign legislators, and could therefore widely differ.

Further problems arise for the operation of the integrated market. If home country standards exceed host country standards, making multinational firms grant home country rights to foreign workforces may place such firms at a local competitive disadvantage compared to host country firms, or to multi-nationals from third countries with lower standards also investing in the host country. If, on the other hand, host country standards are higher, limiting host country workers to home country rights would give advantage to foreign over domestic firms in the host country. Difficulties like these are endemic to arrangements of fragmented citizenship and must inevitably accompany any attempt, motivated by political expediency or by respect for national diversity, to live with a *coordinated patchwork of national citizenship regimes* as an alternative to unified citizenship in a supranational state.

Trying to avoid the complex puzzles of equality and inequality under fragmented citizenship, the directive managed to be passed by creating a *separate system of uniform weak European rights for foreigners*, to exist alongside the *pre-existing systems of differently strong rights for nationals*. Responsibility for whether or not national rights, in home or host countries, are below or above the European rights of subsidiary workforces is thereby handed to national legislators. Fair competition is secured in that all multinational companies, wherever they and their subsidiary plants may be based, have to comply with the same rules concerning the information rights of non-domestic workforces. In this sense, European legislation, taken by itself, does remain competitively neutral. At the same time, national rights remain exposed to competitive pressure, as it is left to the discretion of national policy makers whether they want their domestic standards to be above or below the European standard or, for that matter, the standard of other countries.

Working out the details of the coexistence between national and supranational participation rights is, again, left to national legislation and to the voluntarism of the marketplace. Here, too, what in fact was an admission of defeat by the unsolvable technical complexities and political dilemmas that follow from fragmentation of state capacity and citizenship, is presented as an inventive practical application of the new creed of decentralization and 'subsidiarity'. Indeed even with respect to the substance of European rights, the directive goes out of its way to turn industrial citizenship, from an *institutional condition* of negotiations between employers and workforces, into their *result*. While it does not prevent firms from agreeing to councils with consultation or even co-determination rights, no firm has done so as yet, and all known agreements have remained at or below the statutory minimum of participation rights (Bonneton et al. 1996).

This does not rule out that some firms may in the future institute participation procedures, very likely decentralized ones, that go further than the directive. However, voluntary participation arrangements are of a different quality than obligatory ones, as firms enter into them only if they promise to be pro-competitive. Their presence and structure depends on technological and market conditions, and perhaps on managerial strategy. They can therefore be expected to vary widely, making worker access to participation highly unequal in different countries, sectors, and companies. Legal regulation is precisely to prevent such inequality by neutralizing the impact of markets, establishing participation as a *universal right* rather than a contingent and particularistic benefit of favourable market conditions. To the extent that works councils are institutions of industrial citizenship bringing non-competitive 'social' interests to bear on managerial decision making, the mostly voluntary European works councils are works councils only in name.[25]

The Deficiencies of Coordinated Citizenship

The European Works Councils Directive does not establish integrated European citizenship rights, let alone contribute to supranational state formation, and in the end was no longer intended to. But what does it accomplish in terms of supranational regulation of national industrial citizenship regimes, especially with respect to equal treatment of non-nationals? And to what extent does its studied non-interference with national regimes actually protect these, given their continued exposure to regime competition? History and results of the long conflict over industrial citizenship in Europe impressively confirm the claim that there is *no substitute for unified state capacity* as an institutional condition of advanced forms of citizenship in an integrated economy.

Incomplete Inclusion

In the firms to which it applies, the Directive creates a *dualism* of representative bodies, by adding a European works council to existing national councils. The structure of the former and its relationship to the latter are left to negotiation. In these the representatives of a firm's home country workforce are likely to play the leading role, not only because they will usually represent the majority of the workforce but also because of their long-standing bargaining relations with central management. European works councils can therefore be expected to be heavily *coloured* by the national system of a company's home country. In fact, European works councils in French-based firms are more similar to French works councils than to European works councils in German-based firms, which above all resemble German works councils.[26]

Rather than European institutions proper, European works councils are in reality *international extensions of national systems of workplace representation*. In line with Weiler's model of internationally pooled citizenship, the Directive makes multinational firms include representatives of their foreign-based workforces in an extended version of their domestic representation system. Such inclusion does *not*, however, take place *on equal terms*. The inevitable dominance of home country representatives in the negotiations on the structure and status of European works councils offers them rich opportunities to protect their privileged access to central management. Indeed one reason why so many voluntary agreements on European works councils were concluded before the directive took effect seems to be that up to this time they could be negotiated directly by national unions and workforce representatives in a company's home country, acting also on behalf of the non-national workforce.[27] This may explain why some of these agreements remain below the fall-back standards of the directive, which would have automatically applied only a few months later (although only after a delay of three years; Hall et al. 1995: 31).

The special negotiating body prescribed by the directive must include representatives from all affected plants. It will therefore typically give higher proportional representation to foreigners than to home country nationals. Still, given the minimal statutory rights the directive creates, the effective strength of a European works council in relation to central company management is likely to continue to depend on whether home country workers and unions are willing to invest their political capital in it. It also depends on management, whose resistance to formalization of rights above the legal minimum may in itself be enough to preserve the asymmetry of access between nationals and non-nationals. All in all, the directive does little to check or change the interest of home country workforces, potentially shared with management, in containing the impact of the European works council on industrial relations at headquarters. Indeed it presents them with a temptation to make concessions on the rights of foreign workforces in return for continued privileged access to information and collaborative relations. The unchanged existence, parallel to the European works council, of national representation systems to which only nationals have access further serves to limit the stake of the latter in European-level participation. Here as always, voluntarism does not favour the weaker party.[28]

The consequences of *voluntarism at multinational and institutional dualism at national level* can best be observed in a country like Germany where national participation rights are strong. First, since the directive founds European participation rights only in labour law and disregards company law, workforce representation *on the board* of a large German company will remain confined to its German workforce which, under German co-determination law, elects one-half of the members of the supervisory board from among their ranks. As board-level co-determination exists in national law only, this holds even if the vast majority of a company's workforce is employed outside Germany.

Second, European works councils in German companies will typically coexist with a central works council in German law (*Gesamtbetriebsrat*) which has extensive legal rights to information, consultation, and co-determination (Lecher and Platzer 1996; Niedenhoff 1996). In large firms, all members of the central works council will be full-time, and as a body they are likely to have use of a professional staff. The central works council will be meeting regularly in short periods, perhaps once every two weeks. It will be in daily contact with central company management, and its leading members will at the same time serve as elected workforce representatives on the company's supervisory board. The central works council is also likely to be in close contact with the industrial union that organizes the company, and will be receiving advice from it on a current basis. Unless management wants it otherwise, meetings of the European works council will thus be not much more than extended special sessions of the central works council, especially since most of the members of the latter will also sit on the European council. Usually the agenda of European works council meetings will have been structured by the German central works council in previous contacts with central management, and what management will say at the meeting, under its residual European obligations to inform, will long be known to the German participants.

Generally, the contrast between uniformly weak supranational rights and differently strong national rights may give rise to complex politics. On the labour side, conflict may emerge between workforce representatives in the company's country of origin and from foreign subsidiaries, especially if these try to use their new position aggressively. Where national participation rights are stronger in the country of origin, such conflicts are likely to take a different course than in the reverse case. Generally, subsidiary representatives from countries with strong representation rights would seem to stand a better chance of making themselves heard in European works councils than those from countries where workplace participation is weak, on account of the former's superior resources and experience. Home country representatives confronted with the possibility of well-endowed non-nationals wielding too much influence on a European works council would, therefore, seem to have an incentive to keep the rights of the latter limited, in particular if their own, national rights are strong. Another factor in this context is likely to be the numerical relationship between the company's home country and subsidiary workforces.

All of this reflects the fact that the European works councils of the directive are in fact no more than European extensions of national systems. Within them, the distinction between nationals and non-nationals remains fundamental. While non-nationals are represented only through the European works council, nationals are represented through it and, in addition, their respective national representation system where, in all countries except one, rights are much stronger. As it remains *nationally fragmented*, the European system of workplace representation provides for no more than *second-class industrial citizenship* for non-national workforces.

Continuing Competition

Regime competition persists under the directive and, indeed, is likely to increase, in a variety of ways.

1. Precisely because the directive leaves national participation regimes unchanged, it does nothing to take them out of competition. The increase in bargaining power within national systems that economic integration confers on employers, by enabling them to extract concessions from workforces with threats to relocate work to countries with weaker regimes (Mueller 1996), remains unchecked. To the extent that this leads to a 'hollowing out' of national rights, as a result of workforces abstaining from using them, this trend continues unabated.[29]

2. Another way in which national fragmentation fosters regime competition is by implementation of the directive being left to national legislation. National implementation laws vary with respect to the rights they assign to European works councils and the obligations of employers in relation to these. While such differences are slight, there seem to be tendencies among firms that have a choice—especially firms from outside the European Union—to designate their *Belgian* operations as their European headquarters for the purposes of the directive, affording themselves the advantages the Belgian works council regime offers to management.[30] Accordingly, the German debate on the implementation of the directive was in part structured by the issue of *competitive advantage*, with firms and employers associations clamouring for legal minimalism in line with a strict reading of the directive, to protect German multinationals from having to fulfil more demanding obligations in relation to their European works councils than their foreign competitors.

3. Furthermore, the dualism between weak European and strong national systems may induce multinational companies to seek a stricter distinction between *national issues* that must be dealt with under national participation regimes, and *European issues* that can be discussed with the European works council.[31] Here, regime competition is between the national and the supranational regime coexisting within the same firm, and over the allocation of substance matter between them. Where a European works council exists, demands from home country workforces to be consulted on the company's international business may be more legitimately rejected by management. Indeed the Europeanization of participation as instituted by the directive may accelerate tendencies in companies to split into a multinational 'holding' with a European works council, and national production companies that remain subject to national participation regimes. To the extent that the latter are stronger than the European regime—which all but one of them are—such change would reduce participation rights on balance. Given the fragmented character of European industrial citizenship, management efforts to transfer substance from strong national to weak multinational participation may meet with the support of non-domestic workforces, which stand to gain from any increase in the significance of the weak multinational system, as they have no status in the strong national system in the company's home country. By siding

OXFORD
UNIVERSITY PRESS

Review Copy
from
Oxford University Press
Great Clarendon Street, Oxford OX2 6DP
Telephone: 01865 556767

EUROPEAN CITIZENSHIP
National Legacies and Transnational Projects
Edited by Klaus Eder and Berhard Giesen

0 19 924120 1
Price: £40.00
Publication Date: 1 February 2001

The source of the book should be given as
Oxford University Press

The publisher requests that no review should appear before the publication date and would be grateful for a clipping of your review. Further information on the book or its authors will gladly be given by the Publicity Department.

with central management, foreign workforces may thus be able to improve their access to information, at the expense of the national workforce's access to consultation or co-determination. While this may contribute to evening out the difference between national and multinational participation rights, it would do so by pre-empting the former rather than reinforcing the latter.

4. European works councils are accepted by firms to the extent that they can be regarded as *efficiency-enhancing*. That they can indeed be so regarded was an important reason why a number of European employers were in the end no longer opposed to them and urged their association, UNICE, to mute its opposition. European works councils seem to offer European multinational companies an opportunity to develop a multinational corporate identity and comprehensive, non-parochial human resource management. As their 'customized' institutional design is subject to negotiation in the shadow of the market, they are unlikely to become vestiges of anti-competitive social protection or redistribution, as indicated by the fact that unions have not been able to gain a single European works council agreement providing for participation rights above the legal minimum (Krieger and Bonneton 1995).[32]

Beginning Erosion

As the directive essentially extends national systems of workplace representation beyond national borders, its impact must differ by country, making it difficult at first to assess its overall effect.[33] Especially in countries with high national standards, however, like Germany and the Netherlands, the directive must be expected to reinforce tendencies towards erosion of such standards.[34]

In the German case, this is beginning to happen as a consequence of the European move from company to labour law as the site of industrial citizenship. In late 1995 the European Commission issued a consultative document (Com (95) 547) which, along the lines of the 1989 and 1991 revised proposals of a European Company statute, recommended to resolve the deadlock on European company law by eliminating from current proposals all provisions for workplace participation. In their stead, the Commission suggested, in characteristically opaque language, the adoption a single new instrument on national-level information and consultation. Alternatively, it proposed to designate the European Works Council Directive as that instrument, as all European multinational companies were already covered by it. If successful, this initiative would end for good the quest for integrated European industrial citizenship in corporate governance, in favour of the European works council regime of 'pooled' national citizenship based in labour law. While there is as of now no evidence for this, it may be suspected that employer toleration of the Works Councils Directive was conditional on the Commission's subsequent undoing of the political nexus between the Europeanization of company law and the incorporation in it of participation rights for work-forces.[35]

With the European works councils in place, prospects are that German unions will not for long continue to be able to secure the support of the other European unions for their resistance to European Union company law without strong provisions for co-determination. Increasingly isolated in the ETUC, the DGB may also lose its hold on the German government position on this matter. In fact, anticipating defeat it is presently beginning to lower its sights. Rather than continuing to seek organizational provisions for workforce representation written into the constitution of European corporations (*Organmitbestimmung*), the tendency now is to demand rights for unions to negotiate company-specific participation arrangements for a legally specified list of subjects. Just as under the European Works Council Directive, the concrete form of such participation would be left to the parties at the workplace (Küller 1996). Whether a satisfactory solution will at all be possible along these lines must be more than doubtful given recent experience. But from the perspective of German unions and the German government, it would avoid a long struggle for an, inevitably highly complex, provision in European Company statutes allowing the German legislator to bind German companies to German co-determination even if they chose to incorporate in European law. Given the way European 'pooled sovereignty' works, it is likely that German demands for a special national arrangement would not go unheard. But inevitably that arrangement would be far from watertight. Not only would the unions have to accept compromises and expend valuable political capital in the national arena to get the necessary national legislation passed. It would also be difficult, and probably impossible, to extend the provisions of such legislation to new firms, or to prevent existing firms from moving their seat to more liberal political jurisdictions. The result would inevitably be company-level co-determination turning into a 'grandfather system', like the coal-and-steel version of co-determination in Germany already is.

Remarkably, then, the voluntarism of the European Works Councils Directive is beginning to find its way even into the national system that more than any other relied on statutory law to create strong rights and obligations of industrial citizenship insulated as best as possible from market pressures. That participation arrangements in Germany will slowly become more negotiated and more pro-competitive is now widely regarded as inevitable among German unionists; hopes to export German co-determination to Europe in order to preserve it have effectively been given up.[36] Correspondingly, employer objections to company-law co-determination in Germany now centre mainly on the fact that the system will remain unique in Europe, and may therefore constitute a competitive disadvantage both for German firms and for Germany as an investment site.

Still insufficiently understood is the possibility of an eventual conflict between the voluntarism of the European participation regime and the uniquely German distinction between legally based workplace participation and collective bargaining. Such conflict would become acute if European works councils were to turn into vehicles of some sort of European collective bargaining, dealing with subjects that in Germany are regulated by industrial agreement. This, of course, is exactly the future that unions in other European countries would find attractive. Even short of it, European works councils are likely to assist multinational firms in building company-centred human resource management regimes, helping them loosen their ties with national industrial relations systems, especially those that try to bind them into obligatory sectoral or national regulation. In Germany, this could reinforce the erosion of industry-level collective bargaining and contribute to further divergence of wages and conditions between workers in different firms, especially international and local ones.[37]

In a world of competitively interdependent national industrial orders embedded in an internationalized market economy, regime erosion in countries with high standards is likely to be followed by regime erosion in countries with lower standards. Hopes that the alternative to harmonization at the highest level would be some sort of convergence at a middle level, averaging out national systems by redistributing participation rights from the strong to the weak, seem unfounded given the weakness of European-wide redistributive institutions and the operation of regime competition. Precisely to the extent that participation regimes are not merely market-driven devices for increasing productivity, but are to limit managerial prerogative, not least in order to protect workforces from excessive intensification of work, erosion of a strong regime may *enhance the competitiveness of the firms subject to it*.[38] This explains why firms under competitive pressure tend to seek such erosion. But it also suggests that weaker regimes must then lower their standards in response, or become more productivity-enhancing, to compensate for their loss of *relative competitiveness*. Rather than making national systems 'meet in the middle', if European fragmented sovereignty fails to protect strong national regimes from competitive erosion, it is likely to weaken all regimes, beginning at the top and continuing down to the bottom.[39]

Concluding Remarks

The subject of this paper was the broad institutional conditions that fragmented citizenship under 'pooled sovereignty' (Keohane and Hoffmann 1991) creates for politics in economically integrated Europe. As long as Europe is governed by a constitutional construction under which most Europeans remain foreigners to most other Europeans, and common policies are not backed by the power of a common state, outcomes seem likely that do not fit the optimistic image of inexorable progress towards advanced forms of citizenship divorced from state coercion and based in the common values of a stateless European civil society. Regulating national citizenship through a supranational non-state regime does open up national systems to foreigners, but only in a very limited way. And the price for this seems high as regime competition must be allowed to continue, undermining strong national regimes and, in the longer term, probably all others.

In the perspective of 'policy analysis', workplace participation is just one 'policy area' among others. What the character of integrated Europe as a polity is can therefore be determined, if at all, only by surveying all such areas and somehow aggregating the results. Workplace participation may also be seen as an 'industrial' issue of declining significance in a 'post-industrial' society in which, allegedly, consumer interests take precedence over producer interests (Majone 1993). None of these positions is taken here. Since workplace participation regimes regulate, or may precisely fail to regulate, the extent to which the organization and intensity of work may be governed by market pressures, and since social regulation of the 'effort bargain' at the workplace may be anti-competitive, they present a strong test for the ability of a polity to mediate the impact of competition on social life. Not all 'policy areas' are equally instructive when what is at stake is the relationship, not between institutions, but between politics and markets. Moreover, as markets expand and their competitiveness increases, what institutional resources a society has or has not at its disposal to regulate its 'labour process' would seem to become more rather than less important.

What responses creative human action may devise to new institutional constraints and opportunities, and what it may accomplish in relation to the problems and probabilities these pose, can never be predicted with certainty. All this paper tried to do was explore the *institutional potential* of what Weiler calls the Community, as opposed to the Unity, model of European integration—not to offer a strategic recipe of how to deal with the exigencies of a two-level polity that separates rights of citizenship from state capacity. Indications are that a non-state regime of industrial citizenship rights that is forced to rely heavily on national and managerial voluntarism must accept considerable inequality, as it must allow participation to vary with firms' national origin and corporate strategy. It also seems likely that the industrial order that it will bring about will be more market- and efficiency-driven, more private and less public, and much more internally diverse than the national regimes of the post-war period, with potentially far-reaching consequences for the structure of European societies and their social cohesion. On the other hand, while social science may sometimes be able to understand the conditions of action, its imagination is too limited to pre-empt its results.

NOTES

1. Earlier versions of this paper were presented at a conference on 'Social and Political Citizenship in a World of Migration', European University Institute, European Forum, 1995–96 Project on Citizenship, Florence, Italy, 22–24 Feb. 1996, and to a plenary session of the 1996 meeting of the European Consortium for Sociological Research (ECSR) in Berlin, 27 Aug. 1996.
2. Not to mention the 'scientific' respectability that is gained by shifting to a liberal world view capable of providing analyses with a proper 'micro-foundation'.
3. The way I use the terms, 'international' refers to relations between states; 'transnational', to phenomena that exceed the boundaries of any one state; and 'supranational', to institutions above states that are designed to govern these.
4. Leaving aside his more specific concern with the Maastricht ruling of the Bundesverfassungsgericht (Weiler 1995). I also concentrate on the relationship between, in Weiler's terms, state and citizenship, at the neglect of a third pole that figures importantly in his argument, *ethnos* or *Volk*.
5. I am using the term 'regulation' in the sense of Majone (1993, 1994).
6. The mechanism at work was identified as early as the eighteenth century, by none less than Adam Smith who, as quoted by Streit (1995), points out in the *Wealth of Nations* that 'the proprietor of stock is properly a citizen of the world, and is not necessarily attached to any particular country. He would be apt to abandon the country in which he was exposed to a vexatious inquisition, in order to be assessed a burdensome tax, and would remove his stock to some other country where he could, either carry on his business, or enjoy his fortune more at ease. By removing his stock, he would put an end to all the industry which it had maintained at the country he left. . . . A tax which tended to drive away stock from any particular country, would so far tend to dry up every source of revenue, both to the sovereign and to the society. Not only the profits of stock, but the rent of land, and the wages of labor, would necessarily be more or less diminished by its removal'.
7. On 'status' in the present context, see Streeck (1990).
8. See the present situation in almost all European countries, which are facing both an erosion of their tax base and rising demands on their welfare budgets, forcing them to cut back on citizen entitlements.
9. And it is only this that the paper will show. In particular, it does not try to predict the extent of 'social dumping' in Europe, nor is it to announce a 'race to the bottom'. While the first of these concepts inexplicably limits the impact of regime competition to the migration of production and 'jobs' from high- to low-standard regimes, the second treats time essentially the way economists do: as non-existent. But time matters, and the historical world is sticky and slow-moving. A 'creeping to the bottom' is all one can expect, and it would be bad enough.
10. Exactly the same point can be illustrated drawing on other Acts of European social policy, e.g. the Posted Workers Directive. I will deal with this case elsewhere.
11. See Sturmthal (1964), Rogers and Streeck (1995). This does not apply in Britain where industrial citizenship remained limited to a right of workers to be represented by trade unions through collective bargaining. In most countries of the

European Continent, collective bargaining came to be supplemented by rights of workforces to participate through union-independent workplace representatives in the management of the firm where they are employed. Because of peculiarities of the British legal system, rights to collective bargaining in Britain were never safely enshrined in law, although at the time Marshall was writing they were widely considered as so immovable a fact of industrial life that Marshall could conceive of them as of rights of citizenship. In the Roman law systems of the Continent such rights became much more formally established. This protected them better against changes in political and market power—see the different impact of the changes of the 1980s on industrial relations in, for example, Britain and Germany.

12. On the early history of European workplace participation policy, see Nagels and Sorge (1977), Zügel (1994).
13. Initially the European Works Councils Directive of 1994 was introduced, in 1990, not as social policy legislation, but under Art. 100, as 'vital to the removal of unfair competitive advantage' (McGlynn 1995: 79).
14. On voluntarism in European social policy, see Streeck (1995).
15. On the history, see Eser (1994) and Kolvenbach (1990).
16. On workplace participation in Germany, see Müller-Jentsch (1995), Streeck (1984), Thelen (1991), Turner (1991).
17. On 'institutional nationalism', see my chapter in Marks et al. (1996). Danis and Hoffman (1995: 180), among others, point out that the German features of the proposed legislation did not endear it with non-German unions.
18. In fact it dealt with a third situation as well, where the headquarters is located outside the Community. This became politically important as it mobilized the vigorous and successful opposition of US multinationals. It can, however, be disregarded for present purposes.
19. And thereby effectively reducing European participation rights to a mere annex to national participation systems. This prefigured the 1994 Directive; see below.
20. Art. 54 deals with the removal of barriers for companies choosing their seat!
21. The text of the directive is found in Blanpain and Windey (1994: 118 ff.) and in Hall et al. (1995: 49 ff.).
22. Which it still meant in the Vredeling draft. Under its 1983 version, managements would have had to obtain a view from workforce representatives on planned measures that were likely to have 'severe consequences' for employees. Workforce representatives had thirty days to state their view; within this period the measure in question could not be enacted and litigation could have prolonged the period to sixty days (Zügel 1994: 49). By comparison, while the 1994 Directive does speak of consultation, it defines it simply as 'exchange of views and establishment of dialogue' (Art. 2(f)). In the Annex, where the statutory fallback provisions are spelled out, it is made explicit that even in 'exceptional circumstances affecting the employees' interests to a considerable extent', the requirement to inform the workforce 'shall not affect the prerogatives of the central management' (para. 3). This is clearly below the standard even of the 1989 Social Charter—which is, of course, not legally binding (Danis and Hoffman 1995: 87).
23. According to the responsible EU Commissioner, Padraig Flynn, 'the success of the directive . . . will reside in the fact that its provisions will never need to be implemented' (quoted in TUC n.d.: 16).

24. In this way, an agreement can stand even if negotiated exclusively by the central works council or the union representing the workforce at company headquarters.
25. In the debate on European works councils, unusually muddled even by European standards, the voluntarism of the directive is sometimes defended with reference to the 'Nordic model' of workforce participation, which is based on national industrial agreement, as distinguished from the German, or even 'Germanic', model based on, inevitably, 'rigid' legislation. Critique of the voluntarism of the directive can then be dismissed as expression of an idiosyncratic national preference for law over negotiations, or worse as an imperialistic attempt to impose one 'national culture' on the others. The fact of the matter is, of course, that from the perspective of the individual firm, a strongly normative and effectively enforceable national agreement of the Scandinavian sort is for all practical purposes the same as legislation, as it exempts high standards of participation from inter-firm competition. This is very different in the case of the directive where the voluntarism takes place, not between powerful associations, but exclusively at the level of the individual enterprise. On the relationship between the voluntarism of the directive and the minimalism of European works councils as representative institutions, see Schulten (1996).
26. French European works councils are labour-management forums whereas German European works councils are labour-only bodies. See Bonneton et al. (1996).
27. The frustration on the part of the TUC about the British opt-out seems to be related to the fact that it made British employers less willing to negotiate advance voluntary agreements with British unions only, and indeed with unions as opposed to freely elected workforce representatives (TUC n.d.).
28. Potentially balancing the influence of home-country workforces and unions are the sectoral European union confederations. For these the voluntaristic elements of the European Works Councils Directive represent the first opportunity to insert themselves in bargaining with employers, especially and precisely when councils are created. It is not by accident, however, that unlike the German Works Constitution Act, the directive never mentions unions (Däubler 1995: 156). It remains to be seen who will prevail in the emerging conflict over their respective roles between external (European) unions and internal (national) workforce representatives. For an unusually honest account of some of the tensions that have already arisen, see Gerstenberger-Sztana (1996).
29. For examples, see Mueller and Purcell (1992).
30. In Belgium the directive was transposed in national law by an agreement between the social partners, in accordance with national practice. 'While the agreement, of course, follows the obligations laid down in the Directive, it adds nothing, and seeks to provide as much flexibility as possible . . . in the areas which are left to member states' discretion. Commentators attribute this to a wish on both sides to avoid complex or burdensome requirements and provide an attractive environment for foreign investment and multinationals wishing to establish their European headquarters in Belgium' (*European Industrial Relations Review*, 266 (Mar. 1996): 4).
31. For an initial view on this, see Lecher (1996: 267).
32. The vast majority of the European works councils that existed in 1996 were joint

labour-management bodies chaired by a representative of the employer (Rivest 1996).

33. In other words, this effect is governed by Stanley Hoffmann's (1966) 'logic of diversity'.

34. As yet little is known about the way supranational regulation and international regime competition together affect national social policy, and in particular how the voluntarism of supranational social policy 'softens' the hard obligations on which it is typically based. Very likely, one reason for the liberalizing impact of supranational governance on national regimes is that integration under fragmented sovereignty amounts to a supranational extension of national political arenas—which seems to offer more oportunities to forces and tendencies of liberalization than to their opponents. National regime change would then have to be explained as a consequence of a *dynamic interaction* between the specific political selectivities of national and supranational institutional constraints and opportunities, adding to the effects of interdependence between national systems competitively embedded in an encompassing common market.

35. Already in Jan. 1995, a high official of the German labour ministry had promised German employers that 'the issue of co-determination at European level would be put to rest with the passage of the (European Works Council) Directive' (Hornung-Draus 1995: 90).

36. European works councils themselves tend to be regarded by German unions, not as vehicles for internationalization of interests, but as substructures of international 'networks', not costly as they are funded by multinational companies and the European Commission and usable for limited purposes of information gathering and, above all, international relations among organized worker interests. That European works councils are perceived mainly from a national perspective reflects their correspondence as an institution to a 'logic of national diversity'; exactly the same can be observed in all other countries.

37. The above is not meant to be an exhaustive discussion of the future of industrial relations or workplace participation in Germany; it merely serves to illustrate how certain institutional properties of the emerging European participation regime may erode high national standards. As pointed out, to understand the full dynamic of this process one would have to look in detail at the interaction between ongoing 'endogenous' trends at national level and the dynamics of supranational institutional development. One would also have to factor in the impact of direct regime competition.

38. While strong workplace participation regimes in European countries have turned out to be far from incompatible with firms being competitive *in some respects*, they are also clearly anti-competitive *in others*. For example, German co-determination admits and indeed supports competitive strategies based on product innovation, customization and the use of skilled labour, while making it difficult for firms to achieve competitiveness through process innovation or downsizing. In this way, it serves significant although largely latent social and employment policy functions. Employer dissatisfaction with co-determination is not because it makes firms uncompetitive, which clearly it does not, but because it limits their 'flexibility' under market pressures to explore competitive strategies for which consensus is more difficult to get. Regime competition erodes primarily those elements of

national participation regimes that are anti-competitive; the others remain in place or re-emerge on a voluntary basis. This is another reason why regime erosion is likely to proceed mainly gradually.

39. To the extent, of course, that national regimes are stronger than the supranational regime. This is the case in all European countries subject to the directive. It is not the case in Britain where, however, due to the Maastricht opt-out the directive does not (yet) apply. If it did, Britain would be the only major country where there would be no dualism between the national and the European system of industrial citizenship, as the former does not, or not any more, exist. It is also, and for this reason, the only country where the European Works Council Directive might raise national standards.

Building on this an argument for the general benevolence of European works councils would, however, be somewhat excessive. The main reason for the high regard in which British unions hold European social policy, including the Works Councils Directive, is their own extreme weakness. It was only after the destruction of their shopfloor power under the Thatcher Government that British unions have sought some sort of legal underpinning of their status. The British political system, however, cannot really provide this as there is no written constitution, and any Parliament can with a simple majority undo any law made by its predecessor. This is why, in the absence of a domestic possibility for labour rights to be legally locked in, the British union movement has historically not bothered to seek such rights, and has rejected legally based co-determination through works councils even in periods of political strength when they might have been possible to get.

'Europe', which they have always also rejected, British unions came to embrace only when Thatcher had left them desperately in need for legal rights of organization and recognition—rights that they could secure for themselves regardless of the Conservative majority and that would remain beyond the reach of the 'Westminster system' of parliamentary sovereignty. It was for this objective, and only for it, that British unions developed an interest in supranational legal regulation of their national industrial relations—a distinctly national interest that has little to nothing to do with Europeanizing industrial relations or, for that matter, workplace participation. It also happens to be the case that the voluntarism of the European works council regime meshes well with British traditions, just as the latter are not incompatible with minimal legal rights to union recognition. The fact that no strict distinction is made in the directive between union and workforce representatives, or between co-determination and collective bargaining, further adds to its affinity with the British system. Moreover, company-based industrial relations are by now the rule in Britain.

REFERENCES

ADDISON, J. T., and SIEBERT, W. S. (1991). 'The Social Charter of the European Community: Evolution and Controversies'. *Industrial and Labor Relations Review*, 44: 597–625.

BLANPAIN, R., and WINDEY, P. (1994). *European Works Councils: Information and Consultation of Employees in Multinational Enterprises in Europe.* Leuven: Peters.

BONNETON, P., CARLEY, M., HALL, M., and KRIEGER, H. (1996). *Analysis of Existing Agreements on Information and Consultation in European Multinationals.* Brussels: European Commission.

DÄUBLER, W. (1995). 'Die Richtlinie über Europäische Betriebsräte'. *Arbeit und Arbeitsrecht,* 5: 153–6.

DANIS, JEAN-JACQUES, and HOFFMAN, R. (1995). 'From the Vredeling Directive to the European Works Council Directive: Some Historical Remarks'. *Transfer,* 1: 180–7.

DEVOS, T. (1989). *Multinational Corporations in Democratic Host Countries: U.S. Multinationals and the Vredeling Proposal.* Dartmouth: Aldershot.

ESER, G. (1994). *Arbeitsrecht im multinationalen Unternehmen.* Frankfurt am Main: Peter Lang.

GERSTENBERGER-SZTANA, B. (1996). 'Europäische Betriebsräte in der Metallindustrie: Praktische Erfahrungen des Europäischen Metallgewerkschaftsbundes (EMB)'. *WSI-Mitteilungen.*

HALL, M. (1992). 'Legislating for Employee Participation: A Case Study of the European Works Councils Directive.' Warwick Papers in Industrial Relations, No. 39. Warwick: Industrial Relations Research Unit, School of Industrial and Business Studies, University of Warwick.

—— CARLEY, M., GOLD, M., MARGINSON, P., and SISSON, K. (1995). *European Works Councils: Planning for the Directive.* London: Industrial Relations Services, and Coventry: Industrial Relations Research Unit.

HOFFMANN, S. (1966). 'Obstinate or Obsolete? The Fate of the Nation-State and the Case of Western Europe'. *Daedalus,* 95: 862–915.

HORNUNG-DRAUS, R. (1995). 'Vorrang für betriebsspezifische Gestaltung'. *Der Arbeitgeber,* 47 (3): 89–91.

KEOHANE, R. O., and HOFFMANN, S. (1991). 'Institutional Change in Europe in the 1980s', in R. O. Keohane and S. Hoffmann (eds.), *The New European Community: Decisionmaking and Institutional Change.* Boulder, Colo.: Westview Press, 1–39.

KOLVENBACH, W. (1990). 'Gesellschaftsrecht und Mitbestimmung: Die Vorschläge der EG-Kommission', in R. Birk (ed.), *Die soziale Dimension des europäischen Binnenmarktes.* Baden-Baden: Nomos, 87–102.

KRIEGER, H., and BONNETON, P. (1995). 'Analysis of Existing Voluntary Agreements on Information and Consultation in European Multinationals'. *Transfer,* 1: 188–206.

KÜLLER, D. (1996). 'Gleichwertig, nicht gleichartig'. *Die Mitbestimmung,* 42: 57–9.

LECHER, W. (1996). 'Europäische Betriebsräte: Erfahrungen und Perspektiven'. *Industrielle Beziehungen,* 3: 262–77.

—— and PLATZER, H. (1996). 'Europäische Betriebsräte: Fundament und Instrument europäischer Arbeitsbeziehungen?' *WSI-Mitteilungen.*

MCGLYNN, C. (1995). 'European Works Councils: Towards Industrial Democracy?' *European Law Journal,* 24: 78–84.

MAJONE, G. (1993). 'The European Community between Social Policy and Social Regulation'. *Journal of Common Market Studies,* 31: 153–70.

—— 'Understanding Regulatory Growth in the European Community'. EUI Working Paper SPS No. 94/17. Florence: European University Institute.

MARKS, G., SCHARPF, F. W., SCHMITTER, P. C., and STREECK, W. (1996). *Governance in the European Union*. London: Sage.

MARSHALL, T. H. (1964). *Class, Citizenship, and Social Development*. Garden City, NY: Doubleday.

MUELLER, F. (1996). 'National Stakeholders in the Global Contest for Corporate Investment'. *European Journal of Industrial Relations*, 2: 345–68.

—— and PURCELL, J. (1992). 'The Europeanization of Manufacturing and the Decentralization of Bargaining: Multinational Management Strategies in the European Automobile Industry'. *International Journal of Human Resource Management*, 3: 15–34.

MÜLLER-JENTSCH, W. (1995). 'Germany: From Collective Voice to Co-Management', in J. Rogers and W. Streeck (eds.), *Works Councils: Consultation, Representation, and Cooperation in Industrial Relations*. Chicago: University of Chicago Press, 53–78.

NAGELS, K., and SORGE, A. (1977). *Industrielle Demokratie in Europa*. Frankfurt: Campus.

NIEDENHOFF, H.-U. (1996). 'Der Europäische Betriebsrat aus Arbeitgebersicht'. *WSI-Mitteilungen*.

PUCHALA, D. J. (1972). 'Of Blind Men, Elephants and International Integration'. *Journal of Common Market Studies*, 10: 267–84.

RIVEST, C. (1996). 'Voluntary European Works Councils'. *European Journal of Industrial Relations*, 2: 235–53.

ROGERS, J., and STREECK, W. (eds.) (1995). *Works Councils: Consultation, Representation, and Cooperation in Industrial Relations*. Chicago: University of Chicago Press.

SCHARPF, F. W. (1994). 'Mehrebenenpolitik im vollendeten Binnenmarkt'. *Staatswissenschaften und Staatspraxis*, 5: 475–501.

—— (1996). 'Negative and Positive Integration in the Political Economy of European Welfare States', in G. Marks, F. W. Scharpf, P. C. Schmitter, and W. Streeck (eds.), *Governance in the European Union*. London: Sage, 15–39.

SCHULTEN, T. (1996). 'European Works Councils: Prospects for a New System of European Industrial Relations'. *European Journal of Industrial Relations*, 2: 303–24.

STREECK, W. (1984). 'Co-Determination: The Fourth Decade', in B. Wilpert and A. Sorge (eds.), *International Perspectives on Organizational Democracy*. London: John Wiley & Sons, 391–422.

—— (1989). 'The Social Dimension of the European Economy'. Paper Prepared for the 1989 Meeting of the Andrew Shonfield Association, Florence, 14–15 Sept.

—— (1990). 'Status and Contract as Basic Categories of a Sociological Theory of Industrial Relations', in D. Sugarman and G. Teubner (eds.), *Regulating Corporate Groups in Europe*. Baden-Baden: Nomos, 105–45.

—— (1992). 'National Diversity, Regime Competition and Institutional Deadlock: Problems in Forming a European Industrial Relations System'. *Journal of Public Policy*, 12: 301–30.

—— (1995). 'From Market-Making to State-Building? Reflections on the Political Economy of European Social Policy', in S. Leibfried and P. Pierson (eds.), *European Social Policy: Between Fragmentation and Integration*. Washington, DC: Brookings, 389–431.

STREIT, M. E. (1995). 'Dimensionen des Wettbewerbs—Systemwandel aus ordnungsökonomischer Sicht'. *Zeitschrift für Wirtschaftspolitik*, 44: 113–34.

STURMTHAL, A. F. (1964). *Workers Councils: A Study of Workplace Organization on Both Sides of the Iron Curtain*. Cambridge, Mass.: Harvard University Press.

THELEN, K. A. (1991). *Union of Parts: Labor Politics in Postwar Germany*. Ithaca, NY: Cornell University Press.

TUC (n.d.). *A Trade Unionists' Guide to European Works Councils. A TUC Guide in Conjunction with LRD (funded by the European Commission)*. London: TUC.

TURNER, L. (1991). *Democracy at Work: Changing World Markets and the Future of Labor Relations*. Ithaca, NY: Cornell University Press.

WEILER, J. H. H. (1991). 'The Transformation of Europe'. *Yale Law Journal*, 100: 2403–83.

—— (1995). 'Does Europe Need a Constitution? Reflections on Demos, Telos and the German Maastricht Decision'. *European Law Journal*, 1: 219–58.

ZÜGEL, J. (1994). *Mitwirkung der Arbeitnehmer nach der EU-Richtlinie über die Einsetzung eines Europäischen Betriebsrats*. Studien zum europäischen und internationalen Wirtschaftsrecht Band 3. Frankfurt: Peter Lang.

PART III

Citizenship Participation in a European
Public Space

PART VI

Citizenship Participation and European Identity?

7

Changing Boundaries of Participation in European Public Spheres

Reflections on Citizenship and Civil Society

Yasemin Soysal

The unfolding episodes of world politics in the 1990s have brought intensified attempts to redefine nation-state identities and citizenship. This is clearly linked to a series of world-level developments: large-scale international migration, the political reconfigurations in the former socialist countries, and the emergence of regional and transnational political entities, most clearly observed in the case of the European Union. All these developments are closely associated with the reinvention and reassertion of national(ist) narratives throughout the world: fierce struggles for ethnic or national closures in former Yugoslavia, India, Rwanda, and Ireland; the aggressive vocalization of anti-immigrant groups throughout the United States and Europe; an increasing concern with national sovereignties and borders, exemplified in the reactions of some European governments *vis-à-vis* the advance of the European Union. In addition, the demise of the welfare state, in Europe but also in the United States, increases the stakes of citizenship, which further stirs up restrictionist sentiments and a general attack on citizenship rights.

Such developments have generated a burgeoning literature on the upsurge of exclusionary national identities and citizenships. Although highly dramatic and explosive, these recent developments do not display the complete topography of citizenship in the post-war era. The exclusive focus on current nationalist tendencies, and persistent privileging of the nation state (and national collectivities) as units of analysis in much of sociology, render invisible the significant transformations that have occurred in the post-war era. The broader changes and undercurrents that underlie the contemporary institution and practice of citizenship are commonly overlooked. Alongside the growing emphasis on national identities in 1990s, we are witnessing as well the emergence of new forms of membership, belonging, and participation, which transgress the national order of citizenship.

In my work, I attempt to uncover these new forms and the broader dynamics that occasion their emergence (Soysal 1994, forthcoming). I advance arguments about the changing patterns of participation and collective claims-making in European public spheres. I would like to direct our attention to the emerging forms of solidarity and claims-making—which either remain invisible to the conventional conceptualizations of civil society or are frequently seen as threat to its functioning. I argue that these new forms undermine the conceptual and practical viability of conventional civil society prescriptions, however they do not necessarily imply disengagement from participation in common spheres, or creation of disintegrated civic arenas. On the contrary, they are evidence of a proliferation of new forms of participation, and multiple arenas and levels on which individuals and groups enact their citizenship. I suggest that to provide a meaningful understanding of contemporary formations of citizenship and civil society we need to incorporate these new modes of belonging and patterns of participation into our analytical 'tool-kit'. Drawing upon the experience of post-war immigrants in Europe, and in particular that of Muslims, I elaborate and substantiate these new forms and their implications for enactments of citizenship and participation in public spheres.

Civil Society and Participation in Public Spheres: Assumptions and Tensions

As well as defining certain rights and duties (Marshall 1964), citizenship denotes participatory practices and contestations in the public sphere (Anderson 1983; Orloff 1993; Somers 1993; Tilly 1995a). Through their collective associational, relational activities (formal or informal) in the public sphere, individual citizens mobilize and advance claims. In that sense, a shared public space, within which social actors interact and mobilize, is constitutive of civil society and essential for the exercise of citizenship. Understood as such, civil society is the participatory arena, differentiated from the state and the market, for which the existence of a 'free and equal citizenry' is an underlying requirement (Seligman 1992). And it is the collective participatory and discursive activities of the members of civil societies that create the public sphere.[1]

Civil society assumes the bifurcation of the public and private, which is conventionally articulated as a source of 'tension' in most discussions on the topic (Seligman 1992). This tension between public and private percolates around two different perspectives on civil society.[2] In the communitarian version, the tension is between the individual and the social, individual interests and public concerns. It is the 'social trust and generalized reciprocity', against individual interests, that underlie a meaningful civil society (Putnam 1993). And community-based (associational) activity cultivates and maintains such social trust and cooperation.

More liberal conceptions of civil society see the tension between public civic identities (citizenship) and private social identities of various sorts (religious, ethnic, regional, and sexual). Social identities are relegated to the private sphere, leaving the public sphere free of incompatible identities. In Habermas's rendition, for example, the (political) discursive practice of civil society and identity-formation are separated into clearly differentiated spheres (Calhoun 1994).

As Seligman (1995) argues, these two accounts are not contrasting views. Rather they are the articulation of the same concept with different emphasis. In both versions, communal ties are important, but the basis of such ties are understood differently. In the liberal version, 'noncontractual' forms of social relations are confined to the private, whereas in the communitarian one, they are privileged as the foundation for interaction in the public realm. These differences notwithstanding, the significance assigned to 'communal ties' informs two conjectures that govern civil society formulations. First, civil society is predicated upon a form of solidarity and 'moral sentiments' be they defined by individuals' civic consciousness or collectivities of a 'primordial' type. Second, a territorially bounded public sphere and nationally integrated political community are (implicitly or explicitly) deemed necessary for the realization of civic or communitarian solidarity. Hence, the increasing public expression and mobilization of collective identities inevitably appear as a threat to civil society. The liberal version sees the threat in the reification of (primordially defined) collective identities that undermine the civic unity of the nation. The communal version, on the other hand, identifies the changing boundaries and composition of the national collective as a challenge to civil society (e.g. the introduction of 'nonconventional' identities such as Muslims). These collective identities, argued, intrude upon the national collective by producing, in Seligman's (1992: 164) terms, 'alternative moral boundaries' and alternative social responsibilities.

The assumptions that commonly frame civil society discussions become spurious however, when one takes into account the post-war reconfigurations of sovereignty, citizenship, and national community.[3] These transformations pose a challenge to our conceptions and current prescriptions with regard to how the boundaries of the public sphere are defined; what the basis of social integration within its boundaries is, and who its proper referents as participants are. What this challenge entails is that public spheres are realized intra- or transnationally; solidarities are shaped beyond national boundaries; and the referent is no longer exclusively the national citizen, but increasingly an abstract individual entitled to claim the collective and bring it back to the public sphere as his or her 'natural' right.

In terms of claims-making and participation, I contend that these changes produce two significant constellations. First, nationally bounded social spaces can no longer be assumed self-evident; political communities take shape independently of nationally delimited collectives and at different levels (local, national, transnational). Simply put, the social and political stages of claims-making proliferate not only within but increasingly also beyond the nation state. Second, forms of community, participation, and solidarity that are emerging connect the claims of individuals and groups to broader institutionalized agendas and globally dominant discourses, rather than simply reinvent cultural particularisms. Claims are not only justified by reference to universalistic parameters, but also legitimized with an appeal to loosely defined notions of public good and cast in language that facilitates a host of similar claims by others. I show that Islamic groups appeal to universalistic principles of human rights, draw upon hostcountry and worldlevel repertoires for making claims, and traverse and bridge a diverse set of public places.

These assertions structure my discussion of the changing parameters of collective claimsmaking and participation in public spheres. In the subsequent sections, I discuss three specific processes that have introduced new dynamics for collective claims-making and organizing, and thus for structuring civil societies and practising citizenship, in post-war Europe.

Valorization of Personhood and Individual Rights: The Shifting Boundaries of the Political *vis-à-vis* Citizenship

In the nation-state mode of political community, 'public' and 'people' overlap with 'nation' (Calhoun 1994; Habermas 1995). This postulate strongly figures in our understanding of the legitimacy of claims to rights and participation. National belonging constitutes the source of rights and duties of individuals; and the nationally circumscribed public sphere constitutes the locus of their claims and contentions. The post-war era, however, has witnessed an increasing recasting of (national) citizenship rights as human rights (Soysal 1994; Seligman 1992: 133).[4] Rights that were once associated with belonging to a national community have become increasingly abstract, and are defined and legitimized at the transnational level.

The intensification of transnational discourse and instruments of individual rights crystallizes around the idea of personhood: a conception of human persons in abstract, universal terms, supported by legal, scientific, and popular conventions. As a social code, personhood is not an idealistic, Hegelian notion, but one rooted in highly structured discourses, economies, and politics. This scientifically encoded personness comprises the normative basis of expanding rights. In the post-war era, the rationalized category of personhood, and its canonized international language, Human Rights, has become an imperative in justifying rights and demands for rights, even those of non-nationals in national polities (Soysal 1994).

The valorization of personhood and individual rights expands the boundaries of political community by legitimating individuals' participation and claims beyond national definitions and imbuing them with 'actorhood' (Meyer 1994) independent of membership status in a particular nation state. With the breakdown of the link between the national community and rights have come multiple forms of citizenship that are no longer unequivocally anchored in national political collectivities. These forms, which I have termed 'postnational' (Soysal 1994), are exemplified in the membership of long-term non-citizen immigrants in Western countries;[5] dual citizenship, which violates the traditional notions of loyalty to a single state; European Union citizenship, which breaches the link between the status attached to citizenship and national territory; and regional/local citizenship, which includes collective rights in culturally autonomous regions in Europe.

The post-war reconfiguring of citizenship has significant implications for claims-making and participation in the public sphere. As the old categories that attach individuals to nationally defined status positions and distributory mechanisms become blurred, the nature and locus of struggles for social equality and rights change. Postnational forms of membership require new solidarities and ways of making claims, further problematizing the assumed affinity between national unity and the expansion and acquisition of rights (Cohen and Hanagan 1995).[6]

Naturalization of Collective Identities: Changing Narratives of Belonging

Most discussions of civil society, both liberal and communitarian, assume identity formation as prior to civil society and the constitution of citizenry. Identity formation and politics are not considered as part of the processes of the public sphere (Calhoun 1994). However, the postulate of relegating identity to the private and non-political does not hold, in the face of another post-war development—the redefinition of identities as rights.

Promoted by the works of the UN, UNESCO, the Council of Europe, and the like, as well as by the discipline of anthropology, the universal right to 'one's own culture' has gained political legitimacy, and collective identity has been redefined as a category of human rights.[7] Formerly considered particularistic characteristics of collectivities: culture, language, and standard ethnic traits are now seen as variants of the universal core of humanness and selfhood. Identity represents the 'unchosen'—thus the naturalizing language of kinship, homeland, and territory.[8] One cannot help but have identity.

As a natural attribute and right, identity is exercised in individual and collective actors' narratives and strategies (Abu-Lughod 1991; Somers 1992). In turn, identities proliferate and become more and more expressive, authorizing ethnic nationalisms and non-ethnic subcultures of various sorts (youth, feminist, gay and lesbian, and deaf culture). Identity emerges as an ever pervasive and meaningful discourse of participation, and is enacted as a symbolic, organizational tool for creating new group solidarities and mobilizing resources in national and world polities. Universalistic prescriptions of identity and particularism contest the assumed dichotomy of public and private.[9] Human rights discourse occasions ever increasing demands to maintain distinct group identities, and collective claims. Once institutionalized as natural, the discourse about identities creates the ground for the entry of these collective identities and claims into the public sphere, expressively packing the political with identity.

Emergence of Multi-Level Polities: Transgressing Conventional Loci of Participation

The uniformity and territorial boundedness of public spheres are either taken for granted or asserted as a precondition for functioning participatory democracies. Historically, the principle of nationalism has linked internal democracy with national self-determination, thus with territorially bounded and culturally integrated communities.[10] Thus, the nation state, and its institutions, have delimited the terms of associational, participatory life, and the practice of citizenship. The emergence of multi-level polities, as we observe with the unfolding of the European Union, alters the topography of participation and facilitates new projects of citizenship in the countries of the West.

In its developing form, the European Union exemplifies a political entity in which authority is increasingly dispersed, sovereignty is shared, and jurisdictions overlap.[11] To the extent that the nation state no longer has the sole monopoly of sovereignty, the locus of interest aggregation and articulation (which have been historically linked to the nation state) also shifts. The existence of multi-level polities engenders new frameworks for collective mobilizing and for advancing demands within and beyond national boundaries. The diffusion and sharing of sovereignty among local, national, and transnational political institutions enables new actors, opens up an array of new organizational strategies, and facilitates competition for resources and definitions. Transnational courts and the institutions of the European Union, as well as various nation-state agencies, national courts, and subnational (local) governments, become targets for diverse claims and political action. Despite this gradual but none the less notable advent of 'multiple polities', our conceptual formulations are still confined to the territorial integrity of public spheres. Changes in the locus of claims and participation are thus excluded from analytical agendas.

In the rest of this chapter, I elaborate on the implications of the above-mentioned processes for our concepts and contemporary enactments of claims-making, civic engagement, and political participation, taking examples from organized Islam in Europe.

Organized Islam Enters European Public Spheres

A significant outcome of the post-war labour migration has been Europe's rediscovery of Islam.[12] In response to a vitalization of religious associational life among immigrants, there has arisen a visible interest in Islam as an object of political, cultural curiosity and scientific enquiry. At issue is the compatibility of Islam—its organizational culture and practice—with European categories of democratic participation and citizenship.

Islam in Europe has come to be associated with highly publicized 'affairs' of dramatic content, such as the *foulard* affair and the Rushdie affair. What compounds these events, and the debates around them, is the invoking of religious symbols to make political interventions, by an organized Islam concerned with community-formation and moral boundaries. This politicized Muslim identity poses a manifest difficulty for the elemental principles of liberal democracy, which project public spheres constituted by harmonious political discourses and free of private identities.

One of the main premises in theorizing democratic society is that networks of civic engagement and associations should foster collective 'trust' and 'solidarity' by cutting across social cleavages (Putnam 1993). However, especially in the post-war era, it is precisely on the basis of these 'social cleavages' that the mobilization of civil societies takes place. Authorized by a global discourse of identities as rights, Islam, like other religious belief communities, or ethnic and regional identities, enters into the public sphere as a collective means of making claims. Moreover, the very terms within which national citizenship is construed, by institutionalizing 'nation' as a naturalized cultural entity, inescapably underwrites the engagement of other cultural identities (including Islam) as political agents in the public realm.

Let us consider the following examples. In 1989 the issue of the Islamic *foulard*, or women's headscarf, erupted into a national crisis and debate in France, when three North African students were expelled from school for insisting on wearing their veils in class. The affair revived concerns about the 'laicism principle' of the French state, the definition of freedom of religion in the public school system, and the questions of the integration of immigrant communities. During the debates, the head of the Great Mosque of Paris declared the rules preventing wearing scarfs in school to be discriminatory on the grounds of individual rights. His emphasis was on personal rights, rather than religious traditions or duties: 'If a girl asks to have her hair covered, I believe it is her most basic right' (*Washington Post*, 23 October 1989). In this case, Muslim identity, as indexed by the headscarf, was asserted and authenticized by the very categories and language of the host society. In yet another episode of the *foulard* affair, veiling was represented and defended with adherence to France's principles of laicism and liberty. As reported in Kepel (1994: 205–6, 310–12), on 5 February 1994, about, 1500 students staged a demonstration in Grenoble to support the hunger strike of a Muslim girl named Shehrazad and her newly-converted French Muslim 'sister' Sandra. Shehrazad was expelled from high school because she refused to take off her scarf in gym classes. The centre-piece of the protest was a short street performance to highlight the discrimination directed against Muslim girls. With a twist on multiculturalism, the performers enacted the headmaster's refusing to accept Shehrazad's scarf, while warmly welcoming to school a punk with multicoloured hair, a Catholic in a brown robe, and a Jew with his kipa. The point was unmistakable. The play ended with the slogans of the protesters: 'Yes to Laicism, and to my Scarf!' and 'France is my Liberty, So is my scarf!' For Shehrazad, wearing the scarf was her moral duty as a Muslim; it was a natural act and did not bother her at all. So was her Frenchness. Her protest was framed by the credo 'We are French, Yes! And, Muslim, Too!' along with '*Allah Akbar*—God is Great!' Shehrazad and her supporters, who did not see any contradiction between Islamic and French secular values, mobilized their Muslim identity as a political expression.

When urging Islamic instruction in public schools and the recognition of Muslim family law, during the 1987 national elections, the Islamic associations in Britain asserted the 'natural' right of individuals to their own cultures, to justify their demands. In their election programme they directly invoked the international instruments and conventions on human rights. As such, theirs was a claim for difference affirmed by universalistic and homogenizing ideologies of human rights. And by doing so, they participated in the host country's public space and appropriated its discourses as they mobilized on the basis of their 'difference'.

The closing statement of the fourth European Muslims Conference (July 1990), among other demands, advocated the rights of Muslim women, and the psychological and educational needs of Muslim children. In the declaration, the participants employed a discourse that appropriated the rights of the individual as its central theme. They broached an appeal for the rights of Muslims as 'human beings' and 'equal' members of European societies. Concurrently, they vocalized their demands regarding a Muslim identity, forming solidarities based on being unlike others. On 12 November 1995, which corresponded to the birthday of Fatima, the daughter of the prophet Muhammed, the Shi'ite *Ehlibeyt* mosque in Berlin invited 'all Muslim women' to a celebration of World's Women's Day. Speakers included not only the (male) clergy of the mosque but Muslim women of different nationalities, Turks, Arabs, and Germans. The speeches focused on women's equality and emancipation, locating the gender issue within the realm of religious moral-ity. Islamic vision, as presented to the audience of about 200 women, encap-sulated the very terms of the contemporary gender discourse. Throughout the meeting, all speakers sought to explicate various social identities of women (as wives, mothers, sisters, workers, and professionals). The keynote speaker, a young *imam*, traced 'the question of woman' to the Qur'an: 'We need to iden-tify and investigate the meanings given to social [gender] identities in the Qur'an . . . and then discuss the equality of men and women.' Then, by way of a theological reinterpretation, he placed gender equality in the original script, the creation story: 'We reject the contention that Eve was created from the rib of Adam. This only serves to accept that women come second to men. This is purely a defamation. Adam and Eve were created independently, from the Earth!' Finally, he referred to the Beijing Conference on Women, and claimed as an original teaching of Islam and its culture the assertion that 'women's rights are human rights'. Indignantly he declared, 'In the Beijing conference, when someone said, "women's rights are human rights", thousands of women cheered and clapped. What were they cheering for? We already said that 1,400 years ago! That is our word!' The meeting was an instance of linking the Islamic moral realm to contemporary concerns and discourses about women—speaking to and through them.[13]

With these examples, I aim to show that Islamic groups actively take part in public spheres, making (moral) claims and inserting their identities. Their claims, however, are not simply grounded in the particularities of religious narratives; on the contrary, the claimants appeal to justifications that tran-scend the boundaries of particular groups. The terms they engage are embed-ded in universalistic principles and dominant discourses of equality, emancipation, and individual rights. In that sense, the particular and the universal are not categorically opposed—rather, the particular is interpreted by the universal.[14]

A caveat is necessary here: Muslim groups in Europe obviously do not speak within a uniform discursive framework—though most studies on immigrants assume a uniformity of Islamic discourse. The aforementioned examples by no means exhaust the range of narratives employed by Islamic groups. Again, speaking in support of women's wearing the Islamic veil, a Turkish imam in Nantua declared the practice to be 'God's law', which led to serious divisions within the Turkish immigrant community—and to his deportation from France (Kepel 1994: 306). It is also possible to find Islamic positions which base their claims on religiously codified family laws that sanction status disparity between the genders. These proclamations point to alternative legitimating discourses and scripts.[15] My point here is to delineate the prevalent universalistic forms of claims-making by identity groups that are commonly overlooked, and to elucidate their implications for our theoretical vistas.[16]

Universalistic Discourses of Rights and Identity as the Moral Basis of Public Spheres

Seligman (1992) finds the advent of the 'rights-bearing individual' problematic for civil society prescriptions. This he sees in conflict with 'mutuality and responsibility'—moral elements which underline the classical understandings of civil society. The rights-bearing individual (who has an autonomous, universal ethical standing of his or her own) pursues personal interests 'devoid of a shared, public meaning' (Seligman 1992: 137). The private moves into the public; 'personal is continually projected into and conflated with the public realm' (Seligman 1992: 136). Consequently, the public realm is infused with 'competing moral claims', leading to irreconcilable conflict and undermining the premises of 'trust'.

A related difficulty that Seligman identifies for (Western) attempts to reconstitute civil society is the 'increasing complexity and differentiation of the roles' that individuals are expected to take. This differentiation brings in an 'affect-neutral' and 'instrumental' relationship to the role (1995: 23). Thus, one can no longer talk about a unitary 'moral self' that constitutes the basis of trust. Seligman argues it is this loss of self and the individual that warrants the current reifications of collective identities—especially those identities that are often based on ascribed criteria, such as race, gender, etc.

Seligman (1995: 26) cites an example provided by Wuthnow (1994): a 26-year-old woman, who defines her religious identity as of 'Methodist, Taoist, Native American, Quaker, Russian Orthodox, Buddhist, and Jew'. This display of self appears to Seligman as an epitome of the fragmented individual and 'effectively infinite possibility of self-reflexive regression' of identities. What is not considered here is the possibility of a unitary self, codified in identity narratives as fractured, one whose morality is expressed in discourses that enable such selves. I would argue it is precisely the reification of individual agency and one's rights, and the naturalization of identity as the essence of self, that designates fragmentation as an attribute of the 'holistic' individual. Indeed, the fragmentation of identities emerges as a proper, taken-for-granted prescription and celebrated in personal and public presentations.

In a meeting organized by the German-Turkish Dialogue in Berlin in November 1995 (the theme of the meeting was *Zusammenleben im Alltag*), each speaker started their commentary with an introductory statement of identity. Invariably, the statements included a combination of multiple ethnicities, professional ascription, and gender identification. (A typical one went 'I'm a half-Turkish, half-Albanian Berliner, a woman and a teacher.') Their commitment was not to one of the identities, but to the multiplicity of the identities.[17] As such, these presentations were not examples of decentred, fragmented, but axiomatically integrated selves. If so, Seligman's discontent with the proliferation of identities may not take us far in analysing the changed nature of public sphere and participation.

As these examples show, the narratives of identity, whether they belong to persons or groups, are means for partaking in and contributing to the realization of public spheres. Through such narratives persons attach themselves to available macro-frames and repertoires of making claims and devise strategies of participation. This is indeed the conflation of private with public (as Seligman rightly contends and poses as the dilemma of civil society). However the outcome is not necessarily a public arena devoid of shared meanings, or an arena of disengaged, disintegrated moral claims. What is shared and what constitutes the moral basis of public is the universalistic discourse of rights, and within this framework, the recasting of identity as the natural good.[18] This shared basis is what makes interaction in the public space possible, even when identities are multiple, particularized and set in opposition. What is not possible is that this public be defined as an expression of a closed, bounded community; the emerging public spheres disrupt national constellations. But I will come back to this in the next section.

Here it might also be useful to reinsert an insight into the discussion from the 'new social movements' theory: identities are not a priori defined but in part constituted through participation in public spheres. By a process of interaction, negotiation, and contestation, shared identity definitions and markers are constructed.[19] In civil society debates, identities are assumed to be distinct and fixed, thus in conflict as they enter the public sphere ('threat' of incompatible civil identities). This I reckon has to do with the dominant understandings of identity.

In conceptual formations, otherness and difference are essential corollaries of identity. Identity connotes similarity only when one's own community is considered; it becomes inclusionary to the extent that it creates boundaries to exclude the ones who are not alike. This conceptualization rules out the common grounds and discourses that identity politics generates across collective groups. The process of collective identity formation concurrently assumes and facilitates shared discourses and public spaces. Furthermore, through participation, identities themselves are revised and homogenized. Difference is formalized with reference to common themes, comparable modes of presentation, and routine markers and attributes of culture.

As the examples I cited in the previous section show, Islamic activists redefine and reconstruct religious symbols, such as veiling, as cultural or political expression, and defend them on the grounds of human rights, thereby reproducing and contributing to the host society and global discourses. As they engage in political conflicts and public debate, they join in the same 'discursive medium and frames', and use the same 'symbolic packages' that are available as public discourse independent of their original carriers (Eder 1996: 208).[20]

The Islamic organizations I studied do not justify their demands by reaching back to religious teachings or traditions, but by recourse to the language of rights, and thus of citizenship. By using the 'rights' language they exercise civic projects and link themselves to the broader public good. The projects of citizenship in which they engage are not however necessarily nationally bounded; they are multi-referential, both spatially and symbolically.

Participation Beyond the Bounds of National Spaces

I have so far argued that what increasingly characterizes public spheres is the multi-connectedness of symbols and discourses as opposed to the 'horizontal connectedness' among members of civil societies (Putnam 1993). The 'ties that bind' (Kymlicka 1995) manifest themselves through participation in and by vertical connection to common, universalistic discourses that transcend the national idiom of community. When Islamic associations make demands about veiling in schools, theirs is not a claim for belonging to an existing 'French collectivity' but to the educational system, which they behold as their most natural right. This is not necessarily disengagement from the collective life but an assertion that the collective is no longer bounded by a preordained national community. Their claims concomitantly redefine the national and extend beyond its bounds. I see two complementary aspects to this process of 'extending beyond the national'. First, Islamic organizations initiate and target different level public spheres in pursuing their claims. The mobilization and participation of Muslim communities entail multiple states and political agencies, and trans- and subnational institutions. For example, the issue of the Islamic *foulard* was not simply a matter confined to the discretion of a local school board, but has traversed the realms of local, national, transnational jurisdictions—from local educational authorities to the European Court of Human Rights. Similarly, in 1990, when the local authorities refused to permit the opening of another Islamic primary school, the Islamic Foundation in London took the issue to the European Court of Human Rights. Indeed, more and more, Muslim associations elevate their operations to the European level, establishing umbrella organizations and forums to coordinate their activities and pursue a Europe-wide agenda (Soysal 1994; Kastoryano 1996).[21]

Second, Muslim groups make claims on and attach themselves to multiple communities, intra- and transnational. Muslim immigrant communities do not constitute a diaspora in the classical sense. Not only do they transgress the confines of a unitary national community, in both country of residence and of origin, but they also connect to intensified transnational social spaces, both imagined and otherwise. Recent anthropological work observes that Muslim economic and political activity, while linking immigrant communities to their homelands, at the same time establishes 'transnational communities'. [22]

The transnational connectedness of immigrant communities reveals itself interestingly in their mobilization for voting rights. During the 1995 local elections in Berlin, there was visible activity among immigrants from Turkey, even though a large percentage of them lacked voting rights.[23] Their mobilization served an agenda beyond the immediate act of voting and electing their own representatives. Turkish immigrant groups not only made demands for the right to vote in German and European Union elections but also used Berlin's elections as leverage for the elections in Turkey. Their election platforms focused particularly on the recognition of dual citizenship, eradication of racism and discrimination, and extension of Europe-wide voting rights and free movement rights, along with other local issues relating to youth, education, and the elderly. One consequence of this heightened activity concerning elections was to reignite the debates about the rights of immigrants and (re)place them on Berlin's public agenda. Another was the initiatives taken by the Turkish government to facilitate the participation of Turkish citizens abroad in national elections. Thus, through their politicized mobilization, immigrant groups brought together and effected multi-level agendas, as they positioned themselves in local public spheres.

The cultural expressions of Muslim youth constitute yet another enactment of transnational affiliations and social spaces. Second-generation immigrants appropriate their identity symbols as much from global cultural flows as from the host or home country's cultural practices. As 'youth subcultures', they are increasingly part of the global, in many ways bypassing the national or traditional (Hannerz 1992; Hebdige 1979; Willis 1993). Immigrant rap groups, such as Berlin-based Islamic Force and Cartel, evoke symbols and employ language that replicates Black rap culture. They identify with 'resistance', 'brotherhood', and 'assertion of the self' in the 'universal' message of hip hop. They do not limit themselves to Turkishness or Germanness, or to Islam *per se*.[24] As such, they belong to 'diversely spatialized, partially overlapping or non-overlapping collectives' (Gupta and Ferguson 1992).

National citizenship rights are seen as an instrument to bring political communities into closure (Brubaker 1992). But as the universal individual becomes the norm, and identities are defined as rights, the national closure of political communities (and the public spheres in which they are realized) presents a formidable task. Neither are the range of legitimate discourses solely delimited by national political communities, nor are these discourses reserved only for groups who belong to the national collectivity. Thus, nationally coded public spheres do not hold; new participants permeate public spheres and alter their forms of participation, expediting mobilizations and claims for equity.[25]

Conclusion

The experience of organized Islam in Europe indicates a diversion from the classical forms of participating in the public sphere, mobilizing identities, and making claims. The decolonization and civil rights movements of the 1960s and the early women's movements were to a great extent attempts to redefine individuals as part of the national collectivity. Similarly, labour movements were historically linked to the shaping of a national citizenry. It is no coincidence that the welfare state developed as part of the national project, attaching labour movements to nations (as in Bismarckian Germany). However, the emergent formations of associational activity and collective participation (that is, mobilization of civil societies) are less and less nationally delimited citizenship projects. New collective movements aim to realize (individual) rights and enhance participation through particularistic identities, which are embedded in, and driven by, universalistic and homogenizing discourses of human rights. This shift in focus from national collectivity to particularistic identities does not necessarily signify a decrease in the importance of participation in a 'common civic sphere'. Rather, it indicates the emergence of new bases for participation and the proliferation of forms of mobilization at various levels of polity, which are not imperatively defined by national parameters and delimited by national borders.

Our concepts and theories have yet to incorporate these changes in the institutions of citizenship, rights, and identity, and to address the challenge posed by emergent actors, bordercrossings, and non-conventional mobilizations. Only then can citizenship serve as a meaningful analytical tool for our understandings, and enactments, of effective civic participation.

NOTES

1. As an analytical concept, civil society has recently gained intellectual import as exemplified by the growing literature in political theory and sociology. An incomplete selection includes Alexander (1991, 1992), Benhabib (1992), Calhoun (1992, 1993), Cohen and Arato (1992), Putnam (1993), Seligman (1992), Somers (1993, 1995), Taylor (1990), Walzer (1991), and Wolfe (1989). This scholarly interest is

contemporaneous with the popular adoption of the concept as a political remedy for the recent failures of both 'socialist' and 'capitalist' societies. The literature provides rival definitions of the concept (for an overview, see Calhoun (1993) and Somers (1995)), but I do not intend to engage the complete literature or the varying interpretations of the concept in my discussion. My treatment of civil society and public sphere is most congruent with the definition provided by Somers (1993: 589). Critically adapting from Habermas, she denotes the public sphere as 'a contested participatory site in which actors with overlapping identities as legal subjects, citizens, economic actors, and family and community members (i.e. civil societies), form a public body and engage in negotiations and contestations over political and social life'.

2. I am aware of and in agreement with the critique of the dichotomy of public and private. See Somers (1995), for an effective criticism of the commonly assumed duality of 'public state/private economy'. Although civil society is generally conceptualized distinct from the state, its realization in the public sphere assumes to address the state and its policies. State, civil society, and market constitute overlapping spheres, rather than dualities (Habermas 1962, 1995). This is an important discussion but not the focus of my contribution.

3. See Hobsbawm (1990), Tilly (1990), Meyer (1994), Soysal (1994), Jenson (1994), and Sassen (1991).

4. I use the term 'human rights' in its broad, abstract sense, not necessarily referring to specific international conventions or instruments and their categorical contents.

5. The membership rights of non-citizen immigrants generally consist of full civil rights, social rights (education and many of the welfare benefits), and some political rights (including local voting rights in some countries).

6. The transformations in national citizenship not only have to do with the global intensification of individual rights, but also with liberal ideologies and institutions of free market and trade (Jenson 1994; Sassen 1991). Together, they generate paradoxical consequences for the institution of citizenship. While the ideologies of individualism and liberalism contribute to the dismantling of the welfare state and the elimination of the policy categories based on the collective (e.g. affirmative action and welfare propositions), at the same time, they facilitate the claims of various groups for the collective as justified on the basis of individual rights. Thus, the same transnational processes that lead to new marginalizations and exclusions also create the grounds for new forms of claims-making and participation.

7. A set of transnational legal conventions and institutions guarantees the right to claim identities and self-determination. See e.g. the International Covenant on Economic, Social, Cultural Rights and the International Covenant on Civil and Political Rights. The first article of both covenants proclaims that 'all peoples have the right of self-determination. By virtue of that right, they freely determine their political status and freely pursue their economic, social, and cultural development' (quoted in Dinstein 1976: 106).

8. See Anderson (1983), Appadurai (1991), Yanagisako and Delaney (1995), Douglas (1966, 1986), Herzfeld (1992), Malkki (1992), Gupta and Ferguson (1992), and Soysal (1993).

9. It is argued that the public/private distinction has always been challenged in the history of the modern nation-state and that identity formation has always been a constituent of the public sphere (Calhoun 1993, 1994; Somers 1993; Tilly 1995*b*). I agree with this contention, but I want to make a further point that collective identities are now defined as natural rights of individuals, and thus comprise an inevitable component of their existence in the public sphere.

10. On the relationship between the principle of nationality and public spheres, see Calhoun (1994).

11. See Schmitter (1992) and Marks and McAdam (1996) for the prospect of the European Union as a multi-level polity. Closa (1995) provides a more cautious account.

12. Islamic population in Western Europe has been estimated to be 10 to 13 million, with concentration in France (5 million), Britain (1 million), and Germany (2 million). The associational activity is in rise among Muslim immigrants, but this does not necessarily correspond to increased religious practice. According to a recent survey of 13,000 foreigners in France, 68 per cent of those from Algeria consider themselves to have no religion and only 10 per cent practise Islam regularly (survey conducted by the National Institute of Demographic Studies in France, *NY Times*, 5 May 1995). Another study reports that 40 per cent of Maghrebians surveyed in France and 30 per cent of Turks in Germany report that they are 'non-believers' of God (Bozarslan 1996). A similar trend has been observed in the United States. Americans' engagement with organized religion has increased (Wuthnow 1994) despite a decline in membership in congregations and church attendance (Putnam 1994, reporting from General Social Survey data). Wuthnow's study shows that more than 20 per cent of all American adults are actively involved in some church-related group (Sunday schools, Bible study groups, 'singles' groups, *havurot*, etc.).

13. Establishing linkages between Islamic belief systems and contemporary discourses is not exclusive to the congregation mentioned above. The Alevites, another important Islamic group in Germany, incorporate secularism and equality as essential components of their culture and religious ideals. The prevalence of gender discourse in presentations of Islam is not coincidental, either. Not only the leaders but also Muslim women employ feminist discourse, particularly when they talk about their own identity. In an interview, 23-year-old Fatemeh Amin emphasizes that, through her veil, she 'represents (her) true personality' and avoids being a sexual object. She also blames the failures of Islamic countries regarding women on incorrect interpretations of the Qur'an by men (*Die Tageszeitung*, 4 Oct. 1995).

14. See Hart (1995) for a similar observation on the religious organizations' deployment of local and universal discourses in making social demands (such as for public housing and inner-city resources in the United States). Also see Lamont (1995) for a critique of the scholarly practice of taking the universal/particular dichotomy for granted. Obviously, the distinction between the particular and the universal is not new. Societal groups always use broader discourses than their specific interests (they claim the public good). But here the distinction refers to something else. Historically, for the nation-state model, and for the bourgeoisie involved in nation-building, the universal meant the whole citizenry, bounded by

the national. What is different now, I argue, is that claims are no longer confined to this nationally bounded universality, but expand beyond it.

15. See Parekh (1995) for a discussion on the range of strategies and arguments that can be employed to legitimate the Islamic practice of polygamy.

16. Another caveat is warranted here. Obviously, there is significant variation in the accommodation of the types of claims advanced. While some claims face organizational resistance, others are more readily accepted and incorporated into formal state structures. The educational authorities in Britain, for example, are more willing to accommodate the claims for Islamic dress codes, or even the teaching of immigrant languages in schools. On the other hand, religiously codified family laws (or polygamy, female circumcision) which create status disparity between genders are not viewed as legitimate demands. Here, the principle of gender equality contests the principle of religious equality, both of which are clearly embedded in European citizenships and transnational frameworks. In Europe, the treatment of women is codified in secular laws and institutions, thus the attempts to subject it to religious, private domain generates conflict. In my research, I attempt to untangle the contradictory dynamics among different legitimating discourses and principles, and explain how these dynamics lead to conflicting claims and empowerments in the public sphere.

17. In my research, I repeatedly observe that, contrary to common theoretical expectations, immigrants readily combine apparently conflictual identities (e.g. laicist republican and Muslim) and are firmly committed to the particular identity they evoke.

18. Note that here I am not talking about shared 'values' on rights and identities. Jepperson (1991) usefully clarifies the distinction between shared values and shared discourses.

19. See Laraña, Johnston, and Gusfield (1994), McAdam, McCarthy, and Zald (1988), and Melucci (1989) for an introduction to and Gamson (1995) for a review of this literature. Tambini (1995) provides an illuminating analysis of this process in his study of identity constructions in nationalistic political movements in Ireland and Northern Italy.

20. By emphasizing the commonality of discourses and strategies, I am not taking a naive position and assuming that individuals or groups will bond together and arrive at agreeable positions. Here I diverge from the Habermasian project, according to which the discursive process, when rational, serves to bring reason and will together and create consensus without coercion (Habermas 1992: 12). Public sphere necessarily involves conflicts, contestations, and incoherent outcomes, however rational. In that sense, the role of the discursive participatory process is to focus on agendas of contestation and provide space for strategic action, rather than consensus-building (Eder 1996).

21. Examples of these trans-state networks include the Directorate of Religious Affairs' Turkish Islamic Union, the European National Vision Organization, the Federation of Alevite Unions in Europe, and various other Europe-wide informal networks of mosque organizations.

22. See Kepel (1994) for transnational Muslim communities between Algeria and France, Werbner (1990) between Pakistan and Britain, and Wolbert (1995) between Turkey and Germany. For others, see Watson's (1975) study on the

economic activity and associations of extended Chinese families, spanning London and Hong Kong; Levitt's (1995) study on the mutual transformation of Dominican Republicans' church associational life in Boston and in their villages of origin; and Sassen's (1991) work on global cities.

23. Of 423,000 foreigners living in Berlin, only 54,000 had voting rights (*Die Tageszeitung*, 14–15 Oct. 1995). Of 180,000 immigrants from Turkey, about 10,000 were eligible to vote and 12 were elected to office from various political parties (*Hurriyet*, 24 Oct. 1995). As non-EU foreigners, Turkish immigrants do not have the right to vote in local elections in EU member countries. Neither can they participate in Turkish elections unless they are physically present in the country at the time of the election.

24. The hip-hop community itself is transnationally organized, though invisible to many of us. A 'world conference' of B-boys (a subsection of the international hip-hop community, whose members in Berlin are mainly immigrant youth) was to be held in Santa Barbara, Calif., in Apr. 1996. Europe-wide competitions and networks of hip-hop and rap embrace immigrant youth from England, France, and Germany. The 'Turkish' group Cartel, whose members include three Turks, one German, and one African Spaniard, has brought together the hip-hop scene in Turkey and Germany, while at the same time aiming to be an international success (see the interviews with the group in *Süddeutsche Zeitung Magazin*, 1 Dec. 1995, and *Spex* 1995).

25. Clearly my assertion is not that new participatory projects (based on transnational rights and discourses) indiscriminately supplant the previous forms of claimsmaking (based on and framed by national collectivity). Rather, I am arguing that these emerging forms, and their prominence, should be taken into account in our analyses and theoretical statements, if we want to capture the current dynamics of citizenship.

REFERENCES

ABU-LUGHOD, L. (1991). 'Writing against Culture in Working in the Present', in R. G. Fox (ed.), *Recapturing Anthropology: Working in the Present*. Santa Fe, N. Mex.: School of American Research Press, 137–62.

ALEXANDER, J. C. (1991). 'The Discourse of Civil Society: Citizen and Enemy as Symbolic Classification'. *American Sociological Association*.

—— (1992). 'Citizen and Enemy as Symbolic Classification: On the Polarizing Discourse of Civil Society', in M. Lamont and M. Fournier (eds.), *Cultivating Differences: Symbolic Boundaries and the Making of Inequality*. Chicago: University of Chicago Press, 289–308.

ANDERSON, B. (1983). *Imagined Communities: Reflections on the Origins and Spread of Nationalism*. London: Verso.

APPADURAI, A. (1991). 'Global Ethnoscapes: Notes and Queries for a Transnational Anthropology', in R. G. Fox (ed.), *Recapturing Anthropology: Working in the Present*. Santa Fe, N. Mex.: School of American Research Press, 191–210.

BENHABIB, S. (1992). *Situating the Self: Gender, Community and Postmodernism in Contemporary Ethics.* New York: Routledge.

BOZARSLAN, H. (1996). 'Urban Milieus, Social Movements, and Islam'. Paper presented at the conference on 'Islam in Europe: New Dimensions', Berlin Institute for Comparative Social Research, Jan.

BRUBAKER, W. R. (1992). *Citizenship and Nationhood in France and Germany.* Cambridge, Mass.: Harvard University Press.

CALHOUN, C. (ed.) (1992). *Habermas and the Public Sphere.* Cambridge, Mass.: MIT Press.

—— (1993). 'Civil Society and the Public Sphere'. *Public Culture,* 5: 267–80.

—— (1994). 'Nationalism and the Public Sphere'. *Lectures and Papers in Ethnicity, No. 14.* Toronto: University of Toronto.

Cartel (1995). 'Wir Sind die Deutschen von Morgen'. *Spex,* 11: 32–7.

CLOSA, C. (1995). 'EU Citizenship as the Institutional Basis of a New Social Contract: Some Skeptical Remarks'. EUI Working Papers. Florence.

COHEN, J. L., and ARATO, A. (1992). *Civil Society and Political Theory.* Cambridge, Mass.: MIT Press.

COHEN, M., and HANAGAN, M. (1995). 'Politics, Industrialization and Citizenship: Unemployment Policy in England, France and the United States, 1890–1950'. *International Review of Social History (Supplement 3),* 40: 91–129.

DINSTEIN, Y. (1976). 'Collective Human Rights of Peoples and Minorities'. *International and Comparative Law Quarterly,* 25: 102–20.

DOUGLAS, M. (1966). *Purity and Danger: An Analysis of Concepts of Pollution and Taboo.* London: Penguin.

—— (1986). *How Institutions Think.* Syracuse, NY: Syracuse University Press.

EDER, K. (1996). 'The Institutionalization of Environmentalism: Ecological Discourse and the Second Transformation of the Public Sphere', in S. Lash, B. Szerszinski, and B. Wynne (eds.), *Risk, Modernity and the Environment: Towards a New Ecology.* London: Sage, 203–23.

GAMSON, J. (1995). 'Review Essay on New Social Movements and Identity Politics'. *Contemporary Sociology,* 24: 294–8.

GUPTA, A., and FERGUSON, J. (1992). 'Beyond "Culture": Space, Identity, and the Politics of Difference'. *Cultural Anthropology,* 7: 6–23.

HABERMAS, J. (1962 [1989]). *The Structural Transformation of the Public Sphere.* Cambridge, Mass.: MIT Press.

—— (1995). 'The European Nation-State: Its Achievements and its Limits. On the Past and Future of Sovereignty and Citizenship'. *Rivista Europea di Diritto, Filosofia e Informática,* 2: 27–36.

HANNERZ, U. (1992). *Cultural Complexity: Studies in the Social Organization of Meaning.* New York: Columbia University Press.

—— (1992). 'Further Reflections on the Public Sphere', in C. Calhoun (ed.), Habermas and the Public Sphere. Cambridge, Mass.: MIT Press, 421–61.

HART, S. (1995). 'Cultural Sociology and Social Criticism'. *Newsletter of the Sociology of Culture,* 9 (3): 3–6.

HEBDIGE, D. (1979). *Subculture: The Meaning of Style.* London: Routledge.

Herzfeld, M. (1992). *The Social Production of Difference: Exploring the Symbolic Roots of Western Bureaucracy.* New York: Berg.

HOBSBAWM E. J. (1990). *Nations and Nationalisms since 1780: Programme, Myth, Reality.* New York: Cambridge University Press.

JENSON, J. (1994). 'Mapping, Naming and Remembering: Globalization at the End of the Twentieth Century'. *Review of International Political Economy,* 2: 96–116.

JEPPERSON, R. L. (1991). 'Institutions, Institutional Effects, and Institutionalism', inW. W. Powell and P. J. DiMaggio (eds.), *The New Institutionalism in Organizational Analysis.* Chicago: University of Chicago Press, 143–63.

KASTORYANO, R. (1996). *Negocier l'identité: La France, l'Allemagne et leurs immigrés.* Paris: Armand Colin.

KEPEL, G. (1994). *A l'Ouest d'Allah.* Paris: Seuil.

KYMLICKA, W. (1995). *Multicultural Citizenship: A Liberal Theory of Minority Rights.* Oxford: Clarendon Press.

LAMONT, M. (1995). 'On the Mysteries of Fluid Identities'. *Newsletter of the Sociology of Culture,* 9: 5–7.

LARAÑA, E., JOHNSTON, H., and GUSFIELD, J. R. (eds.) (1994). New Social Movements: From Ideology to Identity. Philadelphia: Temple University Press.

LEVITT, P. (1995). *Transnationalizing Civil and Political Change: The Case of Organizational Ties between the US and the Dominican Republic.* Boston: MIT Press.

MCADAM, D., MCCARTHY, J. D., and ZALD, M. N. (1988). 'Social Movements', in N. J. Smelser (ed.), *Handbook of Sociology.* Newbury Park, Calif.: Sage, 695–737.

MALKKI, L. (1992). 'National Geographic: The Rooting of Peoples and the Territorialization of National Identity among Scholars and Refugees'. *Cultural Anthropology,* 7: 24–44.

MARKS, G., and MCADAM, D. (1996). 'Social Movements and the Changing Structure of Political Opportunity in the European Union'. *West European Politics,* 19: 249–78.

MARSHALL, T. H. (1964). *Class, Citizenship, and Social Development.* Garden City, NY: Doubleday.

MELUCCI, A. (1989). *Nomads of the Present: Social Movements and Individual Needs in Contemporary Society.* Philadelphia: Temple University Press.

MEYER, J. W. (1994). 'Rationalized Environments: Institutional Environments and Organizations', in W. R. Scott and J. W. Meyer (eds.), *Institutional Environments and Organizations: Structural Complexity and Individualism.* Thousand Oaks, Calif.: Sage, 28–54.

ORLOFF, A. S. (1993). 'Gender and the Social Rights of Citizenship'. *American Sociological Review,* 58: 303–28.

PAREKH, B. (1995). 'Cultural Pluralism and the Limits of Diversity'. *Alternatives,* 20: 431–57.

PUTNAM, R. D., with LEONARDI, R. and NANETTI, R. Y. (1993). *Making Democracy Work: Civic Traditions in Modern Italy.* Princeton: Princeton University Press.

—— (1994). 'Bowling Alone: Democracy in America at the End of the Twentieth Century'. Paper, Department of Government, Harvard University.

SASSEN, S. (1991). *Global City.* New York: Princeton University Press.

SCHMITTER, P. C. (1992). 'Interests, Powers, and Functions: Emergent Properties and Unintended Consequences in the European Polity'. Stanford: unpublished paper, Department of Political Science, Stanford University.

SELIGMAN, A. (1992). *The Idea of Civil Society.* Princeton: Princeton University Press.

—— (1995). 'Civil Society and Its Unconditionalities: Public or Private Selves?' Paper presented at the European University Institute, Florence, Dec.

SOMERS, M. R. (1992). 'Narrativity, Narrative Identity, and Social Action: Rethinking English Working Class Formation'. *Social Science History*, 16: 591–630.

—— (1993). 'Citizenship and the Place of the Public Sphere: Law, Community, and Political Culture in the Transition to Democracy'. *American Sociological Review*, 58: 587–620.

—— (1995). 'Narrating and Naturalizing Anglo-American Citizenship Theory: The Place of Political Culture and the Public Sphere'. *Sociological Theory*, 13: 229–74.

SOYSAL, Y. N. (1993). 'Boundaries and Identity: Immigrants in Europe'. *Paper presented at the conference on European Identity and its Conceptual Roots, Harvard University.*

—— (1994). *Limits of Citizenship: Migrants and Postnational Membership in Europe.* Chicago: University of Chicago Press.

—— (1996). 'Boundaries and Identity: Immigrants in Europe'. EUF, No. 96/3. Florence: European University Institute.

TAMBINI, D. (1995). *Convenient Cultures: Nationalism as Political Action in Ireland (1890–1920) and Northern Italy (1980–1994).* Ph.D. thesis. Florence: European University Institute.

TAYLOR, C. (1990). 'Modes of Civil Society'. *Public Culture*, 3: 95–118.

TILLY, C. (1990). *Coercion, Capital, and European States, A.D. 990–1990.* Oxford: Basil Blackwell.

—— (1995a). 'Citizenship, Identity and Social History'. *International Review of Social History (Supplement 3)*, 40: 1–17.

—— (1995b). 'The Emergence of Citizenship in France and Elsewhere'. *International Review of Social History (Supplement 3)*, 40: 223–36.

WALZER, M. (1991). 'The Idea of Civil Society: A Path to Social Reconstruction'. *Dissent*, 28: 293–304.

WATSON, J. L. (1975). *Emigration and the Chinese Lineage: The Mans in Hong Kong and London.* Berkeley: University of California Press.

WERBNER, P. (1990). *The Migration Process: Capital, Gifts and Offerings among British Pakistani.* New York: Berg Publishers.

WILLIS, P. (1993). *Common Culture: Symbolic Work at Play in Everyday Cultures of the Young.* Boulder, Colo.: Westview Press.

WOLBERT, B. (1995). *Der getötete Paß. Rückkehr in die Türkei. Eine ethnologische Migrationsstudie.* Berlin: Akademie Verlag.

WOLFE, A. (1989). *Whose Keeper? Social Science and Moral Obligation.* Berkeley: University of California Press.

WUTHNOW, R. (1994). *Sharing the Journey: Support Groups and America's New Quest for Community.* New York: Free Press.

YANAGISAKO, S., and DELANEY, C. (1995). *Naturalizing Power: Essays in Feminist Cultural Analysis.* New York: Routledge.

8

Requirements of a European Public Sphere

Civil Society, Self, and the Institutionalization of Citizenship

Carlos Closa

The energies devoted to the characterization of European citizenship and the deficiencies in the democratic quality of the EU have been enormous. In the case of citizenship, analysis has been grounded in solid empirical evidence provided by EC law, because of the very fact that citizenship is a juridical institution. Allegedly, analysis has been enriched by historical or national comparisons, since nation states have been the traditional conceptual setting for this institution. EU democracy, on the other hand, has been characteristically and predominately tackled from an orientation towards designing institutional solutions. In either case, the suitability of the conceptual settings provided by nation states for constructing both supranational democracy and citizenship have yet to be proved.

Methodologically, this chapter avoids the model of the nation state under the assumption that naturalization (raising to normative standards of empirical evidence) should be avoided. Since the EU is a political entity in construction and with an undefined end, its analysis requires also *sui generis* elements which are nurtured by a careful blend of empirical evidence and normative (i.e. value-bound) arguments. And the location of these elements should not be projected to the future under an ideal-type final form. Rather, it must be placed in the diffuse arena of the conflict between old and new institutions. Thus, the bulk of the analysis should be placed in the interaction between the level of member states and the EU; i.e. the clash between the old and the new institutions. Whilst some traits of a questioning of the traditional theory of the state can be singled out, a sensible historiographic interpretation recommends the postponement of a substitutive theory of a supranational form of political domination. But equally, history shows that forms of political domination are rooted in earlier ones, like links in a chain (Hintze 1931). Institutions of the new form of political domination will grow undoubtedly from old ones. They will serve as solutions to specific shortcomings in the old institutions and, therefore, they hardly can be material concretions of a theoretical model drawn a priori. Taking citizenship as the example, it is still too early to affirm whether it amounts to a general redefinition of national citizenship in order to make it more compatible with European integration or whether it is a completely new institution.

The argument developed here focuses, first, on the emergence of this new form of political domination, the EU, and the issue of its legitimation. Although democracy is usually singled out as the requirement for formal legitimacy, the crux of the paper is that democracy is intimately connected to its current form, the nation state, and implicitly based on national identity. The difficulties for its adaptation to the EU derive both from questions about the desirability of a European *national* identity and the parallel questions on its feasibility. Lack of an equivalent to national identity also means a difficulty for the concretion of a European public sphere. Alternatively, the empirical ground for a European public sphere may be provided by the growing European civil society. But this requires also a different articulation of the democratic citizens' self. For this purpose, some institutional developments which also serve as a reconfiguration of national citizenship might be highly instrumental.

The State and the EU as Coexistent Forms of Political Domination

The idea that the traditional nation state and the theory on which it is grounded have come under strain is widely accepted. In a 'horizontal' dimension, i.e. its standing *vis-à-vis* other states, the challenge can be illustrated by the questioning of a central piece of the dogma of national sovereignty: the assumption of territorial impenetrability (meaning the exclusion of other law within the sovereign territory of a state) which has been challenged not only by higher international laws but by alternative domestic laws which claim universal applicability by invoking these international principles.

Whilst this development is illustrative of the new context, the interest of this paper is more in the reconfiguration induced by the 'vertical' articulation of the state. Strictly speaking, this vertical reconfiguration is inherent in the nature of the state; thus, examples such as the (promising) realization of a new international order based on human rights with a superior status to constitutional orders is justifiable within juridical monist or quasi-monist conception of the state (where constitutional and international law are perceived as part of the same order in hierarchical relations). Within this vertical restructuring, European integration has acquired the status of being the protagonist rearticulation of the so-called Westphalia system of atomized sovereign states. At this stage, arguments to substantiate this point (the questioning of national sovereignty by European integration) are well known. Evidence provides arguments for alternative and competing explanations on the theoretical value given to this fact.

From a theoretical standpoint, the creation and growth of the EU results in a reorganization of the nation state as the predominant political system, to the point that the whole process has been described as the European rescue of the nation state (Milward 1992). Legal evidence, at least partially, substantiates also a similar argument. Although it is recognized that supremacy of EC law has been solidly established by EC case law and accepted in national legal orders, the question of ultimate validity remains anchored for some in national constitutional provisions which lately allow disposability of membership commitments. This line has been championed by the German Constitutional Court, although it would be naive to assume that this is a single standing on this issue. Central aspects are the ultimate option to recover competencies and the unsettled possibility of withdrawal. Ultimate validity grounded in national settings implies predictability of membership commitments and places legitimacy within the single domestic arenas; in the words of the German Constitutional Court in its Maastricht ruling, *it is first and foremost for the national peoples of the member states who, through their national parliaments, have to provide democratic legitimation. Democratic legitimation necessarily comes about through the feedback of actions of the European institutions into the parliaments of the member states.*

An alternative historical appreciation would allow the thesis to be substantiated that the EU has consolidated itself as a distinctive and relatively autonomous polity. Recovering the neo-functionalist measurement instruments, scope and level (and leaving aside the teleological or finalist implicit element—i.e. the creation of a European federation—and the automatism for which neo-functionalists were condemned), it is evident that from 1957 onwards there has been a significant growth in both. In the legal domain, the counterpart has been the progressive affirmation of the autonomy of the EU legal order which has not only been developed by EJC case law and its progressive interpretation of the treaties as a constitution, but it has been also strengthened by the introduction of explicit constitutional principles such as fundamental rights, the rule of law, and even a basic model of democratic functioning. These two different (and probably, complementary) interpretations, together with complex realistic descriptions, give a sense of uncertainty on the character of the political entity and the conglomerate formed by member states. But empirical evidence, at this stage, permits reference to an emergent and different form of political domination which is coexistent with the former, the nation state, in the same way in which the absolutist state grew within feudalism. The relevant aspect of this parallelism lies in the suggestion for the utilization of historical methodology. Historical analysis of the apparition of the modern state shows the difficulties in dating its emergence. The traditional theory of the state has shown the difficulties in reaching a general agreement on whether the state has always existed or, otherwise, is a characteristic phenomenon of a given historical period, from which the thesis on the continuity and discontinuity of the state derives.

From the experience of concept formation on the notion of state, it seems that conceptualization should be derived from historiographic analysis. The lesson is that whilst it is possible to refer to a historical continuity·of insti-tutionalized forms of political power, what can be termed 'forms of political domination' of which the nation state has been the last manifestation, disagreement appears when prediction and specificity are required as to its future configuration. On the same logical grounds followed until now, the EU, as a suprastatal polity, is the continuation of political domination. Thus, there might be a basic agreement on genre (i.e. political domination) whilst the particular species (i.e. the characterizing concept) remains a question for the future. Philippe Schmitter must be credited with being one of the first authors to place the analysis of the EU in a larger temporal sequence and to name it 'an emerging form of political domination' (Schmitter 1992), although he recognizes that the specific designation of this form is a matter of imagining the future (Schmitter 1996). Thus, conclusive classification by species must await a later stage because the emergence of this form of polit-ical domination can be theoretically sanctioned on two assumptions: the unavoidability or necessity of its final consolidation does not derive natu-rally from its current existence, since extraordinary events or currently unperceived ones may alter the trend altogether. Judgement on the preva-lence of either nation states or the new form has to be placed on the proper temporal scale. Next, assumptions cannot be made on its institutional shape.

The final prevalence of this new form will depend (among other things) on establishing its distinctive legitimacy, whose systematization would have to probably be traced backwards in the future. What can be identified in the present are the normative legitimizing discourses and, consequently the object and the *locus* of these discourses. Starting from the second, the current analyt-ical objective should be focusing on the border line between the emerging new form, the EU (without this implying its final supremacy), and the conflicting elements of the old form, the nation state. The advantages of this strategy is that it provides for a restatement of the initial form (should this prevail in the long run—the idea of mutation) as well as providing for the identification of the foundational elements of the new form. This means that the discourses on the legitimacy of the new form of political domination are closely linked to those legitimizing the former and that the existence of these discourses create, in themselves, a public sphere.

The Justification of Political Domination: States and the EU

The justification of a form of political domination is, as Hermann Heller put it in connection with his discussion of the justification of state, closely linked to its survival in the future. It can be perfectly accepted that, despite its short-comings, states enjoy in general legitimacy, a justification in which its histor-ical existence is not unimportant. Current perception of legitimacy, however, does not rely solely on factual historical constructions. Democracy is a procedural requirement of legitimate law or a condition of validity. As Joseph Weiler put it, formal legitimacy connotes that in the creation of the institution all the requirements of the law are observed; and, any notion of legitimacy must rest on some democratic foundation loosely stated as the people's consent to power structures and processes (Weiler 1991: 2469). Although Weiler admits that formal legitimacy is akin to the juridical concept of formal validity, he states that it distinguishes itself from single legality because it is legality understood in the sense in which it was created by democratic institutions and processes. In normative terms it is highly valuable that legal theorists have gone further than Kelsenian legal positivism to inoculate political values within the concept of validity. But when this applies empirically to the EU, some of the positivistic objections reappear. The terms commonly accepted in the debate are that member states are legit-imate forms of political domination whilst the EU is the subject of a discus-sion on its legitimacy. Validity of the EU political and legal order remains ultimately anchored on the national constitutional provisions of EU member states. Moreover, every ratification act of the several EU treaties must be regarded not only as an affirmation of this specific validity but also as an increase of legitimacy, since it sanctions the acceptance of the EU polity. Still, the question on EU legitimacy remains.

Why? In this context, Kelsen's legal positivism is highly revealing: legal validity cannot provide legitimacy, since this is placed further away in the domain of political theory and political philosophy. The recourse to legal (democratic) validity provides a highly valuable normative objective, for instance, in the terms expressed by Habermas: 'the united will of citizens is bounded, through the mediation of universal and abstract laws, to a demo-cratic legislative *procedure* which ... only admits regulations that guarantee equal liberties for all and everybody: the procedurally correct exercise of popular sovereignty simultaneously secures the liberal principle of legal equality (which grants everybody equal liberties according to general laws)' (Habermas 1994: 11).

But the illusion that procedures by themselves may be enough to legitimate the Union should be avoided. Thus, Weiler argues that, next to formal legitimacy, social legitimacy connotes a broad societal (empirically determined) acceptance of the system. Acceptance of the system is not logically linked to its nature, although Weiler in an effort to inoculate substantive values, argues that social legitimacy embodies an important substantial component: legitimacy is achieved when the government process displays a commitment to, and actively guarantees, 'values that are part of the general political culture, such as justice, freedom, and general welfare' (Weiler 1991: 2469).

In terms of *acceptance*, the capability to provide these values seems to be the main constitutive element of this EU empirical legitimacy. In this sense, the EU involves an instrumentalist dimension which is grounded on a conditional perception: since the starting assumption is that member states secure *most* of the aspects of preferred forms of life, the existence of the EU is tolerable as far as it covers the subsidiary deficits of member states (and, as some theorists have pointed out, the lack of democracy might be instrumental for the efficient functioning of the EU; Merkel 1993). Conditionality is reinforced through the idea of disposability, the principle that member states remain the masters of the treaty. National constitutional rounds and mainly referendums fulfil this function as much as they are also and simultaneously instruments for national democracy.

Thus, the normative component of legitimacy (i.e. democracy) is disconnected from the empirical one. This does not mean a rejection of the democratic character but its replacing in a larger temporal scale, as a goal for the future. Democracy might act as a normative objective but it is uncertain that the kind of institutional arrangements that currently can be qualified as democratic (and which are drawn from the experience of nation states, such as representation and majority principle) might currently be fitting for suprastatal democracy.

In the meantime, it seems more compelling to face the teleological question: For what, or for what not, is this new form of political domination? Apart from federalist thinking calling for a supranational state and proponents of a universal state, the justification is not transcendent to EU self-functioning. In the brief historical time of the existence of the EU, the foundations for its justification can be identified functionally: peace, security, and economic well-being. And it is also evident that, by its very continued existence, the EU has established itself as a de facto political entity with a certain factual legitimacy. This is reflected by the scarce disposition by national public opinion to withdraw from the Union (and corroborated by the fact that withdrawal is also justified mainly by the future shape than by past achievements of the Union).

At this point, some legitimizing aspects (capability to deliver, economic well-being, factual existence) have been identified. Why, then, a discourse on the lack of legitimacy? As it has been mentioned, some authors see the source of the legitimacy deficit in the lack of democracy. Thus, the form to eliminate or diminish the legitimacy problem would be to inoculate democratic procedures and institutions. But this seems contradictory with the criticism made of the state-like features of the EU being a reason for its illegitimacy. A sober and realistic statement could perhaps conclude that facticity plus legitimizing discourses on factual existence might legitimate the emerging form of political domination, acting democracy as a normative objective. This depends on an important qualifier: in as much as opposite discourses do not become encroached in the perception of the people. The formerly mentioned coexistence of forms of political domination is mirrored by a coexistence of normative discourses on its legitimacy or lack of it. This, of course, is a simplification of a more complex reality where discourses can integrate several more refined attitudes. Nevertheless, they provide the polar points between which arguments are organized.

The questioning of EU legitimacy, paradoxically, might provide for the identification of aspects which legitimate the new form of political domination. In fact, these negative discourses generating debate and contestation create a discursive ground on which affirmative discourses on legitimacy might be rooted in the future. Empirically, the question at stake is the viability of a civil society within the EU; the empirical base for this public sphere and the substantive dimension of it.

Public Sphere and Civil Society in the EU

For the sake of clarity in the discussion, it is necessary to trace at least broadly the conceptual differences between civil society and public sphere. Classical sociologists and political theorists constructed the notion of civil society as the counterpart to public power. Both civil society and public power (state) have the same substrate, the population and, originally, the main constitutive element of the civil sphere was the market. Progressively, of course, the civil society has become a richer one where voluntary associations, such as NGOs, have acquired a more protagonist role and a network of functional subsystems has been developed. Although public power can stimulate the development of civil society, its characteristic is precisely its autonomy.

Public spheres are the mediating element between both. The public sphere, in Habermas's model, presupposes a triadic model which explicitly recognizes the normative zone between public power and the market (Somers 1995: 124). Somers reformulates the notion of public sphere as a contested participatory site in which actors with overlapping identities as legal subjects, citizens, economic actors, and family and community members (i.e. civil societies) form a public body and engage in negotiations and contestation over political and social life (Somers 1993: 589).

The arena for this interaction between public power and the market has been traditionally constrained within the boundaries of the nation state, which set the limits for discussions in terms of the language used, the themes raised, and the participating collectivity. In classical democratic practice, the world outside the frontiers of the state was ruled by norms other than the domestic ones. The perception of sharing community was a prerequisite for engaging in discussions and accepting participation and national identity has an essential identifying role. Thus, national identity has performed as the backing element of public spheres.

But before naturalizing this empirical evidence (i.e. raising it to the level of a normative condition for the formation of public spheres), the meaning and contents of national identity should be closely scrutinized. First of all, this, as most social science materials, is an abstraction, a concept created to encapsulate a complex and dense reality. Taken as a whole, national identity is an acceptable (and tractable) reality. The analytical necessity is unveiling the complexity, the connotation of the concept of national identity. Items such as religion, race, culture, language, habits are normally embedded in that broader concept. Some of these were historically elevated to the category of founding stone of national identities at different historical stages: first, religion, in some moments, race, nowadays, language. As result of the historical aberrations that they served to justify, their normative value as founding stones of national identities has been marginalized.

Thus, the contradictory situation is that national identity has been empirically substantiated around essentialist elements. Current normative understandings of identity within advanced societies require that any affirmation of national identity is subject to a process of rationalization of these elements, i.e. checking them against alternative reference values such as human rights to neutralize any potential unacceptable effects in moral terms. Thus, these rarely reach a positive foundation. But still, all referents keep a certain presence as the substrate for the construction of national identities, which occasionally appears as an instinct unifying popular reactions, in events such as sport or occasional political conflicts. The worry is that any attempt to base a European public sphere on the idea of identity would surreptitiously introduce some of these essentialist elements.

The European Civil Society

At the EU level, the first issue to be elucidated is the existence and quality of the civil society. No doubt, there is a growing civil society with active NGOs, market and free circulation of persons and ideas. The source of this civil society must be redressed: first of all to the reconfiguration of nation states themselves which derives not only from the rearticulation between levels of government (regional and suprastatal) but also from the transfer to functional subsystems which are located within the domain of civil society. The actors of civil society do not have any specific compulsion to limit their activities to the national boundaries. For these, there is no formal mechanism which contains and constraints them to the nationally bounded national civil society, they can move freely and link to any of the points of the existing power structure. More specifically, the market and the structure of political opportunities within EU polity provide an area of activity. In fact, William Wallace identified the growth of this European civil society with the concept of informal integration, which consists of those intense patterns of interaction which develop without the intervention of deliberate governmental decisions, following the dynamics of markets, technology, communications networks and social exchange, or the influence of religious, social, or political movements (Wallace 1990: 54), furthermore enriched by practices such as institutional learning and borrowing.

Again, the analogy with national civil society may give a distorted view. Selecting one of the central collective actors in national politics in the social movements of the last two centuries, Sidney Tarrow, taking the nation state as the model, argues that social movements only will become transnational to the extent that they can cohere around supranational institutions and political processes that provide identities, targets, and political opportunities in the same way as the nation state (Tarrow 1994). He points out three reasons for the the lack of supranational development: the invisible way in which the Union implements most of its regulations; the absence of a truly representative body that would attract protest around it because of its supranational policy making; finally, the 'natural' strategic arena is the national one for social movements. Of course, if the nation state is the model to be replicated, it cannot be empirically found in the EU.

Empirically, however, it can be shown how actors are able to mobilize alternative resources to state power, push forward general values and enter an intergovernmental structure to the point of conditioning and finally modifying the positions of national governments. The role of humanitarian NGOs in the discussion on the suppression of asylum rights for EU citizens during the 1996 IGC provides an example of this growing 'non-national' civil society (Closa 1998) and, probably, some further empirical evidence could further corroborate this point. Some of the empirical obstacles for this European civil society have been singled out by Victor Pérez Díaz. He pointed out three different ones; first, the absolute priority of domestic matters combined with the expectation that they should be resolved by national governments; second, the 'performative contradiction' of EU politics where everyday behaviour tends to follow the logic of self-interested nationalism and thus contradicts the rhetoric ideal of a common interest and, finally, the difficulty in convincing a commonality of feelings posed by historical narratives (Pérez Díaz

1994: 17, 1997). These objections are real, but rather than obstacles to European civil society, they are difficulties for the appearance of a truly European contested participatory site, i.e. the European public sphere, and they will be addressed below in the proper argumentative context.

From the normative requirements side, Meyer has suggested some procedural requirements to secure that the autonomy of civil society and, specifically, the functional subsystems, can be redressed towards the re-politization and democratization of the political process. In the direction of the general public sphere, subsystems can help to make more enlightened, more realistic and more fundamental political decisions possible. Then it is the task of the political system to motivate and guide those who bear responsibility within these subsystems to implement the framework decisions in a more committed and responsible way. These two requirements are conditions which depend upon the third requirement which is the instrument for both: the institutionalization or semi-institutionalization of the relationship between subsystems and political system (Meyer 1995).

The European Public Sphere

Once the empirical evidence to sustain the existence of a European civil society and its future feasibility has been identified, it is the procedural moment to turn towards the consideration of the European public sphere. Pertinent questions directing the enquiry are the following: *Is the constitution of a European public sphere possible? What is the value of current configurations of national public spheres as a model for the Union?* A positivistic assessment of the situation would be that the existing form of political domination and civil society and their interplay (which seems unavoidable) would result in a contested participatory site, which would become the European public sphere. But at this point, the diagnosis of the required components of a public sphere seems demolishing: the lack of an organized party system, neither European associations nor citizens movements, no European media, no European-wide discourse on key issues which connects arguments and counter-arguments, and competing opinions and interpretations on a European scale (Grimm 1995; Meyer 1995).

Without fully denying the diagnosis, it should be underlined that its accuracy depends on the measurement bias on which it has been constructed. The summary would be that there is nothing like a *national* public sphere at the European level. Then, the argument proceeds stating that it is doubtful whether there will ever be one and, therefore, finally the option for supranational democracy is questionable. In this line, Preuß states that 'it is an empirical question in the first place whether the populations of the European Union member states share common ideas, values, interests and feelings of unity and social solidarity which have become characteristic of the political and cultural coherence of *nation states* and which are amenable to be represented in common institutions and to be reflected in a common public sphere' (Preuß 1995: 278).

The objection is placed on whether the capability to reconstruct national public spheres at a European level really becomes the empirical issue. It has been discussed above that these national public spheres are firmly backed by national identities which are semi-rationalized results of historical processes. As regards European identity, contemporarily, it does not seem, at this stage, that there is a substrate of European identity consolidated through history, although, in future, this may be traced backwards and analytically reconstructed. In any case, priority should be placed on the normative value assigned to a national-like European identity. Because, to be as close as national identities it would probably have to be nurtured by a similar blend of historical crystallization. If these elements are isolated they demonstrate their normative unsuitability: race-based constructions have proved a moral aberration, religion in a highly neutralized form may still find a place in certain contemporary writings as the amalgamating element (Marquand 1995) but is equally morally unsuitable. In these conditions, the most aseptic component of national identities, language, gains currency as the essential aspect whose absence questions the prospect of a European public sphere. Language offers an example of the link between national public spheres and national identity. On the one hand, the difficulty of constructing a European public sphere is posited as a communication problem, but on the other hand, normative qualifications are also attached to language. It is said, for instance, that democracy is more genuinely participatory within national/linguistic units, since it is assumed that political communication has a large ritualistic component which is typically language-specific. Equally, it is maintained that language-based political units are in fact the most consistent with freedom and equality, since language helps to construct a society of free and equal citizens (Kymlicka 1996). Whilst is undoubtedly true that communication is required for this kind of society, it is difficult to perceive a logical link between freedom and equality and language-based political units.

Sociologists of language have shown how the process of creating national languages has been intrinsically linked to the process of nation-building. The tendency within the EU is the opposite: the consolidation of language (English) for resolving the problem of communication in a situation of diglossia (de Swaan 1993) does not follow from any kind of political imposition. Inversely, member states are actively committed in the defence of their languages to preserve what is perceived as an essential element of national identity vis-à-vis communications requirements. Taking this fact, Laitin argues that the new European 'state' (*sic*) is following a general pattern for the consolidation of states characteristic of the twentieth century which has similar features to what is emerging in India (Laitin 1997). Rather than the assessment of the consolidation of forms of political domination, the interest of this argument lies in the empirical confirmation of the possibility of overcoming the communication requirements within it.

Communication requirements serve, of course, substantive issues. Meyer argues that there is nothing like a European-wide discourse on the key issues of the European agenda which connects the arguments and counterarguments, competing opinions and interpretations on a European scale, so that arguments from various national, regional, or sectoral quarters of the EU regularly, continually and in a sufficiently structured manner can meet and form something like a European public opinion (Meyer 1995: 126). But appreciation may diverge; for instance, monetary union currently provides an example of such a widely discussed topic. The difference is, of course, that discussions and arguments are much more fragmented than has been the case nationally. The evaluation of their quality and prospects are a matter of perspective, not a matter of comparison with national arguments and discussions. Thus, if these objections are met and the requirements for a European public sphere emerge, its feasibility seems a distinct possibility. As to its most salient feature, it is doubtful whether it will be based on anything similar to 'national identities'. To the objections from a normative point of view pointed out above, which make very unpalatable the national reconstruction at the European level, some empirical facts can be added, for instance, the lack of coincidence between institutional frontiers, on the one hand, and the arena for the activity of civil society and the emerging values, on the other. Next, there are prospects for an ongoing conflictuality between national identities and the development of a new focus on political discourse.

Thus, the normative minimalist construction fits with empirical developments. Close national identities would have to be substituted by a wider reality, where identity lacks substantial components: 'une identité dont la définition n'est jamais considérée comme simplement donnée, ni liée à un contenu fixe sémantiquement, mais constamment reformulée dans le cadre d'une discussion démocratique' [an identity the definition of which is never simply given nor bound to a fixed semantic space, but which is reformulated continuously through democratic debate] (Berten 1992: 82). Habermas has argued that the possible substitute for national identity might be a liberal political culture which recognizes democratic citizenship as the mechanism for securing preferred forms of life (Habermas 1995). But the influence of the national model also permeates writers who have shown a preference for the minimalist programme of seeking a substitute for a foundational mythology. Thus, Gamberale tries also to identify a European public identity by splitting the national component based on kinship from the political component based on association, but then he goes on to identify the foundational political experience of European political identity in European resistance and the struggle against Fascism

(Gamberale 1997). Precisely, one of the attractions of the EU is the possibility to evade these mythological foundational elements; an option which has been followed, for instance, in the design of a European currency. Thus, the eventual characteristics of the European public sphere are its lack of foundational mythological components as well as a highly reflexive attitude. In comparison with former models of political domination, the process of construction of the EU has been a highly deliberative one, where new creations, such as the statute of EU citizenship have been discussed by actors. In this sense, it is a highly reflexive construction. It is precisely this deliberative process around policies, institutions, and rights which constitutes the European public sphere. But its principal dimension, at this stage, it is the conflict with institutions and policies of the previous form of political domination, the state and the necessity to subject either of them to rational justification. These requirements put heavy psychological demands on individual citizens.

The Internal Public Spaces of European Citizens

So far, the discussion of the background theme, supranational democracy, has postponed institutional designs to concentrate on the arena for the formation of legitimizing values, the public sphere. But the discussion should go a step forward and consider the prospective necessity of a revision of the qualifications of individual citizens. This is an unavoidable task, since the supporting net of national identity has been questioned normatively and empirically as the foundation of the European public sphere. The burden of democratic processes is then transferred to the capability of individual citizens to engage in a non-essentialist conception of community. The inquiry requires the consideration of two different and interlinked aspects. On the one hand, scrutiny of the democratic credentials of the individual self in a national context, on the other hand, the evaluation of the suitability of this inherited self for a supranational form of democracy.

On the Democratic Quality of Internal Public Spaces of Citizens

Regarding the first question, national democracies are built on the assumption of a 'democratic' citizen, a point which deserves closer scrutiny. The abstraction of an ideal citizen is at least modified by the consideration of the situated man (Bourdeau). This citizen brings into their inner public sphere their material conditions as well as inherited values. The inner public space can be defined as a mental internal space where essential aspects of political identity, fundamental elements of citizenship morality are reflected. National democracies are built on an assumption (which becomes a matter of fact) of congruence between outer public and inner public spheres. In general terms, it could be argued that there is not a single causal direction in which public power or political systems shape inner public spaces or, inversely, inner public spaces produce a determinate form of public power or political systems. This later link was established in the theorization of civic culture, which looked for a substitute for the older idea of the 'national character'.

It has been argued above that national identities are a historical crystallization which is not merely the result of a democratic process. Thus, it is reasonable to assume that, at the national level, processes of socialization mix democratic values with those which are embedded in national political cultures. It is assumed that, to maintain coherence between inner and outer public spheres, individual citizens may proceed simply through an uncritical acceptance of some received elements of national identity on which their behaviour is rooted. Perception of the nation as the framework for solidarity, for instance, eliminates the necessity for a permanent internal democratic process of discussion on the moral foundation of the community. And it is also highly coherent with inherited identity elements such as ancestry, language, or religion.

What may be concluded is that the inner self of democratic individuals is not *naturally* a democratic one in the sense that received values are internally scrutinized to co-validate their validity in accordance with democratic procedures. This provides ground for the authoritarian affirmation of inherited values: by default, they are true and good and the new values have to be proved. Whilst this second postulate is not incompatible with democracy, the worry lies in the possibility of an authoritarian retreat to national values. Gamberale, following Bobbio, has pointed out that all the elements of the so-called Ur-Fascism (irrationalism, sense of the outsider, etc.) are not exclusive to a totalitarian form of government and identity, but that they derive from the kinship model of national identity (Gamberale 1997: 42). Thus, the inner self of democratic individuals is not fully dominated by a highly reflexive instance. As far as there is no institutional referent to which discourses on any of these components cling, discussions are not a natural product of democratic inner spaces.

Conditions for Inner Self Construction of a European Public Sphere

Grounded in such inner spaces of individual citizens, the construction of a European public sphere is conditioned by two characteristics. First, the capability of integrating, in a legitimate way through an internal democratic or pluralistic process of will formation, non-national values. This implies the question to what extent elements of inner public spaces which would not resist democratic scrutiny gain currency and are projected to the outer public sphere. Since congruence between inner and outer public spaces is assumed in national democracies, it might be presumed that individuals normally adopt the procedural rules of the institutional framework of reference, i.e. the national one. This leads towards the assumption of a differential treatment: whilst the inner self may be subject to the democratic exigencies of procedural rules in dealing with issues and conflicts pertaining to the national framework of reference, the arena outside this domain permits the expression of another kind of value inherited through socialization, which may even lead to the final point of reconstructing the other as the enemy.

The second characteristic is the empirical priority of the national identitarian component in the construction of inner public spaces. Its previous existence conveyed the normative necessity that, for individuals and public authority, it is the EU which has to prove its value. And this despite the acceptance of mutual influence between both the inner and outer public sphere, which may lead to the affirmation that, in the long run, individuals may accept the values deriving from the existence of certain suprastatal institutions. Following this reasoning, it has been suggested that the people of Europe would acquiesce to the factual existence of the kind of political structures associated with a political community (Howe 1995: 34), such as citizenship. It is probably true that facticity carries also an implicit acceptance. Coming back to the argument, the issue deriving from the priority of the national identitarian component is that the locus of the performative contradictions of EU politics (where everyday behaviour tends to follow the logic of self-interested nationalism and contradicts thus the rhetoric ideal of a common interest) is not only constructed within the institutional setting but also within inner public spaces.

These two characteristics, the individual capability to manage democratically inner public spaces and the empirical priority of national identities within them, form the equipment of individual citizens to deal with the new public exigencies, which are induced not only by the European integration process but also by the increasing complexity of current society and politics. These exigencies are, respectively, territorial and functional.

Dimensions of Inner Public Spaces: Territorial and Functional

The territorial dimension attracts wider attention mainly in a vertical structuration because it is referred to an institutional setting: the simultaneous restructuration of European nation states through European integration and regionalization processes. Regarding the inner self, the issue is the way individuals articulate internally its link with different layers of political institutions, regional, national, and supranational. Elizabeth Meehan was one of the first to refer to multiple identities within the context of the EU: members of the community have different allegiances to an 'increasingly complex configuration of common supra-national institutions, states, national and transnational voluntary associations, regions and allegiances to regions' (Meehan 1993). But realism also advises the underlining of the possible sources of conflict. In current writing, there is a presumption in favour of regions as the closest arena to citizens. Closeness of course implies accessibility to political institutions and processes. In this specific sense, regionalization is an interesting development to be welcomed. But the assumptions derived should be treated more cautiously. There is, first, a participatory assumption; in this line, Gamberale shows his preference for the small size and local nature of the 'commune' which allows for real self-determination and participation in public life (Gamberale 1997: 43). This perception is not a new one; it can be traced back to Rousseau's model of participatory democracy through positive liberty, drawing inspiration from the small size of the Greek city state or the Geneva government. In this respect, even communitarianists are ready to accept that the model of active and engaged citizen is flawed, as it does not correspond to the real life of many citizens. This is partly due to the decreased influence of the individual citizen in the political process of the modern state, but also to the fact that individuals pursue interests and values other than politics (Walzer 1992).

There is, second, an assumption on competence; in this line, Meyer states that political regions represent the life sphere in which the common citizen is 'anchored' and feels 'competent' when it comes to political argument. A second statement follows: this is the sphere of life with which citizens identify and with respect to which they can develop a vivid sense of responsibility and common concern (Meyer 1995). A secondary objection would be that it seems that the strength of anchorage and competence would be mediated by themes, media coverage, etc. For example, territorial closeness does not underlie the almost universal concern with certain themes (such as President Clinton's private affairs). However, the main objection which can be raised to this conception is the lack of clarity about the form in which physical closeness and accessibility is transformed into anchorage and competence. The priority of regional levels for individuals is not self-evident, particularly if the weight of national identities constructed at the nation-state level as the predominant substrate for linking individuals to the political community is taken into account.

This presumption in favour of the facility to develop competence in relation to a specific territorial level is permeated by a positive evaluation of the kind of substantial identity provided at this level. This statement is made clearer, perhaps, by a comparison between the positive connotations of regionalism with the concept of localism which often has a negative connotation implying an incapability and/or lack of will to deal with complex and transcendent political issues. Equally, parochialism was the term chosen by Almond and Verba in order to describe the lack of civic culture skills required for democracy. Thus, it seems that there are two different points conflated: on the one hand, the many options for participation offered by different levels of public authority territorially organized and justifiable merely on subsidiarity grounds. On the other hand, the stimulus to forms of identity fostered from each territorial public authority and a judgement on the value of these. Thus, two elements appear conflated in this positive evaluation of regions: the territorial closeness and the facility to develop identitarian links with territorial levels. Whilst the persuasiveness of accessibility renders normatively acceptable the politicization of lower territorial levels, this might lead towards the reconstruction of a new form of identitarian politics. The regional level can be regarded as a substitute (in exclusivist regionalist identities) or complement (in nested identities) to the national (and eventually supranational one); but the outstanding fact is an implicit uncritical reconstruction of the old form of (national) identity on a different territorial base. Justification of this process goes further than 'closeness' or mere subsidiarity, as it is demonstrated in some cases: to foster the attachment in individual citizens to conscious policies of national construction (in which the mythification of the past and of the future in the classical nationalist tradition) is systematically applied by regional institutions. Thus, whilst the initial justification for the territorial institutional setting was closeness to citizens, this is finally twisted towards an endorsement of similar policies of identity construction which are criticized at the national level and normatively unacceptable at the European level. Finally, it is identity which justifies political participation. This squares the circle and the identitarian model of the nation state is projected to other levels. So far, the issue has been treated as an articulation of the relations of individuals with public spaces in a vertical dimension. But the priority granted to the vertical dimension when the idea of multiple identities is constructed neglects an important and essential second dimension: the horizontal, or the way in which individuals perceive the other in a similar territorial standing. The vision of conflicts between communities is perhaps usual in composite states such as Belgium or Spain but it would be unavoidable in a highly plural community such as the EU, not least because EU member states have been historically the external referent for each other, consolidating a national perception in front of the enemy. In this context, one of the greater difficulties for connecting the inner self of citizens with the construction of a European public sphere is the difficulty of a convincing commonality of feelings posed by historical narratives (Pérez Díaz 1994: 17).

In fact, rather than commonality of feelings, it seems that the requirement for a rational connection among citizens is to introduce a consciousness of lacking an enemy. Historical narratives probably foster or reinforce mythical elements of national identities and individuals find it expedient to actualize the substrate of national identity as a self-affirming or reinforcing mechanism; this substrate is embedded in the logic of constructing the external enemy which is the distillation of the past. Visceral popular reactions expressed in sports events and occasional political crises reflect this intuitive identitarian construction. It provides an alternative form of knowledge to a merely analytical process led by reason and logic. The fear and incapability of individuals in dealing with a complex external would nurture this.

So far, the territorial framework has been the centrepiece for the construction of identities, but there exists also a functional component. For instance, within the EU where the market has the central role, objective alignments appear which bring together consumers and producers. Moreover, it could perhaps be demonstrated empirically that anchorage and competence are also influenced by a highly complex environment where, for instance, certain policy communities (fishing, agriculture, environment) may develop these elements of anchorage and competence of individual citizens in a non-specific territorially bounded arena. Progressively, the development of a European civil society will provide functional referents for individuals. So far, these functional identities have only an accessory character in relation to territorial identities.

Multiple identity is an attractive label to present a highly complex situation for individual citizens. It is a self that is integrated by several internal pieces which are not really under its dominance. In this context, the outstanding issue is not the possibility of multiple identities but the settlements reached to accommodate them. Since the reflexivity within inner public spaces of individual citizens becomes a requirement for their engagement in the European public sphere, this means that the several territorial layers and the functional dimension will have to be integrated within inner spaces. The inner public space of a democratic citizen would have to deal with this multi-level complexity where the main problem is located in the tendency towards a permanent conflict between levels and a concomitant tendency towards the authoritarian imposition of either of them. The crucial issue is, of course, the visions of the horizontal other and the vertical other. In this instability, a harmonious coexistence will be an option as far as identity does not crystallize around a single territorial level. In this context, institutions provide an important referent, as may EU citizenship.

The Contribution of European Citizenship

It was mentioned in the previous section that institutions provide a reference frame for inner public spaces as well as for the European public sphere. Thus, in this last section, the task is to explore how a concrete and specific institution, European citizenship, relates to both. The initial argument is to maintain that it is wrong to assume that the creation and development of European citizenship should not create problems of compatibility with existing national and cultural identities because it would not affect matters of identity in the first place. The former assumption is a literal translation of the TEU provisions safeguarding national identities. Art. F2 states, 'The Union shall respect the national identities of its member states.' No doubt, this provision provides a moral standard for the Union's behaviour, but it would be naïve to assume that there will be no effects on national identities. The principle orients towards institutional developments that are normatively compatible with national settings. But normative compatibility does not go hand-in-hand with institutional congruence. Normative acceptability has to be constructed discursively within each member state through democratic procedures and, in this way, the pre-democratic, pre-legal, or pre-political substrate of national identity has to become the object of public discussion and must prove its validity. Supranational institutions provide a highly useful instrument for engaging in discourses on national and supranational institutions.

This may be exemplified by EU citizenship. Basically, the essential element for EU citizenship to become the institutional foundation of a European civil society and public sphere is the way in which it is conceived within national citizenship, the way in which institutional and legal arrangements are made and, most importantly, the kind of discourses which are developed in this process. The individual practice of rights provides the anchorage for the way in which the self relates to institutions. Thus, for instance, freedom of movement and residence is normally taken as the most complete single right. But its practical realization once again shows the performative contradictions currently associated with the integration process: difficulties in daily routines with different requirements for nationals and non-nationals still foster the self-perception of being a foreigner.

In this realm, the implementation of EU citizenship by Spanish authorities might be highly illustrative not least because it was the leading advocate of EU citizenship. Among the several issues discussed within the Spanish national setting, naturalization law featured some exclusivist discourses. Attempts to change stringent Spanish conditions have been rejected on grounds that this would be an extremely generous move if it were not reciprocally followed by other member states. The exclusivist and effectivist (i.e. existence of effective links with the naturalizing country) perception of Spanish nationality was unveiled during parliamentary discussions.

Also, the implementation of specific rights related to the condition of EU citizenship has aimed at similar protectionist and exclusivist attitudes and discourses. Thus, regarding freedom of residence, the EU citizen is required to meet a series of conditions which give title to a residence card, all economic conditions: to be economically active or to be self-employed. The right to social services or the right to reside in Spain without economic activity is bound with possession of economic resources for self-maintenance or to be a student with economic resources. Spanish implemented legislation has not moved one inch further towards an unqualified right of movement and residence.

Similarly, the implementation of voting rights in local elections showed a surprising nationalistic reaction by the Spanish government. Despite having local elections in May 1995 and despite the petitions of several local governments with significant shares of EU citizens as residents, the government passed to the parliament a Royal Decree which obviated the directive on voting rights in local elections. The Decree referred to the traditional reciprocity principle for foreigners enrolling on the electoral register if an agreement had been concluded with their states and the residence conditions had been fulfilled.

Concluding Remarks

The conclusion must be necessarily modest. This chapter has argued the feasibility of a European public sphere as the arena for constructing the legitimacy of an emerging form of political domination (whose empirical existence albeit in a uncharacteristic form seems beyond question). But attention should be concentrated on the interplay between the old and the new forms. Citizens are equipped within their inner self with a repertory drawn from the national setting which enjoys a presumption of goodness. The acceptable normative way to proceed is that certain institutions that cannot be rejected normatively have to confront their inherited values with a process of re-deliberation to prove their goodness. European citizenship is a founding stone in this process.

REFERENCES

Berten, A. (1992). 'Identité européenne, une ou multiple? Réflexion sur les processus de formation de l'identité', in J. Lenoble and N. Dewandre (eds.), *L'Europe au soir du siècle: Identité et démocratie*. Paris: Editions Esprit, 81–97.

Closa, C. (1998). 'International Limits to National Claims in EU Constitutional Negotiations: The Spanish Government and the Asylum Right for EU Citizens'. *International Negotiations*, 3 (3): 1–23.

GAMBERALE, C. (1997). 'European Citizenship and Political Identity'. *Space and Polity*, 1: 37–59.

GRIMM, D. (1995). 'Does Europe Need a Constitution?' *European Law Journal*, 1: 282–302.

HABERMAS, J. (1994). 'Human Rights and Popular Sovereignty: The Liberal and Republican Versions'. *Ratio Juris*, 7: 1–13.

—— (1995). 'The European Nation-State: Its Achievements and its Limits. On the Past and Future of Sovereignty and Citizenship'. *Rivista Europea di Diritto, Filosofía e Informática*, 2: 27–36.

HINTZE, O. (1931/1968). *Esencia y transformación del Estado moderno, en Historia de las formas políticas: Spanish translation of chapters of 'Staat und Verfassung' and 'Soziologie und Geschichte'*. Madrid: Revista de Occidente.

HOWE, P. (1995). 'A Community of Europeans: The Requisite Underpinnings'. *Journal of Common Market Studies*, 33: 27–45.

KYMLICKA, W. (1996). 'Identity, Language and Democracy: Commentary on Veit Bader'. Prepared for the Conference on 'Social and Political Citizenship in an Age of Migration'.

LAITIN, D. D. (1997). 'The Cultural Identities of a European State'. *Politics and Society*, 25: 277–302.

MARQUAND, D. (1995). 'Reinventing Federalism: Europe and the Left', in D. Miliband (ed.), *Reinventing the Left*. London: Polity Press, 219–30.

MEEHAN, E. (1993). *Citizenship and the European Community*. London: Sage.

MERKEL, W. (1993). 'Integration and Democracy in the European Community: The Contours of a Dilemma'. Institute Juan March Working Paper 1993/42 41. Madrid: Center for Advanced Studies in Social Sciences.

MEYER, T. (1995). 'European Public Sphere and Societal Politics', in M. Teló (ed.), *Democratie et construction européenne*. Brussels: Editions de l'Université de Bruxelles, 123–40.

MILWARD, A. S. (1992). *The European Rescue of the Nation State*. London: Routledge.

PÉREZ DÍAZ, V. M. (1994). 'The Challenge of the European Public Sphere'. ASP Research Paper 4/1994. Madrid.

—— (1997). *La esfera pública y la sociedad civil*. Madrid: Taurus.

PREUß, U. K. (1995). 'Problems of a Concept of European Citizenship'. *European Law Journal*, 1: 267–81.

SCHMITTER, P. C. (1992). 'La Comunidad Europea como forma emergente de dominación política', in J. Benedicto and J. Reineses (eds.), of Sovereignty and Citizensh*Las transformaciones de lo político*. Madrid: Alianza.

—— (1996). 'Imagining the Future of the Euro-Polity with the Help of New Concepts', in G. Marks, F. W. Scharpf, P. C. Schmitter, and W. Streeck (eds.), *Governance in the European Union*. London: Sage, 121–65.

SOMERS, M. R. (1993). 'Citizenship and the Place of the Public Sphere: Law, Community, and Political Culture in the Transition to Democracy'. *American Sociological Review*, 58: 587–620.

—— (1995). 'What's Political or Cultural about Political Culture and the Public Sphere? Toward an Historical Sociology of Concept Formation'. *Sociological Theory*, 13: 113–44.

SWAAN, A. DE (1993). *Der sorgende Staat: Wohlfahrt, Gesundheit und Bildung in Europa und den USA der Neuzeit.* Frankfurt: Campus.

TARROW, S. (1994). 'Social Movements in Europe: Movement Society or Europeanization of Conflict?' EUI Working Paper RSC 94/8. Florence: EUI.

WALLACE, W. (1990). *The Dynamics of European Integration.* London: Pinter.

WALZER, M. (1992). 'The Civil Society Argument', in C. Mouffe (ed.), *Dimensions of Radical Democracy.* London: Verso, 89–107.

WEILER, J. (1991). 'The Transformation of Europe'. *Yale Law Journal,* 100: 2403–83.

PART IV

Postnational Projects of Belonging

The Question of a European Identity

9

The European Union

Economic and Political Integration and Cultural Plurality

M. Rainer Lepsius

Europe is difficult to define. There is no clear geographical or historical border with Asia. The Russian Empire, in colonizing Siberia and subjugating the peoples and cultures of Central Asia went way beyond the boundaries of Europe. Neither the Urals nor the Sea of Okhotsk are political and cultural borders. The European states have lost their overseas empires while Russia has maintained its continental empire. Yet Russia is a European power, a 'wing power' and, at least since the time of Peter the Great, a part of European culture. This also applies to the USA, the second 'wing power' of Europe. Where is the western border of Europe? It is true that the Atlantic separates Europe from America, but only geographically, not culturally or politically and economically.

To what should a European identity relate? To the cultural traditions of old Europe, to political principles, economic ties, to similarities in social structure and daily life? It is possible to find numerous criteria to construct similarities and differences in cultural identity on the European semi-continent. Even without taking its colonial expansion into account, there exists wide variety within Europe.

The development of identity assumes an object which understands itself to be a unit, differentiates itself from others and describes itself as such. For groups, the objects of identity are institutionalized concepts of order which have a normative content and which structure social action. Usually, several concepts of a cultural order play a role in collective identity. Linguistic culture, aesthetic culture, political culture, religious culture, professional culture—all these are aspects of collective identities relating to differing objects. Cultural identity is, to this extent, always heterogeneous and contains conflicting concepts of order. The differing degree of homogenization of identity depends upon the orders which become objects in the development of identity, and the power which such objects have as norms and structures of action. A church representing a state religion will shape aesthetic standards and structure everyday life. If there is, in addition, a uniform language and little social-structural differentiation, then there will be a high level of cultural homogeneity. Such cultural homogenization was dominated by the political system of the European nation states as they developed in the nineteenth century. Cultural identities were remoulded along nation-state lines. The political nation also became an elevated object in forming cultural identity. Leaving aside cultural minorities who reject the state order under which they live, for example the Basques, the cultural identities in Europe were formed by states.

For the development of a European identity a normative concept of order that structures social action is needed as an object of reference. Considering the strength of the European nation state, Europe should also present a relatively strong institutionalized order. For as long as this is not the case concepts such as 'European thinking', 'The West', and 'European Cultural Heritage' remain ideas without sufficient reference to concrete concepts of a cultural order. 'European culture' is a conglomeration of cultures which have been formed by the nation state. There exists competition between the European cultures using national labels. Cultural policies promote this in order to ascribe cultural achievements and symbolizations to the state. The situation is changing with the development of the European Community. The idea of European unity has lead to a specific type of institutionalization. The Council of Ministers, the Commission, Parliament, and Court form a new supranational regime which has binding authority in extended areas of competence. Thus, an object has arisen which possesses a normative content and which structures social action in the member countries. If a specific reference is needed in order to create a European identity, then it has come into being through the development of the European Union. To what extent this has created, or will create, a European cultural identity will be examined in the following.

I

The process of the 'communitarization' of European nation states began in 1951 and has progressed steadily since then. There have occasionally been great steps forward. This process is by no means complete. It is necessary to differentiate between two trends: the territorial expansion of the area of jurisdiction and the extension of competence, as regards content, of the organizations of the European Community.

The European Coal and Steel Community, founded in 1951, comprised of only six countries: France, the Federal Republic of Germany, Italy, Belgium, Luxembourg, and the Netherlands. The 'Northern expansion' came about in 1973 through the entry of Great Britain, Ireland, and Denmark. It was not yet possible to speak seriously about 'Europe'. Only Western Europe was integrated into the Community. Following the 'Southern expansion' through the admission of Greece in 1981 and Spain and Portugal in 1986, Europe west of the 'Iron Curtain' became integrated into the European Community. Only a few countries were missing, among those were Austria, Sweden, and Finland who were bound by their neutrality. These countries entered the Community in 1995 following the collapse of the Soviet Union. Switzerland, Iceland, and Norway remain outside. Nevertheless, with these exceptions, the process of communitarization has, in a period of forty-five years, embraced the Europe which found itself outside the influence of the Soviet Union. The European Union is currently made up of 370 million people from fifteen states. 'Eastern expansion' remains to be seen. Of the former Eastern Block countries only the GDR, through its entry into the Federal Republic, has been included in the European Union. Poland, the Czech Republic, Slovakia, and Hungary are candidates for entry. Slovenia and the Baltic states are potential candidates. Wherever the eastern border will finally be, the changing millennium will see a new Europe with common political institutions. An integrated economic system will enter history as an institutionalized economic-political regime.

Similarly to the area of jurisdiction, the scope of competence of the European bodies has also extended during the forty-five years of their existence. The European Coal and Steel Community communitarized the coal and steel industries, which were at the time two central branches of the economy. But these remained only two industries which could be isolated from their respective national economic system. The European Economic Community arose from the European Coal and Steel Community following the Treaty of Rome in 1959. The scope of competence of the EEC was considerably extended. Not only agricultural policy was subordinated to a European regime, the next target for integration was a customs union. Thus began extensive intervention in the national regulation of foreign trade. European organizations undertook the representation of foreign trade for the member states in respect of third parties; a new actor had taken its place on the international stage. Following on from the customs union, the next step was the creation of a common internal market in 1986. The criteria were the so-called four freedoms, i.e. the full free movement of people, goods, services, and capital. The attraction of a large market and the target of increased competition promised increased welfare for all member states. European legislation intervened extensively in national economic law, 70 per cent of which is today determined by European norms. At the same time an extension into further political fields took place, e.g. vocational training regulations, product norms, and competition and environmental law. Finally, the Maastricht Treaty of 1991 concluded the development of the European Community into the European Union by creating an economic and monetary union and thereby regulating the currency, monetary, and budgetary policies of the member states. In addition, responsibilities were taken over in the areas of domestic and judicial policy (immigration and asylum regulation, fighting organized crime), transport, and industry policy (individual projects had long been supported by the structural fund), research and technology policy and social policy. Furthermore, the harmonization of foreign and defence policy should lead to the European Union being an effective representative of European policy in international relations. Once the agreements made at Maastricht have been put into effect, the European Union will be, in its areas of competence and degree of effectiveness, an institutionalized regime. The member states will have formally transferred a considerable part of their jurisdiction to the EU and its regulation will substantively limit their remaining areas of competence. A new European order will emerge above the nation states.

The process of European communitarization has over the years altered the character of the Community. The original conception was of a 'rational purpose coalition' ('*Zweckverband*') which had been given limited tasks by the member states to be dealt with jointly with little material restraints on the action competence of the members. Out of this arose a regime which had independent authority for implementing rules in all the areas for which the Community has taken over responsibility. This created an irreversible density of regulation from which the member states could no longer extricate themselves. Now the Union is making efforts to assume the central coordinating competence for economic, defence, and foreign policy, encompassing the most vital matters of the member states. Central national institutions are losing their creative power. In this way, for example, the Federal Cartel Authority has become subordinate to the European Commission. As a result of monetary union the Bundesbank has lost its jurisdiction for independent monetary policy, and the budgetary policy of the national parliaments will be bound by criteria for monetary stability administered at a European level. The German Federal Constitutional Court and the other upper courts are subordinate to the jurisdiction of the European courts: Community law has precedence over national law. This development had already been taken into account by the amendment to the German constitution revising Art. 23 dated 21 December 1992. This authorized the Federal Government to transfer sovereignty to the European Union as long as the 'democratic, constitutional, social, and federal principles', the principle of 'subsidiarity', and a 'guarantee of basic legal protection largely comparable with this constitution' were complied with. The principle of the opening of the constitution in relation to the European Union is thus established. Germany has lost parts of its sovereignty, not only de facto but also normatively. This also holds for the other member states. It is true that the European Union is not yet a 'state', however it is moving towards being a state-like political regime.

The first hypothesis is as follows: the process of European integration has brought into being a new economic-political order with a normative content and immediate effect on the living conditions of the people who live within its area of judiciary and competence. Thus, Europe has become a concrete object of reference for a collective identity. The formation of institutions precedes the formation of consciousness. This is because as long as all essential interests are formed and represented by nation-state processes, there is no need for an identification which extends beyond the nation state and no need for a collective self-description on the European level.

II

The European Community has legitimized itself primarily due to criteria of economic efficiency and long rejected more comprehensive ideas of a cultural order. The process of economic integration substituted, to a certain extent, general and diffuse values as principles of a cultural order. Thus, the definition of objectives and decision-making processes were largely freed from national orders based on political, social, and cultural values. Criteria of efficiency could be instrumentally directed at specific targets: the customs union, the creation of a large internal market, and the making of a competitive market. The intended and unintended consequences associated with these decisions were left to the socio-political systems of the member states. Thus, the European Community could concentrate on well delimited policy fields and continue to present itself as a 'specific administrative union', although it had long outgrown this status. Until Maastricht, constitutional debates were effectively avoided. Furthermore, they had not been raised by the public.

Additionally, the frequently raised problem concerning the deficiencies in democratic legitimacy failed to lead to a discussion of the problems of the new supranational regime. The governments of the member states were the 'masters of the contracts', their representatives in the Council of Ministers were responsible for decision making, and the fundamental decisions of the state and government leaders were determined in the European Council in direct and personal negotiations. For them no democratic deficit resulted, they were legitimized through their national systems, and together they constrained within narrow boundaries the right of participation of the directly elected European Parliament. Only the cooperation of functional elites was necessary for the development of the programmes. These elites possessed a large degree of autonomy over the public and the interests of nation states because they could ground the validity of their decisions on criteria of economic efficiency. This autonomy was further promoted by the monopoly that the staff of the Commission had in the drafting of legislation. The Council of Ministers decides, and the European Parliament always debates laws and regulations which have already been voted upon and instrumentally prepared by expert staff according to criteria of economic rationality. As long as these could be successfully isolated from other political, social, and cultural values and concepts of order, a sufficient capacity for compromise existed. The belief in welfare benefits for all participants justified integration policy without recourse to non-economic values.

The second hypothesis is: an agreement on the regulation of economic exchange relations was sufficient justification for segmentary communitarization based on criteria of economic efficiency. A more extensive sense of identity did not form and was also unnecessary.

III

The most recent 'Eurobarometer 43' of the European Commission showed that in April and May 1995, on average of only 6 per cent of the respondents described themselves as European, a further 9 per cent described themselves as European and belonging to their nation. The overwhelming majority perceived themselves, and described themselves, as belonging to their nation state. At the same time around 70 per cent wished for more extensive unification, 56 per cent agreed with their country's membership in the European Union and 47 per cent recognized advantages for their country. These averages vary considerably in the individual nations. The citizens of the old 'community of six' appear to be the most European, they have known the European regime for by far the longest. The approval of Europe seems to be more instrumental than affective. However, a normative core exists. Of the British—with their consistently distanced attitude—only 24 per cent would regret the dissolving of the Community, nevertheless 56 per cent gave the Community their approval. It could be said that instrumental aims are associated with the European Community, but not value-based identifications. In addition, the European Community has neither a comprehensive nor the highest competence as in the case of the nation states. There exist in addition to the Community further transnational regimes of great influence: the United Nations, the GATT, the World Trade Organisation (WTO), the World Bank, the International Monetary Fund (IMF), the summit conferences of the G7 among others. In these regimes the nation states remain the sole representatives of national interests. Supranational 'communitarized' political fields exist next to those which are coordinated internationally. There is also the wide field of transnational interests which are not institutionalized politically, especially in the markets for finance, goods, and services. It is true that the nation states lose competence, they subordinate themselves to being branches of a supranational regime that can increasingly, through majority decisions, assert itself against national preferences. The nation states remain, nevertheless, the representatives of legitimate democratic national interest. Above all, they provide the formal framework for the most important integration processes of societies: a collective self-description produced in direct communication; legal agreements about the distribution of national product including tax and contribution burdens; the attribution of achievements and deficits to the political, economic, and social collective actors.

The third hypothesis: the European Community offers no comprehensive reference for the creation of a collective identity. Within the multiplicity of supranational regimes the European Community continually gains importance, however it has not yet replaced the nation state.

IV

A new level of European integration has been reached with the Maastricht Treaty and the transformation from European Community to European Union. This has given rise to far-reaching consequences and contingencies. Limits to nation-state policy making, arising through the stability criteria for monetary union in areas such as monetary policy, subsidies, and public-sector budget deficits are imminent. In other words, the nation states will lose some power over the means for a specifically national policy of cultural order. Socio-political measures can only be taken within the limits of the earning power of the national taxation and expenditure system. Measures such as politically motivated exchange-rate changes and inflationary state indebtedness are no longer available. Also the pressure of international competition has a depressing effect on earned income and transfer income. The higher the degree of interconnection in the European Union becomes, the more likely it is that there will be an increasing financial equalization between the member states. In the light of the considerable differences in the welfare of the Mediterranean countries and even greater differences regarding the Eastern European candidates for membership, the wealthy nations' capacity for distributive policies will be greatly reduced. On the other hand, with increasing unemployment, domestic socio-political expenditure will increase considerably. Therefore, it should be expected that there will be increasing domestic conflict regarding distribution.

The current strategy of the European Community finds, in the transformation to the European Union, its limits in two ways. On the one hand, the increasing competence of the Union goes beyond its previously legitimizing criteria of economic efficiency. On the other hand, it reduces the possibilities of the European Union to leave it to the member states to cope with the consequences of integration policy as these now have a reduced capacity to adjust. The relief that Community policy has enjoyed, due to the isolation of the criteria of economic efficiency from the usual political, social, and cultural goals, and the externalization of the contingencies from their area of responsibility, will be considerably reduced.

It follows that there is a sequence of consequences that will lead to the politicization of the European Union. The relative immunity of the European organizations from diffuse expectations which they enjoyed while they concentrated
their efforts on the creation of the internal market and free competition, is
diminishing. This results in the search for other legitimizing values in order to
secure agreement for the extension of competence. It is true that environmental policy, the coordination of security policy measures, and research and technology policy still have considerable plausibility in terms of general and
transnational criteria of efficiency. However, this is no longer the case when
European decisions and regulations intervene directly in the area of social
policy. Distribution, and especially decisions concerning redistribution belong
to the most sensitive political areas, particularly in times of economic stagnation
or even decline. Complex intermediary systems of will formation, compromise,
and resulting temporary agreements are needed. To date, these systems have
functioned only at the level of the nation state with its national concepts of solidarity, equal citizenship, and welfare provisions at the level of subsistence according to some poverty line. The prestige as well as the socio-political identity of
the nation states rest on the socio-political mediation processes between differing interests and interest groups and the ensuing legitimacy for the output of
these mediation and negotiation processes. The more the European Union
materially intervenes in this process of the structuring and self-legitimization of
society, or formally restricts the ability to act at the level of the nation state, the
more it will become drawn into distributive struggles. The European Union will
thereby become not only politicized but also potentially threatened by de-legit-
imization. This is why the Union needs, in addition to constitutional reform, the
development of concepts of order for the 'social space of Europe', normative
concepts of European social solidarity through which, given considerable internal inequality, a common identity could be developed.

The fourth hypothesis: 'Europe' will become politicized by the transition
from European Community to European Union. From this follows not only a
greater need for legitimacy, but also the development of new concepts of
cultural order for the European welfare state. The potential for both conflicts
of interest and conflicts of ideals of order are far greater here than in the area
of market regulation and equality in competition. New values and new
concepts of cultural order have, however, not appeared. They would also be
much more controversial than European competition and market regulations.

V

Only here has the construct 'Europe' become the immediate target of diverse
and controversial interests, expectations, and demands. A critical situation

arises regarding the creation of a European identity. Relative welfare benefits can no longer be ascribed directly to the deregulation of national policies. The benefits are directed also in reverse, to the securing and maintenance of nation-state competence to defend against levelling. Therefore, after Maastricht, Europe has a dual task: on the one hand, to develop and normatively recharge new criteria of European solidarity, on the other hand, to shore up the loyalty of the citizen towards the nation states. If the first of these does not take place, the European Union will not gain sufficient value-based legitimacy for its extended competence. Should the second task not succeed, the European Union will lose the capacity to arrive at compromise in distributive conflicts.

The criteria of European solidarity can only be segmentary. The strategy used in the creation of European nation states in the eighteenth and nineteenth centuries, namely political and social mobilization for the creation of a nation cannot serve as an analogy. A uniform European nation can be created neither through cultural and ethnic homogeneity nor by the idea of equal civil rights. On the one hand, the member states are historically formed ethnic-cultural units and democratically organized civil societies which have long had the quality of nation states. On the other hand, the European Union lacks the pre-democratic regimes' potential for oppression and levelling which formed homogeneous nations largely through authoritarianism. The member nations of the European Union are in themselves politically, socially, and culturally homogeneous peoples and bearers of the idea of the sovereignty of the people.

The European Union will not create a 'Nation of Europe', it will present a segmentary 'communitarization' of political management, a regime alongside others. In addition, at the European level two adjacent principles apply: the principle of the supranational development of objectives, decision-making, and implementation and the principle of international cooperation. The essential difference is that in the first case—above all in the extension of the principle of majority—no final jurisdiction can be given to the member states, since they also have no independent right of implementation in respect of measures decided by a majority, whereas in the second case each state keeps its own autonomy of action also in respect of common agreements and retains autonomy within this framework. Whereas a supranational regime is foreseen in the Maastricht agreement for monetary policy, foreign and defence policy remain within international coordination. 'Europe' represents both a dimension of supranationality and a dimension of coordinated nation states. What is characteristic of Europe is an intertwining of supranationality and nationality with differing proportions depending upon the 'degree of communitarization' of the various policy fields.

Moreover, the basis for European civil rights is being created. These are founded in the European Convention on Human Rights as a kind of catalogue of fundamental rights for all those belonging to the member states of the Community. They are made concrete by the freedom of movement requirements within the Community, and recently, through the right to take part in community and European elections in each member state of the Community, without possessing the nationality of the respective state. These are important beginnings for the extension of civil rights beyond the nation state. Nevertheless, European civil rights do not refer to a European people but to nationals of the member states. European civil rights can only be enjoyed through being the citizen of a member state. However, it should be stressed that the possibility of legal claims by individuals has been established outside of the legislature of the nation states and that such claims can be sanctioned external to national jurisdiction by the European Court of Human Rights.

The fifth hypothesis: even after the foundation of the European Union established at Maastricht, no European people will arise which would describe itself as such and create a corresponding identity. The debate on identity which relates to the nation states will open itself. Alongside the nation state a new concept of order will emerge with normative ideals that have effects on action orientations. It will become an inclusive unit for expectations and demands and through this also a reference for the creation of feelings of belonging and identity. The creation of identity within the nation states, which until now has already been multi-dimensional will become more complex and multifarious due to an additional scale of reference.

VI

The whole system of political integration within the European Union has been described as a 'a dynamic multi-level system'. This relates to the procedural character of the interaction of differing politically constituted levels of control, from the communes to the regions (in Germany also the Federal States) and nation states to the European Union, and finally to the trans-European regimes of NATO and the United Nations. The intertwining of this multi-level system arises from the nation states. They take part at all levels without being able to autonomously control the decisions taken. This differentiation and plurality of levels of control limits the creation of a specifically European identity. This identity can only refer to functional relations which are controlled at a European level. This includes the creation of a European 'solidarity concept' necessary for European financial equalization in order to legitimize the asymmetries between national taxation revenue and European tax spending. The second point of reference could be a common foreign and defence policy similar to the model of the nineteenth-century nation states. In all likelihood a European 'intervention force' will not be a conscripted army.

Great Britain already has a professional army recruited from volunteers, and shortly France will convert to such a system. Thus, universal compulsory military service is removed as a reference for identification with Europe. Furthermore, neither European foreign nor defence policy can be made independently. The dependency on the military, political, and economic strength of the United States is evident. There is no autonomous European defence policy which would allow a European identity based on the principle of self-defence. Neither will the European Parliament become a general and comprehensive democratic parliamentary representative of the Europeans because the central functions of the state provision of services and conflict mediation remain with the national parliaments. To this extent the European Parliament is also only a segmentary representation of the European peoples, not the central representation of the European people.

The pluralization of regimes and the overlapping of levels of decision making complicate the identity-forming perception of the 'dynamic multi-level system'. The respective competences become blurred and their complexity remains undifferentiated. This is demonstrated in the nation states' tendency to attribute positive events to their own efforts and to present negative events as being beyond their power, i.e. as being a problem at the European level, the level of the world market or in international power constellations. No clear differentiation of competence exists between the European and national level. The principle of subsidiarity obscures a clear division of functions due to case by case judgement of the effective allocation of competence. What already appears in the relationship between the German Länder and the Federal Republic, namely political and financial links which are no longer clearly accountable, also exists in the relationship between the nation state and the European Union. Such relationships make it unclear to whom expectations are addressed and to whom responsibility should be allocated. Diffuse relationships of dependency dissolve links with values and 'fundamentalist' orientations towards primary interests legitimized by basic democracy take their place. A regressive form of identity is a plausible reaction to no longer clearly identifiable efficiency criteria within a complex multi-level system. The widespread aversion to the Federal State in the USA serves as a warning of a similar development in the European Union. Neither the 3,000 'Eurocrats' of the Commission, the around 10,000 'Euro Lobbyists', nor the 567 European Parliamentarians can create or secure the necessary institutional trust.

A hierarchically clear separation between the European and the nation-state level of the member states will not take place simply as a result of political intertwining. It cannot therefore be assumed that a European consciousness can incorporate or even absorb the existing identification with the nation states. Furthermore the control functions transferred to the European level no longer have final jurisdiction, even when in some policy fields their highest jurisdiction is to be found in European organizations. Similar to the nation states, the power of the European Union is limited principally by the globalization of markets (especially the capital market) by the environmental dynamic and security risks arising from the potential for blackmail from violent minorities. Also the European Union is not sovereign, in the way that a nation state in the nineteenth century could assume itself to be. A multiplicity of inner European and international negotiating relationships and mediating committees attempt to structure these global interdependencies. The European Union plays only a limited role within these. The United States is decisive in security policy. International economic policy cannot be controlled without the Americans, Japanese, and Asians, and environmental problems affect the whole planet. But even those problems which lay close to Europe such as the restructuring of the Russian empire or cooperation with the non-European Mediterranean countries present responsibilities which greatly exceed European capabilities.

The systems of negotiation created are only loosely connected to processes of consensus formation on values. They are occupied primarily with partial questions that are to be solved instrumentally. The more they experience cultural dissensus over value, the greater their effectiveness. Expert staff are homogenized by clear and specific criteria of efficiency. This, however, does not found an identity-based value community. Complex networks of negotiation lack transparency and are decoupled from consensus-generating procedures of legitimization.

The dispersed control functions in the interconnected arenas of negotiation that are characteristic of the 'dynamic multi-level system' need to be linked. 'Systems' which become independent, each with its own action rationality and the tendency to externalize the contingency of its activities, prevent the attribution of responsibility for decision making and political action. Neither arise from the subject areas as such, both are the result of institutionalized concepts of values—i.e. of normatively desired political allocation of competence. Such concepts have so far been provided only by national constitutional states. These have the institutional prerequisites for the construction of responsibilities and liabilities, even when the causal attributions of a decision remain blurred or conceal themselves in the functionality of systems. A normative construction of responsibility and liability is, however, necessary for the creation of identity, together with a system of sanctions in order to implement such attribution of responsibility and liability. The system which is to date the most suitable order is the parliamentary system of government with undivided budgetary sovereignty over public funds. As the proportion of public spending in the member states, including social security, lies between 40 per cent and 50 per cent of gross national product, budgetary jurisdiction remains the most important instrument for negotiation between differing interests and values. Through budgetary disposition, operational relations are established between incommensurable aims and heterogeneous value concepts. Thus, they are made transparent and debatable in public. This is why the parliaments are the central location for the linkage of heterogeneous efficiency criteria and resulting from this the location for the creation of 'solidarity norms'. Budget restrictions make necessary the formation of preferences and justification of the preferences made. Each budget overspent is sanctioned, either through debt or an increase in taxation and duty—in each case publicly visible and requiring justification. Also when the causal attribution of responsibility to the government for an event is occasionally fictitious, because the government could not influence it, there remains an incumbent expectation of action which can be sanctioned by the public through elections. In this way the nation state—limited in its actions—remains the central location for the social construction of objects of identification and norms of solidarity via the collective identities which can be created in the struggle between interests and differing value preferences.

The sixth hypothesis: in the 'dynamic multi-level system' the traditional picture of hierarchically positioned representatives of competence with a clear territorially-based universal competence is being dissolved. Collective concepts of identity are directed towards normatively constructed units with constituted bodies, competences, and responsibilities. They are still to be found in their most transparent form and with the greatest chance of participation within the framework of the national constitutional state. Insofar as their possibility to act becomes fictitious, this should be identified but not, however, referred to uncontrollable agencies, networks of negotiating relationships, or 'powers'. The greater these externalizations of competences become, the more the space shrinks upon which identities can be built. 'European' identity does not therefore separate itself from nation-state identity in the sense of a hierarchical superordinate level of identification, it connects itself with the nation state identification of the member states of the European Union. The control functions organized 'Europe-wide' change the self-description of the nation-state—they enter it without replacing it. This results in the construction of a nation-state identity which no longer conforms with the understanding of the nineteenth century.

VII

From its beginning, European 'communitarization' omitted culture. This was reserved for the nation states. It is true that numerous European initiatives are directed towards the cultural area, however this will not lead to the introduction of a cultural identity. Exchange programmes for students and school children, joint research associations, annually changing European 'Cities of

Culture', and the recognition of qualifications refer to the better understanding of national cultures—not a European culture.

Language is the central medium of cultural identity. In the Europe of the
fifteen there are eleven official languages, to which can be added recognized
regional languages such as Catalonian. Following expansion in the East this
variety would be increased by at least four, possibly seven, languages. It is true
that these languages are differently widespread and have differing functional
importance, yet normatively they are all equal. Only English and French claim
the status of a lingua franca, and this duality already demonstrates the
complexity of uniform communication. English is dominant in economics,
technology, and science, although not resulting from Europe's own dynamic
but rather due to the existing dominance of the USA in these areas. English is
a global linguistic medium, not a specifically European medium. There is also
the increasing importance of non-linguistic codes which have no specifically
European basis. The importance of the national languages does not decrease,
because communication among the speech communities can only result from
the use of these languages. The native language is the immediately accessible
medium of information and communication from which cognitive and
emotive symbols of identification arise. Therefore, the right of use of the
native language is also the basis of all participation, consensus formation, and
legitimation. The cultural integration of Europe is primarily a task of translation which, for a small part of the European population, can be made easier
through the mutual use of a lingua franca. Cultural identities remain linguis-
tically bound, above all in those areas which have a high level of semantic
differentiation.

The cultural plurality expressed in the variety of languages is constitutive
of Europe. It is supplemented through the differing religious traditions and
furthermore through like-minded communities. Not all of these cultural
differentiations are identical with national boundaries, they extend partly
beyond them. This is due to immigration which creates homogeneous subcultures and minorities in various European countries—especially through
Muslim immigrants. Uniformity extending beyond borders can also be found
in the standards of everyday culture and in the principles of political culture.
Given that all European cultures, including those of the large nation states, are
European minority cultures none can bow towards a majority decision. They
demand a 'protection for minorities' in the sense that they can determine the
shape of their development themselves and will not allow themselves to be
majoritized. The fundamental problem in the area of cultural autonomy lies
in the degree to which values which apply within the communities are
compatible with those which define the socio-cultural environment of their
autonomy. For the European Union it is therefore important that values
underlying 'communitarized' control functions are capable of being communicated with as many European cultures as possible. This was easier as long as

they were primarily limited to the standardization of rules regulating the market, the conditions of competition, and the regulation of free movement because such regulations touched only peripherally on the self-concept of cultural orders. Economic categories have already reached a high degree of differentiation from 'culture', though this would change if European legislation were to interfere with morally defined orientations of action. It is advisable to leave such value conflicts to the nation states to solve, even if inequalities in certain areas emerge between the member states which are not compatible with market homogeneity. This includes, for instance, national differences in statutory frameworks for the rights of employees, organization of television broadcasters, social security systems, etc. With the creation of homogeneous partial orders in Europe conflicts arise between specific values which require a complex form of institutionalization without reducing the space for cultural autonomy. Considerable differences also exist between democratic nation states in the area of political culture, especially regarding the concept of the state or the idea of federalism which cannot be homogenized and which, at the same time, have considerable importance for the legitimacy of the European Union.

A common flag and an anthem without words, an additional imprint on passports and common printed currency symbolize the new concept of order that is 'Europe', whose content will incrementally become more concrete. A new symbolic reference arises in addition to those multiple identifications which already exist, yet it does so without dissolving the others. The problem is not the variety, rather the communication of identities.

The seventh thesis: European cultural identity is a conglomeration of identifications with differing value spheres. A homogenization of these cultures is not necessary for the European Union. To link criteria of economic efficiency at the European level with the nationally defined value spheres linked to law and political will formation is sufficient. European cultural policy is therefore primarily 'translation policy'.

VIII

The result of these considerations can be summarized. In the European Union an object of reference for a European identity has arisen. This object can be seen as a 'segmentary communitarization' of economic-political control functions bearing a primarily instrumental character. A more extensive identity construction has not yet appeared, because the nation states are the essential bearers of the ability to make decisions and holders of legitimacy in the European Union. The primary addressee for the realization of value spheres is therefore the nation states. They are moreover the guarantors of the autonomy of the cultures formed by the nation state. Cultures cannot comply with majority decisions which are not borne by the cultural community itself. European culture will therefore continue to be a conglomerate of nation-state cultures.

Two new developments will arise. First, the unity of the nation state will become more open, i.e. references to Europe should be more intensively built into the national self-image without leading to the formation of a hierarchically superior European identity. Second, some dimensions will differentiate themselves from the national self-understanding. The economy and law, the most strongly institutionalized value spheres in the European Union, will become more European, other areas less so. On the whole it is to be expected that nation building, which up to now has dominated cultural self-images, will lose integrative importance. The self-description of collectivities will be formed more strongly through other value spheres. The differentiation of functional relations leads also to a differentiation of value spheres whose importance for cultural identity depends on the degree of their institutionalization, on the agreement with their normative content and on the degree of value realization which is expected. The differentiation of functions should therefore not lead to a levelling of value differences which should rather be mutually mediated. To this extent the cultural identity of Europe must be continually created in part. It is not something which already exists either through tradition or destiny.

REFERENCES

BACH, M. (1993). 'Vom Zweckverband zum technokratischen Regime: Politische Legitimation und institutionelle Verselbständigung in der Europäischen Gemeinschaft', in H. A. Winkler and H. Kaelble (eds.), *Nationalismus—Nationalitäten—Supranationalität*. Stuttgart: Klett-Cotta, 288–308.

DEUTSCH, K. W. (1953). *Nationalism and Social Communication: An Inquiry into the Foundations of Nationality*. Cambridge, Mass.: MIT Press.

European Commission (1995). *Eurobarometer*, vol. 43. Brussels.

GELLNER, E. (1991). *Nationalismus und Moderne*. Berlin: Rotbuch.

GEPHART, W. (1993). 'Partikulare Identitäten und die Grenzen der Gemeinschaftsbildung in Europa', in B. Schäfers (ed.), *Lebensverhältnisse und Konflikte im neuen Europa: Verhandlungen des 26. Deutschen Soziologentages in Düsseldorf*. Frankfurt: Campus, 459–66.

GERHARDS, J. (1993). 'Westeuropäische Integration und die Schwierigkeiten der Entstehung einer europäischen Öffentlichkeit'. *Zeitschrift für Soziologie*, 22: 96–110.

GIESEN, B. (ed.) (1991). *Nationale und kulturelle Identität: Studien zur Entwicklung des kollektiven Bewußtseins in der Neuzeit*. Frankfurt: Suhrkamp.

—— (1993). 'Intellektuelle, Politiker und Experten: Problem der Konstruktion einer europäischen Identität', in B. Schäfers (ed.), *Lebensverhältnisse und Konflikte im neuen Europa: Verhandlungen des 26. Deutschen Soziologentages in Düsseldorf.* Frankfurt: Campus, 492–504.

GRIMM, D. (1995). 'Braucht Europa eine Verfassung?' *Juristische Zeitung,* 50: 581–91.

HALLER, M. (1993). 'Alte und neue soziale Ungleichheiten als Herausforderungen für die Sozialpolitik in Europa', in B. Schäfers (ed.), *Lebensverhältnisse und Konflikte im neuen Europa: Verhandlungen des 26. Deutschen Soziologentages in Düsseldorf.* Frankfurt: Campus, 206–17.

HÉRITIER, A., et al. (eds.) (1994). *Die Veränderung von Staatlichkeit in Europa. Ein regulativer Wettbewerb: Deutschland, Großbritannien und Frankreich in der Europäischen Union.* Opladen: Leske + Budrich.

JACHTENFUCHS, M., and KOHLER-KOCH, B. (1996). 'Regieren im dynamischen Mehrebenensystem', in M. Jachtenfuchs and B. Kohler-Koch (eds.), *Europäische Integration.* Opladen: Leske + Budrich, 15–44.

KAELBLE, H. (1987). *Auf dem Weg zur einer europäischen Gesellschaft? Eine Sozialgeschichte Westeuropas 1889–1980.* Munich: Beck.

LEPSIUS, M. R. (1986). ' "Ethnos oder Demos": Zur Anwendung zweier Kategorien von Emerich Francis auf das nationale Selbstverständnis der Bundesrepublik und auf die Europäische Vereinigung'. *Kölner Zeitschrift für Soziologie und Sozialpsychologie,* 38: 751–9.

—— (1993). 'Nationalstaat oder Nationalitätenstaat als Modell für die Weiterentwicklung der Europäischen Gemeinschaft', in M. R. Lepsius (ed.), *Demokratie in Deutschland.* Göttingen: Vandenhoeck & Ruprecht, 265–85.

MÜNCH, R. (1993). *Das Projekt Europa. Zwischen Nationalstaat, regionaler Autonomie und Weltgesellschaft.* Frankfurt: Suhrkamp.

SCHARPF, F. W. (1985). 'Die Politikverflechtungsfalle: Europäische Integration und deutscher Föderalismus im Vergleich'. *Politische Vierteljahresschrift,* 26: 323–56.

—— (1991). 'Die Handlungsfähigkeit des Staates am Ende des 20. Jahrhunderts'. MPIFG Discussion Paper 91/10. Cologne.

SCHULTE, B. (1993). 'Die Entwicklung der europäischen Sozialpolitik', in H. A. Winkler and H. Kaelble (eds.), *Nationalismus—Nationalitäten—Supranationalität.* Stuttgart: Klett-Cotta, 261–87.

10

Integration through Culture?

The Paradox of the Search for a European Identity

Klaus Eder

European Identity: A Theoretical Approach to an Empty Symbolism

A Sociological Perspective on European Identity

European identity is on the agenda—a European consciousness is called for. Scientists, intellectuals, and politicians have started to provide recipes to create it. Historical memories of a common European experience are re-mobilized. The repertoire of symbols and metaphors has become the object of interest and curiosity in the humanities which allows what is required to be found: a collective identity. What results is what sociologists call a social construction of reality. Europe is going to be invented, and the discourse set in motion is to be expected to have real consequences.

Historical experience, however, of the 'making of a nation' and the construction of a nation by intellectuals in particular (Giesen 1993) should prevent us from joining such discourses without some reflective hesitation. We should rather objectify such discourses, find reflexive distance to such processes of identity construction and analyse the costs and eventual perverse effects of such social constructions. Historical experience with nation-building has provided us with the necessary experience to under-stand these processes and gain a reflexive distance. A first step in this direc-tion is conceptual work that aims at avoiding incorrect antagonistic positions in the discourse on collective identity formation. A fashionable dichotomy is the opposition of identity and difference. This is an empty conceptual device. We do not have to deal with the identical and the differ-ent, but with the paradox that any identity is the identification of something by separating it from the rest. Identity is marking difference. What has been marked as identical might still be quite different. Identity and difference are the two sides of the same coin. Thus, the discourse on European identity in terms of an option between identity or difference does not make sense. The question is rather how much and which difference is permitted by symbolic markers of an identity.

What is defined as identical by symbolic markers can be analysed in three respects. The first is the simplest: symbolic markers imply a normative definition of inclusion and exclusion. The included needs an additional quality: it has to be loved. To guarantee such affective stability, a third element is needed: the symbolic representation of the normatively and emotionally shared. This can be a tree, a spirit hidden in a bird, a hardly readable text, a national spirit or ancestor. The variability of such symbolic representations is endless. Human history is a laboratory producing symbolic devices for such purposes. Thus, a first account of what collective identity is can be given. It is something the content of which is contingent, with which exists a diffuse affective relation and which fulfils the function of defining who belongs and who does not.

The specificity of the discourse on European identity will be looked at by such analytical means. The affirmative discourse on European identity searches for a substance that is collectively shared. This is necessary the more such an identity has to compete with national constructions of a collective identity. However, such a strategy of identity-building turns the logic of identity construction on its head: it tries to determine in advance what the result of a process of social construction is. This contributes to an illusion about the function of constructing collective identity: to confound the substance with the result of a constructive effort. Such an illusion is costly as the modern history of national identity formation has shown. The new history of constructing a European identity seems to continue the national tradition.

Against such an affirmative discourse a critical account of the costs of this history of constructing national identities is proposed. Such a reflexive distance is undertaken in the following.

A Conflict-Theoretical Approach to European Identity

'Doing things together', as Howard Becker (1986) said, presupposes a shared knowledge of the world that we call culture. This claim is partly right. For 'doing things together' can be thought of as happening without symbols, such as by coordinating behavioural schemata through gestural mechanisms. Shared knowledge in this case is either inherited or fixed through imprinting, a case that we would probably not define as a form of culture. There is an additional element that allows us to identify the specificity of culture. Culture—we assume—is there when a shared knowledge can be contested. Culture presupposes that consensus can be transformed into dissensus, that shared knowledge has to be verified and eventually to be reorganized in order to be acceptable as shared knowledge.[1] Within such a cultural context the coordination of behavioural schemata requires specific rules, namely coordination through norms and values which allow the transformation of dissensus into consensus. Dissensus is the constitutive property of culture.[2] Without dissensus we do not need to construct a shared world. Culture would be superfluous. Dissensus is the key to answering the question how social order is possible.

To explain the emergence of culture from dissensus does not rule out the possibility of dissensus about this culture. Culture, however, tends towards closing itself off and cutting out dissensus. What is shared is emphasized, stressed, and often overstressed. A first form of such overstressing is ideological closure by formulating higher values. A second form is ritual enactment of the shared culture by staging a symbolic order as a second nature. Religion well serves this function of stabilizing the shared world and neutralizing dissensus as deviation from the correct belief. Even here we find another way out of this stability: the orthodox and the heterodox interpretation of what is to be taken as the shared world. Such dissensus is highly precarious as the religious wars in early modern Europe have shown.

The paradox of sharing a culture is a consensus which triggers dissensus. The solution to this paradox is to interpret dissensus as a mechanism of variation for avoiding the impossible which is to reach a consensus. In such a conception, consensus has the function of producing variation in social reproduction. This paradox has been rarely looked at. From Durkheim to Parsons and Habermas the aspect of consensus has been emphasized thus privileging theories of integration. From (the early) Marx to (the early) Dahrendorf and to Touraine the aspect of dissensus has been emphasized thus privileging theories of conflict over theories of integration.[3]

A way out of this theoretical impasse has been the attempt to think of society without culture. Society is here seen as a system of interaction which results from maximizing behaviour. The economic theory of social action (Becker 1976; Coleman 1990) has argued that society reproduces itself beyond consensus and dissensus. The classical theory of social action was thus undermined. If there are no norms and values that exist independently of interests,[4] then social order and social conflict are equally the outcome of pursuing rationally one's interests. Cultural factors such as ideological constructions or moral convictions are nothing more than an *Überbau* of the given preference structure of individuals.

The central argument against the economic theory of social action[5] is that social actors also act by following norms and values, the validity of which cannot be reduced to the motive of being in one's interest. Actors accept norms not because they are in their interest, but because they are collectively shared and thought of as being valid independently of one's interest. Norms and values are practised and a rational motivation can only be attributed *post hoc*. Rational motivation then is a rationalization of the fact that actors simply follow collectively shared norms. The simplest rationalization is that norms and values correspond to one's own interests.[6] Instead of being the starting point of social action, interests and rational motives are the outcome of social action, the outcome of a process of internalizing and rationalizing action.

To account for the emergence of social action we are forced to explain the phenomenon that norms and values are shared. They are shared because they are embedded and enacted in symbols, rituals, and beliefs. Contrary to the classical assumption of culture as a closed system of norms and values based on a rational or functional consensus, the starting point of an explanation here is that a social consensus is grounded in symbols, rituals, and beliefs (Wuthnow 1987). Such a consensus is precarious in two ways: first, because the cultural system is itself a system with logical inconsistencies and contradictions; second, because the staging of consensus serves as a medium for the maintenance of conflictualization of a social order.

Culture is needed in any society. How much is needed is an empirical question. Loosely integrated societies need less culture; strongly integrated societies need a great deal of culture. Put differently: the more groups are socially linked, the more culture is necessary. Culture serves as a medium for knotting different groups together. This problem is especially virulent when societies reconstitute themselves. The historically recumbent experiment is the formation of nation states in Europe.[7]

A further experiment occurs today again in Europe, where nation states search for a higher social order. The following thesis is, that to the extent that integration beyond the nation state continues, cultural factors become central to this process. Europe needs therefore culture that allows the finding of a transnational order based on the assumption (or fiction) of a consensus. However, such a consensus on a common European culture is the object of a complex dissensus that is constitutive of this transnational society.

Economic theory will claim that the reciprocal advantage of the nation states is enough to produce a European society. Europe is explained in accordance with this theory as a purposive association, that calls itself in a euphemizing way a 'community'. This is not only a theory, but also a political option.[8] The alternative theory is that the constitution of a society in Europe needs much culture in order to go beyond the social order of nation states (more exactly: nation-state organized societies). How much culture is needed to generate such a transnational social order, and whether the existing cultural repertoire is suitable for this constructive task is an empirical question.

Behind this empirical question lurks the theoretical question regarding the meaning and role of culture in the production of a social order. A reconstruction of cultural processes—this contradicts the theoretical thesis of economic theory—is the key to the explanation of the formation of a European society. The theoretical question raised by the historic case of 'Europe' brings in two complementary questions: How much consensus must be presupposed to produce a modern social order? And how much dissensus is needed to bring about such an order?

Reconstructing and Constructing a European Culture

European Culture: The Ritual Enactment of an Idol

The modern nation state is founded on the idea of a nationally shared culture. 'Getting one's history wrong' has been the basis of constructing a national culture. It is not historical truth that shapes the collective memory and stories. What counts is the process through which collective experiences are remembered. This phenomenon also holds for the idea of a European culture, which is produced by those looking for a European society beyond the idea of a Europe of reciprocal advantages (well separated from the rest of the world).[9] European culture does not exist as a homogeneous unit, as a culture of commonalties. To make this culture the basis of a European society is to invent it as a common culture. To paraphrase: 'to get Europe's history wrong' is in addition the condition for the manufacture of consensus as the start and the medium for dissensus over this culture. To falsely invent history as a construction by intellectuals is the basis of a shared collective identity.

This paradox earmarks the present search for a European culture. This culture is reinvented against the facts. It is based on fictional claims which are put into question. It is searched for in attitudes, in historical literature, in monuments. It is euphemized and therefore provokes the thematization of the 'different sides' of this culture such as its good and bad, its bright and dark sides. In the process of communicating these sides of European culture a new collective experience emerges: that of the difference between the past and the experience of its reconstruction. A new culture emerges from the communication of the traditions. To what extent this communicative dissolution of old traditions leads to a new culture which might overarch the dissensus purported by the past is to be investigated.

The Double Tradition of European Culture

The cultural sociology and cultural history of Europe bring forth its deep ambivalence.[10] The cultural system linked to the idea of a European culture is neither integrated nor an integrating system; rather it is characterized by deep internal tensions. These tensions are not only surface variations of a common culture; they are better referred to as heterodox and orthodox manifestations of a common cultural tradition; they indicate a contradictory code of European culture. This theory can be developed looking at the syncretistic form of this culture which is the result of two historic sources: of the Jewish and of the Greek tradition. The deep-seated ambivalence of modern culture can be found—as will be discussed in the following[11]—in the Greek and Jewish cultures that, through the Christianization of Europe, constitute the cultural heritage of Europe. The two sources of Europe's cultural evolution[12] are found in Greek and Jewish tradition. Both have equally shaped the complex cultural evolution of Europe.

The key to an understanding of the basic code underlying this evolution can be found in the specific symbolic representation of power, especially in the symbolism of power related to 'blood'.[13] Ancient Greek society legitimized its form of political power by *bloody sacrificial rites*. These sacrificial Delphic rites enact the symbolic order of society. The social system is held together by this symbolic order on which a democratic order (in fact an intellectual invention of later Greek history!) could be founded. Sound evidence for the dominance of the bloody model underlying Greek culture comes from the cultural orientations of those social groups opposed to it. Most important were the Pythagorean groups who distinguished themselves by their vegetarianism, a value orientation clearly opposed to the bloody rituals (Detienne 1979). Vegetarianism here is a symbolic rejection of the dominant culture, a ritual reversal of the dominant culture. Logically, persecuting these vegetarian groups became the way to reinstate the dominant culture.

Jewish society, on the other hand, was characterized by a cultural tradition that succeeded in institutionalizing ritual restrictions on shedding blood. This has been the decisive difference between the Jews and their neighbours. The non-sacrifice of Isaac is the key myth marking the historical point when the Jews began to abstain from human sacrifice even while their neighbours continued to practise it. Increasingly, the Jews restricted the shedding of blood. This restriction was rationalized by the myth of a *non-bloody paradise*. Because in reality it was impossible to circumvent bloodshed completely, rules of ritual purity became enormously important. These rules put strong conditions on the practice of bloody sacrifice and other practices concerning animals and other forms of nature. The rules became more and more complicated as social life increased in complexity. The unique canon of dietary prohibitions and rules characteristic of Jewish society thus represents a cultural tradition that has tried to limit the use of an Other being (be it human, animal, or nature as such) as a mere object. It favours instead a culture that puts symbolic limits upon such uses.[14]

Jewish obsession with *ritual purity* explains why its political society never really developed the social dynamism characteristic of Greek or Roman society. Yet, the tradition had tremendous cultural validity, and intervention from outside could not change it. The Jews were never mobilized by political elites in the way neighbouring societies were. The Romans knew exactly why they were trying to force the Jews to eat pork. It would have been the best way to destroy the symbolic basis of their culture. The early Christians also belong within this cultural code. The Romans saw them as a radical Jewish sect.[15] The cultural basis for their persecution was—like the persecution of the Jews later in European culture—rooted in the cultural divide that distinguished them from, and even opposed them to, the bloody tradition of Greco-Roman culture.

The culture of Europe has a complex heritage. On the one hand, we have the Greeks, whose society mobilized its social, economic, and political dynamic by putting rather loosely structured controls upon the use of power. On the other hand, we have the Jews, whose society integrated its economic, political, and social dynamic into a cultural world that put rigid limits upon the use of power.

The reconstruction of a dual tradition of European culture allows us to broaden our conception of European culture. Both the dominant Greek and the latent Jewish traditions have contributed to the process of its cultural evolution. Christianity, as the symbolic system mediating between and blending these two traditions, has not only reproduced but also intensified this constellation of two traditions in one culture. The cyclical outbreaks of protest and rebellion, of 'heterodoxy', in Christian culture against the dominant orthodox traditions can be interpreted as attempts to reverse the relationship between the two cultural traditions.[16]

The Greek model became dominant in shaping the development of European society. Because the Jewish model contradicts the Greek model, it has been circumscribed. In the extreme it was shut up in ghettos and persecuted. This dynamic of European culture has had costly effects. Its history is the history of suppressing the 'non-bloody' tradition by the 'bloody' one within modern culture. Nevertheless, the 'non-bloody' tradition has, despite its bloody suppression, remained part of the 'collective unconsciousness' of European culture.[17]

The interpretation of the cultural code of modern European culture offered above allows us to understand some practices and movements in modern European history that are based on contradictory cultural traditions. This 'heritage' forces modern society to confront the other cultural tradition that has up to now remained outside the discourse on modernity and modernization. The 'collective unconsciousness' has begun to be discussed publicly and shared collectively. This process of discovering and uncovering a latent tradition in the cultural evolution of modernity has put into question the universalism of European culture. At the same time it has produced a new idea: the idea that the unity of a culture does not consist in the universality of its values, but in the reflexive distance and in the reflexive practices that are based on the values of a culture. This leads modern culture to a new way of posing the problem of a shared culture and identity: Is cultural integration possible through the communication of difference?

Cultural Integration through Communicating Cultural Diversity?

Although the code of cultural traditions in Europe represents a contradictory mixture of incompatible traditions, it obviously furthermore fulfils social-integrative functions. From what has been said it follows that it is not the internal cohesion of a cultural code which makes social integration possible. It is not the semantic meaning dimension of culture but the pragmatic function of culture that explains the role of culture in the process of social integration. What integrates is the fact that traditions are good for communication. Traditions are good in order to represent identity and difference. This is the pragmatic function of cultural traditions.[18]

This theoretical perspective is supported by the observation that modern societies have become an object of public communication to the extent that the authority of tradition vanishes. This does not mean that everybody would start to engage in such communication of meaning, as enlightenment thinkers expected. It only means that institutions of authority no longer monopolize the communication of culture.[19] Communication is handed over to a public sphere.[20]

A shared understanding can thus be identified, not because of history but because institutions of communication have emerged which define what should be communicated as a shared culture. The question of social integration thus moves from the question of meaning to the question of institutions which communicate meanings in such a way that they reach the members of society and can be read by all. The technical requirements for such communication are given by the development of the European media landscape. What its 'cultural' use is has to be clarified.

The Formation of the Nation and its Aftermath

A good example is the formation of the nation as an emergent meaning system in the nineteenth century. The nation has already been described by Deutsch (1953) as a system of communication which generates commonness: the density of the communication is linked to the formation of nation states. The communication of what is shared is constitutive of the nation: commonness is produced and reproduced in everyday communication. This specific modern commonness is no longer based on the identification with a representative symbolic figure (the sovereign representing, as king or emperor, the whole) but on an artificial community produced through communication that could refer to any sign: language, ancestry, or religion.[21] To the extent that the nation loses its capacity to symbolize the shared world, alternative symbols appear: local identities, on the one hand, transnational identities on the other. The symbols of commonness multiply; issue-specific political identities are added and widen the repertoire of symbolic markings towards non-ascriptive forms which generate new contingencies in the production of symbols that stand for a shared culture. In this world of postmodern identity designs it becomes less and less possible to represent what is shared. The reciprocal presentation of images replaces well-defined collective identities.

And yet a shared world emerges: the commonness of an audience that observes not only the staging and communication of these identities, but also participates in this staging and communication. From this follow interesting empirical questions: Who listens to whom and when? Who participates and when? Are there temporal cycles? Which role do selective mechanisms such as social status, political power, and cultural expressiveness play? To what extent is the modern media of mass-communication able to control these mechanisms? The crucial theoretical point is that the production of consensus and dissensus does no longer depend on the content. It depends on nothing but communication. Content becomes contingent with the development of modern culture. It is dependent on economic cycles, on political instabilities, and 'postmodern' cultural fashions.

These considerations provide a framework which goes beyond the idea of social integration through common values with the ambivalence of modern culture (Bauman 1990, 1992) that figures so prominently in the analysis of the dynamics of cultural change of modern society. It can also deal with the emergent forms of social order that develop in the postmodern patchwork of identity construction. The example of Europe offers for this new form of constructing a social order beyond the idea of a social order based on shared values, a historical laboratory, and an evolutionary new solution.

The Cultural Representation of European Integration

Europe as a Case of a Postnational Collective Identity

In the 'postmodern' condition the idea of a European society and even more so of a European collective identity seems to be rather atavistic. The discourse about Europe appears at first sight as a discourse that tries to translate the national symbolism simply into a transnational symbolism. However this interpretation would be too simple. For Europe is no longer as obvious as the nation has been. In a world of controversial interpretations of the national its invocation will run into difficulties.[22]

So we are confronted with the search for a common denominator that is different from the model that underlies the construction of a national identity. This search gives a meaning to the discourse on Europe that goes beyond

Europe. The search for a European identity is an example of the attempt to create a common concern out of the interest-based relations of citizens. These interests are of a double nature: not only material, but also ideal interests shape social relations (as Max Weber has formulated). Europe is more than the Europe of the bourgeois. However, this 'more' is hard to define because there is no real referent. The theoretical solution of this paradox is the radicalization of the idea of social integration through communication: social order emerges where people raise their voices and fight to be heard.

Beyond Interest-Based Collective Action

Ideal Interests have to do with ideas. Ideas exist in a linguistic form, they are the referents to the outside world contained in symbols. Now such reference to the world is symbolically loaded in different ways. There are areas where the communicative element plays a rather secondary role. Such are questions of a more socio-political order.[23] To which extent mobility should be fostered, which social rights people should have, can be handled with minimal communicative skills. Interests do not need much interpretation and justification. Distributive questions are solved through strategic games. Issues of identity and difference need more communicative action. Identity exists only by being talked into the world. Such issues exist only through communication. This explains why a common language has been so important in the construction of national identities, why nation-building has been important in providing a meaningful context for material interests and for bargaining such interests. The communicative form of togetherness presupposes a shared language. This is not the case in Europe. Not even the dominance of English is given because of the role of French in administrative matters and the growing global importance of Spanish. Culture cannot integrate because the medium is missing: a common shared language. The globalization of culture has moved therefore to other linguistic media such as music.[24] A different medium is pictorial language, the recognition of symbols through film and television.[25] This form of meaning without words produces a common culture beyond cultures separated by national languages. And yet this does not mean that this could ground an emerging European culture. We have to deal with life forms that do no longer bind their cultural expression to national languages—the cultural split of the world is reproduced in a transnational symbolism: between those who identify with these transnational symbols and those who refuse them. Where linguistic culture and symbolic forms coincide, they reinforce each other reciprocally. The historic example for it is nationalism as a cultural movement that bound together the linguistic community and the symbolic community and thus was able to create clear border markers to the outside world. As soon as pure interest-bargaining is overcome[26] and interests are linked to collectively shared symbolic forms, the double face of culture becomes visible: to provoke dissensus. This dissensus is in the end inevitable because interest-bargaining cannot be restricted to pure interests. It mixes with motives that have to do with the protection of an identity, with the feeling of recognition of oneself by others.[27] This connection earmarks the self-destructive logic of the welfare state in Europe: the experience of being a competitor in the market of social rights leads to the closure of group-specific identities, to a dynamic of the cultivation of the distance to the others up to their cultural devaluation. Shared culture generates cultural difference and fractures the social order. It fulfils a social function against social integration.[28]

Due to the expansion of socio-political and economic forms of interest-bargaining beyond the borders of the nation state, social systems are generated which extend the sphere of interests beyond nationally defined borders. This is integration through economic integration. The aim is to create the conditions for effective bargaining of interests, to create equilibria for such bargaining systems. A system based on reciprocal interests emerges. But this system does not work so smoothly. Culture intervenes and produces disequilibria. Even the attempt to keep culture out makes it come back. Therefore culture is taken up intentionally and strategically without it being known what the consequences will be. The culture that returns is the culture of identity, an 'ethnic revival' as Smith (1981) has called it.

The Ethnic Revival: Limits of Postnational Identities

The movement that results from the search for a common culture counteracts the intention of the searcher. The intention is to found European unification on a unity which also exists in the mind of the people, i.e. to give Western Europe a cultural identity. The result of these attempts is—paradoxically—boundary marking on all levels, especially regional ones. Regional boundary symbols and local relationships are rediscovered, regional identities revived and put against national and supranational forms of integration. The Europe of 'ethnic communities' is a conservative attempt to restore symbolic borders that national memory had already forgotten. Even in a century of 'communism' the imposition of de-traditionalizing ideologies in Eastern Europe did not succeed in such forgetting. Beyond the national borders new symbolic borders, justified as the defence of the West, the Occident, or Christianity against the 'other', are rediscovered. Dissensus is provoked by otherness, by a competing cultural consensus that is to be explained in the most divisive case by religious differences, in the superficial case by aesthetic differences, in the normal everyday case by social differences.[29]

The ethnonationalism that has emerged, especially in the East European countries, no longer allows the differentiation between primordial differences and artificial differences. It re-mobilizes old symbolic markings and designs new symbolic borders. 'Old' meanings experience a renaissance, in which the 'Old' is rethought and enriched with new meanings. The 'Old' is only a medium for the allegation of a commonness, a trigger for collective bargaining which is decoupled in the course of its realization from what it set into motion. In this process the symbols of primordial commonness continue to change, up to the point of no connection to the real world. They become a mere social construction. The regionalism that dominates in West European societies is similar regarding the reference to primordial loyalties. However the national impetus is missing. There is no longer an attempt to construct politically a cultural commonness. The Europe of ethnic communities can therefore easily be integrated into transnational arrangements, without provoking too much conflict.[30] This forces us to question the expectation of an optimistic modernization theory which assumes a convergence of the particular towards the universal in the development of modern society. Even the critical variant which saw colonialism and imperialism as destructive elements of cultural variety has become obsolete. The plea for the particular wins over this destructive power and destroys at the same time the cultural other. The optimism of enlightenment with the idea of rationality through free and equal people communicating with each other is demolished by the experience of closing communication, exclusion through communication, and the reduction of communication to impoverished forms of communicative relationships. The emphasis on cultural diversity and its use as an argument against universalism provide the intellectual support needed. The discourse of intercultural communication is the reaction to the argument that cultural differences can no longer be bridged by communication. However, everyday life goes on. Modern society is split into cultural units, and between these units interest-based interaction develops.[31] The present stage of the development of modernity produces a paradox: cultural heterogeneity coupled with the de-cultivation of social relations between these units. This is valid for Europe in two ways: as heterogenization with regard to national and regional symbols and as heterogenization through immigration movements from different cultures (especially the Islamic world). The European answer is of a double nature. The real answer is the attempt to construct a context of economic interests. The ideological answer is the call for a European tradition, for a European identity. Both answers are inadequate. The first, because interests cannot be separated from identity-related issues, and the second, because it is founded on a harmonizing illusion.

From this further questions emerge: Does this alternative describe the only options that enable the constitution of a modern social order? Or is there an alternative option? Is there a form of social integration between interest-based bargaining and cultural consensus, between the break-up of communication and communicative steering of the world, which is not based on reciprocal benefit or shared values? This is also a theoretical question regarding the forms of a modern social order in a globalizing and heterogenizing world.

Theoretical Implications: Integration Beyond Consent

Integration through Dissent?

The seductive power of rationalist thought that has grasped modern social science, is, finally, founded on the longing for a peaceful world. Modern rationalist social theory has turned Hobbes upside down. The rationale coordination of egoistic interests is the mechanism that generates social order. The social contract suffices—together with some regulating authorities. However, the world does fit that idea. Ideas mobilize actors; they follow reasons that are enough reason for them to sacrifice themselves for others. On the other hand, each idealization of culture as 'liberating' is likewise illusory. It often produces the opposite. So we end up in the paradoxical situation of participating in the production of culture whose function it is to dissociate. The culturalist thinking that has entered the social sciences as a countermovement to rationalist individualism underrates the pacifying power of rationalist thought and overrates the integrative power of symbols which implies to underrate the polemogenic function of symbolic identification (Eder 1994).

Both, rational action and symbolically oriented action, are elements through which social integration is generated. The first generates dilemmas, the latter generates dispute. Strategic action leads into dilemmas which are to be civilized through common reciprocal interests. Symbolically oriented action leads to dispute because it provokes symbolic markers of difference and raises the question of identity. Social integration therefore ends in dilemmatic situations or it ends in dissent. If we accept that social situations are necessarily dependent on symbolic forms (and rational action represents a counterfactual idealization), then prisoner dilemmas or other paradoxes of rational collective action have to be transformed into dissent.[32] This, however, signifies that dissent is in the end inevitable. If, however, this is inevitable, then it is necessary to ventilate an alternative theoretical idea, namely that social integration is possible through dissent, or even the idea that social integration is only possible through dissent. There exist some theoretical ideas of this type. One is the theoretical position of Touraine who proposed to give up the idea of society and replace it by the idea of historical action systems (Touraine 1978, 1984, 1992). Society, Touraine argues, is a historical action system within which actors fight about the orientation of social change. This obviously is a countermodel to thinking of society as a social order. The reason to conceive society in this way is the increasing importance of social movements and the historical obsolescence of bourgeois society as the organizational form of public collective action.

The theoretical question is whether dissent can be conceptualized as an organizational principle of social processes. In a reinterpretation of a classic argument by Schelsky, this is the question of whether permanent communication can be institutionalized in a society (Schelsky 1965). Institutionalization means making sure that dissensus on consensus is generated and that the emerging dissensus is transformed into a new temporary consensus which again sets into motion the cycle of generating dissent.

Such a theoretical idea provides the ground for a minimalist conception of a collective identity which will be presented in the following. The institutionalization of a collective identity can be thought of in the present phase of modernity only as a reflexive one. 'Minimalist' means, in this context, that there is no longer a substantialist representation of a shared culture. Culture is the result of a political management of meaning, of *'gestion du sens'* (Dobry 1986, 1990) as the mechanism of constructing a collective identity in the age of postnationalism. This does not mean that there is no longer nationalism. This only means that also nationalism has become a useful, easily available, and mobilizing idea suitable for the construction of collective identities. The fluidification of traditions does not end in their dissolution, but in their unrestricted availability for political purposes. That traditions nevertheless work, or are functional for the reproduction of modern societies might appear first of all as a paradoxical allegation. This obvious paradox is dissolved in two steps: first with a theoretical argument, namely a critique of the neo-classical theory of culture; second, with a minimalist conception of European identity.

Can Dissent be Institutionalized?

The problem of the symbolic demarcation of cultures from each other (their incommensurability would only be the extreme case of this phenomenon) brings us back to the question of whether these cultures could be thought of as parts of society. Obviously society is more than the addition of cultural life-worlds. However the thesis of cultural consensus as the integrative mechanism of society beyond the bare addition of the units is incorrect.[33] It lacks the identification of the mechanism that holds together the incommensurable and the differentiated without assuming a cultural consensus. Obviously, it is neither culture conceived as a system of shared norms and values nor the shared interpretation of the world nor the consensus over principles of human life. Culture is less and more. Culture is as well a medium for communication as it is constitutive of communication. It is through culture that social relationships can be reproduced such that one's own peculiarity can be related to the particularity of the other.

This argument can take Wuthnow's criticism of neo-classical theories of culture (the phenomenological, hermeneutic, and ethnomethodological variants of sociological theory) as a starting point (Wuthnow 1987). He argues against the neo-classical tradition of the sociology of culture that culture can only be understood within the context of processes of communication. Culture is staged; there is no cultural representation of society that does not stage what it represents. It is often through rituals that culture stages the representations of society. Wuthnow speaks of a 'dramaturgical' concept of culture. Culture is always theatre. Swidler (1986) in a similar way argues against Parsons and uses as an example Weber's thesis regarding the Protestant spirit. Why—Swidler asks—do norms and goals of action produced by ideas (such as the idea of a predestination) continue to have effects even when the original idea, here the theory of predestination, is no longer valid? If Calvinistic ideas do mould the Protestant Ethos, why then does the Ethos survive the ideas that generated it? This effect is not part of the ideas of the Calvinists. What endures is obviously not the ideas, but the type and manner of how social action has been institutionalized. Culture is not an entity that orients action, but an instrument (a tool-kit) that is used to construct strategies of action. There is finally Bourdieu (1980) who supports such a conception of culture. He understands culture as a mode of using symbols, such as symbols of taste, status symbols, or symbols representing the morally good and valued, and introduces an important concept: namely the concept of 'strategy'. Culture is the medium of group-specific strategies of dealings with each other.[34]

A still different line of extending the neo-classical theory of culture is found in 'cultural theory' (Thompson, Ellis, and Wildavsky 1990). This theory argues that culture varies with different lifeforms, that culture therefore is basically not homogeneous, but heterogeneous. This theory tries to heterogenize what the established sociological eye homogenizes.[35] This leads to a theory of culture as a mechanism of drawing borders (or of difference production) and leads away from the classical assumption of a theory of culture as the mechanism of social integration.

These sociological interpretations of culture as a medium of collective action open a theoretical perspective in which dissensus becomes a constitutive element of society. Thus, a first important point of a systematic criticism of a mere interpretative sociology of culture and a step in the direction of a 'post-classical' theory of culture is made. The answer to the question of why social actors can act together is thus far from the classical and idealizing assumption that shared values and norms are the basis of social order.

The criticism of the assumption that norms and values enable social integration does not imply the assumption that norms and values are superfluous, that they are secondary rationalizations or derivatives. Norms and values do not determine action; they define a space of possible actions and constrain the space of possible action. One has to mobilize good reasons for one's own actions, if one's motives of action are to be recognized by the others. These good reasons (respectively their recognizability as good reasons) are culturally predefined and part of shared collective knowledge. To the extent that motives of action must be substantiated, this knowledge is mobilized and reconstructed according to the requirements of the situation. In modern times the speed of this reconstruction has exponentially increased, with the effect that the perception of a collectively shared and recognized knowledge is to be made within increasingly shorter time periods. The consequence is that the idea of a collectively shared knowledge no longer has a social basis. What is lasting, is only more change. What remains identical in change is the process of communication. Social order in modern society is bound to the evolutionary speeding up of the communicative reproduction of culture. The 'post-classical' theory has drawn the consequence that culture is the medium and consequence of communication. Sharing a culture is given by the mere fact of communicating with each other. Where this communication network is extended beyond established cultures, intercultural communication emerges that produces again a shared culture. Thus, intercultural communication becomes a mechanism of the formation of new collectively shared cultures. The case of Europe is exemplary. In intercultural communication between national cultures a new system of communication emerges that assembles continuities of old cultures and makes them part of a different system of communication. However a shared world as the basis of a collective identity remains contingent. This is the starting point for what is to be developed in the following: a plea for a minimalist conception of a European identity.

A Minimalist Conception of a European Identity

What are the options for the construction of a European identity? Which is the collective identity commensurate for Europe? We are faced with minimalist and maximalist options. The maximalist option is the attempt to think of European identity as being analogous to national identity. That this is an unstable option under the condition of reflexive modernity, is an implication of the foregoing discussion. It is nevertheless a possible, although presumably high-cost path. European identity in this maximalist conception would be defined by its difference to neighbouring cultures. Constructing the difference to political Islam could be one such way. Independent of the costs of this strategy of demarcation, this solution is also structurally unstable, because this form of the demarcation necessarily provokes in reflexive modernity a new dissensus,[36] which runs against the temporary consensus over a shared culture in Europe and triggers only a new attempt to transform dissensus into consensus. The question remains, how one could think of a minimalist option of constructing a European identity.

A minimalist conception implies, first of all, that the prescriptive function of boundary marking is restricted to legal forms of inclusion and exclusion. This would, on the one hand, generate flexibility in defining boundaries and, on the other hand, would subject these boundary definitions to the universalist principles of the rule of law.[37] Europe would then be first of all a legal community which defines who is to be included into the processes of communication of this society. Social charters, the Schengen agreement, agrarian policies are—beyond their obvious interest-base—attempts to construct spaces of action in which guarantees for free communication, for the free movement of commodities, persons, and services up to and including thought, are institutionally given.

The further question, how to give this legal community a collective meaning, to provide it with affective casts, necessitates however historic new answers. The social carriers of meaning production have changed. Shared meanings that could make up a collective identity are less and less produced by intellectuals. The historic model of the nation created by intellectuals (Giesen 1993) no longer grasps empirical processes. The meaning attributed to the emerging legal community is created by professionals. The professionalization of meaning production changes the conditions of production and reproduction of meaning. The attribution of meaning to the emerging European legal community is left to professional management of meaning. This mode of constructing symbolic representations follows less the idea of intellectual argument than the idea of emotional persuasion as it is practised in advertising. Its logic is to neutralize negative images and to test possible positive images. If the images work, then they generate the necessary affective effects of belonging or bonding. Because affective relationships become volatile under such conditions (which minimizes the potential costs of symbolic exclusion!), the effect of emotional bonding has to be worked upon permanently. This is the historically new phenomenon of permanent identity work and identity communication.

Europe is a candidate for such a novel case of a postmodern identity construction where reflexivity and contingency of symbolic representations and the hard normative reality of legal exclusion together constitute a 'community'. This novel model does what Renan has assumed counterfactually: that a common culture, a collective identity is produced in the '*plébiscite de tous les jours*'. Identity then is no longer disembedded from politics, no longer conceived as a higher order of reality than politics or something that 'underlies' politics. Identity becomes politics. If politics, and that constitutes the specific modernity and historic peculiarity of Europe, becomes the politics of networks of professional collective actors, then the making of identity becomes daily political business. The search for a European identity disenchants in the course of its realization the idea of collective identity itself. Disenchantment forces the discourse on collective identity to a minimalist conception of collective identity. Europe has no other options, and this is the particular historic experiment of the political construction of a European society.

NOTES

1. For a theoretical formulation of this problematic see Miller (1986, 1992).
2. A theoretical justification is given in Eder (1994).
3. Alexander (1989, 1990) has linked the aspect of integration with assumptions about the integrative function of symbols and rituals. For a further development of the conflict-theoretical position, see Miller (1992) who emphasizes the integrative function of dissensus.
4. This critical argument has been taken up by Hechter (1990). Institutions are explained by a rationalistic theory of action which accounts as well for the emergence as for the reproduction of institutions. Elster (1989) is critical of such attempts to explain norms by rational preferences and explaining norms as something without a rational motivation. The theoretical foundations are made explicit in Coleman (1990).
5. This argument at least takes culture as a social fact. This is a theoretical and empirical, not a methodological argument against methodological individualism.
6. It is one of the central theoretical insights of Habermas (1984, 1987), that this type of validity claim constitutes the most simple case of rationality and that the collective validity of norms has to be based on more encompassing claims.
7. See for more recent cultural-sociological research on the making of the nation state Anderson (1991) and Smith (1986, 1991).
8. Namely the option of those who wish a society which is as little European as possible and argue for the nation state as the social form best suited to a modern society. This also contains the germs of a new political conservativism.
9. See the contributions to Weidenfeld (1985), esp. Löwenthal and the introduction by Weidenfeld.
10. The link between ambivalence and modernity is the topic of Bauman´s work (Bauman 1990, 1992). The following arguments add some further historical evidence to it.
11. A general theoretical account of the idea of a social and cultural construction of nature can be found in Eder (1996).
12. This point has been made systematically within the context of the evolutionary theory of Parsons who talks about 'seedbed-societies'. See Parsons (1971).
13. For the relevance of the blood symbolism in general, see Loeb (1974).
14. A central characteristic of Jewish culture has been its lack of missionary activities. This can be explained not simply by the special relationship with God as a chosen people which is already a consequence of a specific structural characteristic of this

culture. This characteristic is the attempt to preserve in worldly matters the memory of a different world, the paradise. It is this specific utopian character that did not produce the motivation to look for a this-worldly realization of the telos of a chosen people. The telos is securing the continuity with a paradisaic past in which men, even beasts were equal beings, a world without blood. A discussion and more detailed interpretation of these Jewish practices can be found in Eder (1996) with further references.

15. This claim is supported by the interpreters of the scriptures found in Israel some sixty years ago and kept secret until very recently.

16. The movements associated with, for example, St Francis and John Hus are carriers of a cultural orientation opposed to that institutionalized in orthodox Christian culture. The love of animals and the discursive-egalitarian relationship with them that St Francis preached and practised, on the one hand, the vegetarianism in the Hussite movement, on the other, are indicators of a 'non-bloody' culture, a culture based upon an unbloody image of the relationship of nature with culture. The reaction to such heterodoxies, reinstalling the dominant Greek tradition, has been the establishment of church and state power, a formal-rational institutional apparatus, which not only allowed but needed the persecutions of heretics, witches, and Jews, bloody sacrifices for a culture based on them for its own reproduction. It even started to destroy itself—for which the destruction wreaked by religious wars are the proof. This 'bloody' culture is also the one that contained the modern instrumentalist relationship of man with nature. I have discussed these ideas more at length in Eder (1996).

17. The concepts of 'bloody' and 'non-bloody' are used to convey the metaphorical representation of the ideas that shape a culture. The centrality of blood symbolism in cultures, established by cultural anthropologists (Loeb 1974), allows us to justify the use of these metaphors. This does not imply, however, that 'bloody' cultures produce more aggressive individuals than 'non-bloody' ones. This psychological fallacy, widespread in much traditional sociology-of-culture literature, is to be rejected. Rather, we claim that societies organized on the basis of the 'bloody' code have institutions that canalize human interests and ideals in a way that produces expansionist and missionary cultures including all the horrors and persecutions that can be part of such cultural biases.

18. This theoretical perspective can be linked either to philosophical theories (Habermas 1984, 1987) or to cultural-anthropological theories (Leach 1976).

19. For this argument, see Habermas (1989 [1962], 1992). The element of a deliberative public sphere has gained a new momentum in the debate on civil society. See the contributions to this debate in Calhoun (1992).

20. Important here are the mass media. For a general discussion, see J. B. Thompson (1996). The empirical debate however has criticized the simple critical model of an endangered public space. For the public is not only the object of mass-mediated communication but also its conscious consumer which selects what it likes.

21. The history of modern national and nationalist movements shows that the choice of symbolic markers of community can have quite different political consequences. The state of the art on this topic is barely coverable. For an orientation, see Smith (1981, 1991) and Anderson (1991).

22. The actual phenomenon of a renaissance of the national is linked to the mobilization

of strong external borders. The reference to old ethnic and religious particularities is easily transformed into violent forms (up to war and terror) of dealing with the 'Other'. Also the renaissance of Islam indicates this component.

23. Social policy has become the object of bargaining where reciprocal understanding can be assumed. All actors follow social roles in a well-defined ritual process. Contrary to that, in the last century the symbolic aspect of social policy had been the starting point of powerful ideological currents and fights.

24. See esp. the 'music channels' which are 'understood' at least by the next generation. However, also on the political level music is used as a transnational language. For an analysis of musical campaigns on contested political issues by Amnesty International or Greenpeace, see Lahusen (1996).

25. An interesting case is advertising which develops a transnational language and succeeds in keeping a national colouring.

26. This means in theoretical terms that the members of a society behave in such a way that no longer allows an explanation of their preferences (or their development) in a rational way. This is the limit of mere strategic action. Taking preferences as given, the question of rational motivation then becomes the mere and pale question of empirical motivation in a given situation.

27. This is the topic of the recent philosophical critique of utilitarianism (Taylor 1989; Rawls 1991).

28. Insofar as mere interest-based action has an eirenic function (Eder 1994). It avoids the element of dissociation which is characteristic of culture. It reduces conflict to a mere difference of interests which can be dissolved in different ways and transformed into cooperation. This is the issue in rational choice theories.

29. This implies different starting points for the generation of consensus. Social differences can be corrected. People can get used to bodily appearances; aesthetic judgements are part of fashions; social images, prestige can wander from one group to another and move the basis of dissent. Religious differences are harder to deal with. They can only be overcome by secularization—but then you have the risk of competing secular ideologies.

30. This regionalism is fostered by the Commission of the European Communities. Regionalism undermines national interests and national decision makers and complicates rules of coordination in such a way that a coordinating instance (the Commission) becomes indispensable.

31. One of the new conservative critiques of the project of European integration is that a shared European culture cannot be realized. Therefore such 'communities' can be based only on the principle of reciprocal advantages. This makes the European project the object of interest constellations, the more economic and political power differences exist, the more unstable they become.

32. This theory can be deduced formally from levering the constraints of interaction in the prisoner dilemma, namely the possibility of communication among the participants. As soon as people can talk with each other they can start to agree on shared advantages or normative obligations or they dissent. Here again the ambivalent character of culture becomes obvious.

33. This argument has already been formulated by the theory of subculture without raising the implications for sociological theory.

34. Bourdieu tries to show how social classes use different strategies of representing

themselves and calls these class-specific strategies '*habitus*'. These *habitus* increase in number the more Bourdieu is forced to differentiate class fractions (the most famous example is the petty bourgeoisie and its taste which is the imitation of a taste believed to be the taste of the dominant classes. The problem into which Bourdieu runs is the theoretical openness of his conception of strategy. He is less a utilitarianist (the common misunderstanding) than an empiricist. There are as many *habitus* as there are classifiable groups of people.

35. The main rule of the 'cultural method', as the cultural theory claims, is: cultures are life forms. A life form is a mode of linking social structures (group/grid) with a cultural bias. This theory links thus social interaction (systems of communication) and symbolic elements (types of cultural bias) in a way in which culture is neither conceived independently of social interactions nor are social interactions conceived independently of culture.

36. See Salvatore (1997) who reconstructs the discursive field of political Islam in the European/American context and in the Islamic context and shows the contradictory unity of this field.

37. This is the central argument of Habermas (1992).

REFERENCES

ALEXANDER, J. C. (1989). *Structure and Meaning: Rethinking Classical Sociology*. New York: Columbia University Press.

—— (1990). 'Analytic Debates: Understanding the Relative Autonomy of Culture', in J. C. Alexander and S. Seidman (eds.), *Culture and Society: Contemporary Debates*. Cambridge: Cambridge University Press, 1–27.

ANDERSON, B. (1991). *Imagined Communities: Reflections on the Origins and Spread of Nationalism* (2nd edn.). London: Verso.

BAUMAN, Z. (1990). 'Modernity and Ambivalence'. *Theory, Culture and Society*, 7: 239–60.

—— (1992). *Modernity and Ambivalence*. Cambridge: Polity Press.

BECKER, G. S. (1976). *The Economic Approach to Human Behavior*. Chicago: University of Chicago Press.

BECKER, H. S. (1986). 'Culture: A Sociological View', in H. S. Becker (ed.), *Doing Things Together*. Evanston, Ill.: Northwestern University Press, 11–24.

BOURDIEU, P. (1980). *Le Sens pratique*. Paris: Minuit.

CALHOUN, C. J. (ed.) (1992). *Habermas and the Public Sphere*. Cambridge, Mass.: MIT Press.

COLEMAN, J. S. (1990). *Foundations of Social Theory*. Cambridge, Mass.: Belknap Press.

DETIENNE, M. (1979). 'Pratique culinaires et esprit de sacrifice', in M. Detienne and J.-P. Vernant (eds.), *La Cuisine du sacrifice en pays grec*. Paris: Gallimard, 7–35.

DEUTSCH, K. W. (1953). *Nationalism and Sociass.*A: MIT Press.

DOBRY, M. (1986). *Sociologie des crises politiques*. Paris: Presses de la Fondation Nationale des Sciences Politiques.

—— (1990). 'Calcul, concurrence et gestion du sens', in P. Fauvre (ed.), *La*

Manifestation. Paris: Presses de la Fondation Nationale des Sciences Politiques, 357–87.

EDER, K. (1994). 'Das Paradox der Kultur: Jenseits einer Konsensustheorie der Kultur'. *Paragrana: Internationale Zeitschrift für Historische Anthropologie*, 3: 148–73.

—— (1996). *The Social Construction of Nature: A Sociology of Ecological Enlightenment*. London: Sage.

ELSTER, J. (1989). *The Cement of Society: A Study of Social Order*. New York: Cambridge University Press.

GIESEN, B. (1993). *Die Intellektuellen und die Nation: Eine deutsche Achsenzeit*. Frankfurt: Suhrkamp.

HABERMAS, J. (1984). *The Theory of Communicative Action, i. Reason and the Rationalization of Society*. Vol. I. Boston: Beacon Press.

—— (1987). *The Theory of Communicative Action, ii. Lifeworld and System: A Critique of Functionalist Reason. Volume II*. Boston: Beacon Press.

—— (1989 [1962]). *The Structural Transformation of the Public Sphere: An Inquiry into a Category of Bourgeois Society*. Cambridge, Mass.: MIT Press.

—— (1992). 'Further Reflections on the Public Sphere', in C. Calhoun (ed.), *Habermas and the Public Sphere*. Cambridge, Mass.: MIT Press, 421–61.

HECHTER, M. (1990). 'The Emergence of Cooperative Social Institutions', in M. Hechter, K.-D. Opp, and R. Wippler (eds.), *Social Institutions: Their Emergence, Maintenance and Effects*. New York: Aldine de Gruyter, 13–34.

LAHUSEN, C. (1996). *The Rhetoric of Moral Protest: Public Campaigns, Celebrity Endorsement and Political Mobilization*. Berlin/New York: de Gruyter.

LEACH, E. (1976). *Culture and Communication: The Logic by which Symbols are Connected*. Cambridge: Cambridge University Press.

LOEB, E. M. (1974 [1923]). *The Blood Sacrifice Complex*. Millwood, NY: Kraus Reprint.

Miller, M. (1986). *Kollektive Lernprozesse: Studien zur Grundlegung einer soziologischen Lerntheorie*. Frankfurt: Suhrkamp.

—— (1992). 'Rationaler Dissens: Zur gesellschaftlichen Funktion sozialer Konflikte', in H.-J. Giegel (ed.), *Kommunikation und Konsens in modernen Gesellschaften*. Frankfurt: Suhrkamp, 31–58.

PARSONS, T. (1971). *The System of Modern Societies*. Englewood Cliffs, NJ: Prentice Hall.

RAWLS, J. (1991). *Political Liberalism*. New York: Columbia University Press.

SALVATORE, A. (1997). *Islam and the Political Discourse of Modernity*. Reading, Berkshire: Ithaka.

SCHELSKY, H. (1965). *Auf der Suche nach Wirklichkeit: Gesammelte Aufsätze*. Cologne/Düsseldorf: Eugen Diederichs.

SMITH, A. D. (1981). *The Ethnic Revival*. Cambridge: Cambridge University Press.

—— (1986). *The Ethnic Origins of Nations*. Oxford: Basil Blackwell.

—— (1991). *National Identity*. Harmondsworth: Penguin.

SWIDLER, A. (1986). 'Culture in Action: Symbols and Strategies'. *American Sociological Review*, 51: 273–86.

TAYLOR, C. (1989). *Sources of the Self: The Making of the Modern Identity*. Cambridge, Mass.: Harvard University Press.

THOMPSON, J. B. (1996). *The Media and Modernity: A Social Theory of the Media*. Cambridge: Polity Press.

THOMPSON, M., ELLIS, R., and WILDAVSKY, A. (1990). *Cultural Theory, or, Why All That is Permanent is Bias*. Boulder, Colo.: Westview Press.

TOURAINE, A. (1978). *La voix et le regard*. Paris: Seuil.

—— (1984). *Le retour de l'acteur*. Paris: Fayard.

—— (1992). *Critique de la modernité*. Paris: Fayard.

WEIDENFELD, W. (ed.) (1985). *Die Identität Europas: Fragen, Positionen, Perspektiven*. Munich: Hanser.

WUTHNOW, R. (1987). *Meaning and Moral Order: Explorations in Cultural Analysis*. Berkeley: University of California Press.

11

CONCLUSION

Citizenship and the Making of a European Society

From the Political to the Social Integration of Europe

Klaus Eder and Bernhard Giesen

The Challenge of European Citizenship

Europe is more than a system of legal norms and rules and political institutions which regulate European citizenship. Europe is also a symbolic space where projections and memories, the collective experiences and identifications of the people of Europe are represented. Europe has a cultural meaning.

There are three different motives in addressing European citizenship as being more than an administrative matter. It is first of all a concept which raises moral concerns about justice and democracy, and which conveys a sense of transnational universalism. These non-legal elements of citizenship are at the basis of the hope and despair that accompany the discourse on European citizenship. The expectations in terms of political participation and social justice put on national citizenship provoke the question of whether European citizenship can realize what national citizenship rights have succeeded in doing: the creation of a largely stable system of political freedom and social justice.[1]

A second motive is to project onto European citizenship all those hopes that are contained but not put into practice in national citizenship. By challenging unjustified inequalities between the peoples of Europe, the project of a democratic Europe gains ground.[2] Europe appears as a call for social and democratic transformations, a space for the realization of the universalistic claims inherent in the project of a democratic and just society.

A third motive results from the tension between the challenge and the claim of universalism on the one hand, and the factual and mostly inevitable exclusion of others as outsiders of the community. This forms the debate on the boundaries of Europe, the thrust for inclusion beyond the criterion of

membership in a national community.[3] The search for a collective representation of the people of Europe again is torn between the traditional conception of national identity as the unifying symbolic basis of people in Europe
and the optimistic idea of a postnational society emerging from the increasing cultural heterogeneity of the people in Europe.

Thus, the realist description of Europe in terms of a regulatory political
institution gives us only a partial idea of what is at stake in the debate on
European citizenship.[4] Beyond the political administration of Europe there
are social relations that carry with them normative expectations and values.
This (not Brussels' bureaucracy) has created the semantic surplus in the
debate on European citizenship. To disclose the semantic load of this concept
we have to go back to the specific social arrangements and discursive traditions that have left their imprint on this debate.

Europe: The Second New Nation?

The project of a European citizenship is exceptional because it tries to integrate a society through a system of citizenship rights beyond the nation state.
Since the nineteenth century, conceptions of citizenship have been closely
associated with the idea of the nation and its political form, the nation state.
Following the vein of this almost inseparable connection between citizenship
and the nation state, European citizenship can be conceived as a simple extension of the nation-state model leading to a more encompassing unit to which
different European nations shift part of their sovereign rights. Similar to the
United States of America, the first new nation, the nations of the new
European Community would not merge entirely their communal ties of
belonging and completely subsume their national origin. Instead the
European Community would engender hyphenated collective identities such
as European-French in contrast to Canadian-French, or European-German in
contrast to American-German. This transfer of the American model to the
European Community will, however, not create a strong European identity.
Europe will, of course, not emerge as the second new nation by just relabelling
collective identities. In order to answer the question of whether citizenship is
feasible without and beyond the traditional nation state, we will outline
different institutional types of citizenship that have emerged in the course of
European history. We will focus on the structural similarities between these
historical types and the situation of contemporary Europe as well as on the
barriers that impede a simple transfer of these models to the European
Community. As we have already hinted at above, Europe has always transcended its diverse institutional arrangements of political organization. The
idea of Europe was engendered by an encompassing and overarching cultural

movement that stipulated an embracing unity beyond the confines of political boundaries and mundane reasoning. This conception of Europe emerged out of the fundamental opposition between the fragmented and scattered political map, the world of strategic reason and the this-worldly art of politics, on the one hand, and the thrust for a universal community, for salvation, for transcendence, on the other. This axial tension between the mundane order of politics and the sacred order of another world is at the core of European politics and impinges also on claims on and conflicts about citizenship (Eisenstadt 1987). By referring to the unity of the transcendental world, European society could provide a basis for a collective identity beyond the reach and range of political authority. Although rooted in an other-worldly sphere, this collective identity had to be represented in the mundane realm. In the third part of these concluding remarks we will outline different historical institutions that claimed this representation.

Our conjecture is that European citizenship might be conceived as a new pattern of this representation of the sacred in the mundane order of politics, as a mediating interface between the pragmatic exigencies of political organization, on the one hand, and the ideal of human rights, on the other. In this respect European citizenship, even if it seems to be a new problem might indeed continue a particular European heritage. In contrast and distinction to the mundane political order it assumes a society that is supported by a universalist claim, by some transcendental vision of itself. Before we turn to this cultural construction of society we will outline briefly the institutional options for citizenship as they emerged in the course of European history.

From Citizenship in Europe to European Citizenship: A Historical Perspective

European history has provided a limited repertory of institutional solutions for the relation between political order and citizenship. Although, today, the nation state and national citizenship is frequently treated as the basic paradigm of this relationship, it is certainly not the only one and there are serious objections to the simple transfer of the model to the European level. In order to allow for a historically enriched perspective on the European Leviathan and its counterpart, European citizenship, we will briefly outline the model of the city republic, the model of traditional empires, the model of enlightened absolutism, and the model of the nation state in terms of some basic structural features: center-periphery relationships, boundary construction, and political sovereignty, cultural homogeneity, and civil rights. This discussion will allow us to assess more clearly the novelty and the historical embeddedness of the idea of European citizenship.

The European City State

The European city state, as it emerged in late medieval times, is commonly regarded as the institutional seedbed for the idea of citizenship. It imagined the citizenry as a community of free and equal political individuals who, living on a special territory, are endowed with special rights and privileges. Indeed, it was Italian city states such as Florence and Venice, northern cities such as Lübeck and Hamburg, central German cities such as Magdeburg and Nürnberg, Flemish cities such Bruges and Gent, that were the first to develop not only a communal, even republican spirit, but also a strong constitutional frame for citizenship—sometimes on their own without the protection of a powerful prince as in the case of Florence and Venice, sometimes on the basis of special privileges granted by the emperor as in the case of the German '*Freie Reichsstädte*', but sometimes also in successful opposition to the princely powers of the Burgundian duke and, later on, the Spanish emperor as in the case of Bruges and other cities.

In all these cases citizenship was a special privilege granted to a relatively small part of the cities' actual population. Although not entirely inaccessible to outsiders, the status of full political citizenship was highly exclusive and compares distinctively with respect to the open and inclusive nature of the city as a marketplace that aimed at attracting as many merchants and traders, buyers and labourers as possible. Monetary and banking institutions, the protection of property, public safety and the legal supervision of contracts, treaties of cooperation and association between different cities such as the '*Hanse*' cities, and even a trend towards a unified jurisdiction and constitutional frame opened up large spaces of safe and accountable commercial exchange, but never allowed for a new centralized political sovereignty above the city governments.

The political order of these city leagues and associations was clearly polycentric. The conception of citizenship as a republican corporation mirrored in a certain way the exclusivity of the aristocratic world outside of the city walls. Because citizenship was the privilege of a few, citizens could assume responsibility and engage in political debates and decisions. It was the deliberating assembly of mostly patrician citizens that was considered as the source of the authentic political will, of sovereign power, and of cultural splendour. Based on the aristocratic and exclusive nature of citizenship, the city could open its gates to a multitude of immigrants and foreigners and allow for a vast range of internal cultural heterogeneity. Contemporary intergovernmentalists occasionally present the early modern city constitutions as a promising paradigm for a liberal avenue to European citizenship (Majone 1998*b*). There are, of course, some striking similarities between the early modern city leagues and the contemporary European Community: the dissociation between a fragmented and multilayered political order, on the one hand, and an expansive and unifying market dynamic, on the other; the presence of non-national workers who are excluded from participating in national elections; or the diversity of languages within the Community and the elitist nature of governance. But there are also strong barriers impeding an easy transfer of the city league model to the level of contemporary Europe.

The first barrier against a transfer of the city model is that the early modern city states were not fully sovereign in the strict sense of the term. They were certainly not subject to a strong, stable, and omnipresent princely authority controlling their internal affairs, but remain embedded in the embracing occidental order of the Holy Roman Empire. Some might argue that American domination provides a substitute for this embracing political order in which Europe is embedded as a middle-level institution. The American military interventions in order to re-establish peace in the Balkans might support such a view to some degree. However, most Europeans will strongly object to being reduced to the status of an American province. If it comes to the question of empire, Europe claims its own hegemonic space. The second barrier against the transfer of the city league paradigm to contemporary Europe results from the exclusive structure of early modern citizenship. After the great democratic revolutions—well reflected by Marshall's typology of citizenship (Marshall 1950)—the coalescence of legal, political, and social citizenship has ascended to the position of an unquestionable moral trope of the democratic discourse. Even if there are serious institutional reasons for a separation of different spheres of citizenship and even if a graded form of citizenship is actually inevitable, public discourse is bound to universalist inclusion and will hardly endorse any rigid pattern of civic exclusion. Therefore the paradigm of early modern city republics may well represent the praxis of a weak European citizenship, but it will hardly provide a public striving for strong European citizenship.

The Traditional Empire

The second historical paradigm of citizenship is provided by traditional empires that are based on a strong centre embodied in the person of the emperor, administered by a large bureaucracy and carried by a dominant ethnic or national group. Around the centre extends a graded and stratified belt of various nations that accept more or less voluntarily the authority of the ruler. We have called this political order and its corresponding model of citizenship the Habsburg model, but pre-revolutionary Russia and the British colonial empire may as well serve as illustrations. Empires have, by definition, changing and insecure frontiers instead of sharply demarcated and stable boundaries that are typical for the modern nation state. After a period of expansion or conquest this frontier is protected against invasions of unruly barbarian peoples by a zone of military fortresses or fortifications like the great wall of Song China or the limes in the Roman Empire. Usually, the degree of political control decreases in relation to the spatial distance from the centre. Although the centre tries to expand its control by road construction, reports of local officials, letters of the ruler, and occasional visits, the representatives of political authority and the local leaders at the periphery are relatively independent from the direct supervision of the centre. This graded structure of control has its counterpart in a stratification of membership rights and benefits between the carriers of the centre and groups at the periphery. While citizenship in city states was limited with respect to the range of economic exchange, the economic networks in empires remain mostly within the political frontiers that ensure safety and legal protection.

In order to integrate newly conquered peoples, the political system of empires has to allow for the internal coexistence of various national groups, ethnic and religious communities, languages, and cultures. The basic rights of citizenship in empires are therefore inclusive and decoupled from ethnic or religious ties. Citizenship in the mature Roman, in the British or Habsburg empires is no longer confined to a tiny elite of the core nation. This constitutive multiculturalism of empires comes, however, at a price: it is not the peoples of the empire, but the person of the emperor who is the sovereign political subject—the integrative bond of the empire is provided by the sacredness of the rulers' personal or dynastic authority, and not by the constitutional rules which the citizens have agreed upon or by a public debate about the common good. This does not prevent a close link between the ruler and the people. The emperor represents the people and the people can conceive their collective identity by referring to the all-embracing authority of the ruler. The titles of the prince (King of England, King of Scotland, Emperor of India, King of Egypt) reflect the diversity of his nations and peoples. The ruler warrants peace among them and grants citizenship rights to every subject who recognizes his authority and respects his commands. However, these nations are not sovereign carriers of a political will. The citizen of an empire is primarily a subject of the ruler, a servant to the master, a member of a heteronomous political order, a citizen in a Hobbesian Leviathan.

Because of the distance between centre and periphery and the diversity of languages and cultures within the empire, the public spheres of empires are fragmented and dissected. In contrast to the public space of the city states that allowed even for direct communication between the citizens, deliberation about the common good in empires is mostly confined to the arcane debates at the court of the ruler. The main mode of bridging the gap between the arcanum of the ruler and the public space of the citizens consists in ritual public appearances of the ruler or in his visits to the remote parts of the empire. It is his visible and triumphant presence that strengthens and reassures his authority.

And it is the lack of a charismatic central authority that—among other barriers—prevents the modelling of contemporary Europe according to the Habsburg model. Contemporary Europe has, indeed, many of the constitutive features of an empire—a strong distinction between a group of core nations, the original six nations of the Rome treaty, and a group of new members at the periphery, shifting and expansive frontiers, a tendency towards fortification against invasions from lesser developed nations, internal multiculturalism, and religious pluralism, a fragmented public sphere and a strong bureaucracy, a central authority that has to face and to fight local authorities at the periphery and weak institutions of transnational political participation from below. But it certainly lacks a charismatic embodiment of a transnational political authority. Charismatic leaders in post-war Europe like Churchill and de Gaulle, as well as socialist reformers like Willy Brandt, Felipe Gonzales, or Tony Blair appeal to a national public audience and rarely address the European Community. The paramount importance of a democratic constitution of the European body politic as well as the precarious balance of powers between the different European nations engenders a special sensitivity with respect to a charismatic leadership for the European Community as a whole. The fact that the electorate is national instead of European and the linguistic fragmentation of the European public sphere support this reluctance to claim European leadership. But the vacancy at the level of European leadership has its counterpart in the pale and weak constitution of a European citizenry. Thus, Europe not only has to find a substitute for the charismatic ruler, but it has also to construct (and educate) its citizens.

Enlightened Absolutism

In contrast to the traditional empires that were based on the diversity of nations, the enlightened absolutism of the modern territorial state aimed at the construction of a uniform citizenry. Here, too, the political sovereign was the prince and not the people, here, too, the citizen was imagined as a passive subject of the ruler and here, too, the centre is regarded as the source of identity, authenticity, and innovation. But the mission of the ruler was not just to establish and to expand a realm of peace for his subjects. Instead, it was to extend the rule of law, to modernize the state and its institutions and to extract as many taxes as possible from a limited population.

This turn inwards resulted from a change in the nature of boundaries. The boundaries of modern states are no longer diffuse zones of unstable and insecure power relations between civilization and barbarism, but clear demarcations between similar territorial units. Beyond the boundary there was another autonomous state. Although wars and treaties could change them, boundaries were in general stable and resisted crossing and transgression. For an increase of resources the ruler could turn to conquer colonies outside of Europe or further demographic and economic growth within the confines of his territory. In order to support economic activity in a mercantilist system, the immigration of skilled foreign groups had to be encouraged and the emigration of skilled labour had to be prevented. Above all, the absolutist monarch wanted his population to be sedentary and accountable, comparable and taxable. Citizenship in enlightened absolutism results from this attempt to construct the people as objects which could be perceived and accounted by the expanding legal and fiscal institutions of the state. Its dynamics can be described as internal inclusion. The citizen in enlightened absolutism was, however, not only an object of accounting, taxation, and policing, but also a subject who had to be educated and enlightened in order to respect the law, to engage in the development of science and technology, to stimulate trade and crafts and the production of goods. Law and education became the core arenas of citizenship in enlightened absolutism. The image of the prince as well as the conception of the citizen differed profoundly from traditional absolutism. The ruler was no longer the representation of god or the mundane embodiment of the sacred, but the representation of reason and the moving force of progress. The people were turned from a diversity of local peasants and craftsmen into unified and equal citizens of a state. Enlightened absolutism discarded not only local and regional differences, but disregarded also the religious and ethnic diversity of the citizens—they were banned from the public sphere of the state and enclosed in the privacy of the citizens. The public–private distinction became the core institutional device for coping with cultural diversity in enlightened absolutism.

Again, there are some striking institutional similarities between the political order of enlightened absolutism and the current state of the European Union: the strong bureaucratic centre that claims to represent reason and rationality; the rhetoric of progress and modernization; the attempt to stimulate economic growth as the prime motive of political integration; the institutional protection of a large internal market against imports; the bureaucratic standardization of products and services; the thrust to overcome the diversity of national and local identities and to turn the people of different nations into European citizens; the insensitivity of the centre with respect to collective movements of the people; the internal multiculturalism; the penetration of the local lifeworlds by legal regulations of the centre; and the weakening resistance of the traditional powers.

The institutional analogies between enlightened absolutism and today's European administration and governance are, indeed, striking. But they cannot blur a major and decisive difference. In contrast to the regimes of the eighteenth century, today's political orders are based on an entirely different conception of sovereignty and a complete reversal of the centre-periphery relationship. It is no longer the monarch, but the people who are considered as the authentic source of the political will. The ruler and the citizens have changed places—it is not the enlightened ruler who instructs and constructs the nation, but the nation that elects and constructs the government. Riots and revolts of the people against their ruler were quite common in the eighteenth century, but they occurred as unruly outbursts of discontent. Those who rioted against the authority of the enlightened ruler were no longer regarded as citizens but as outlaws who by their very action challenged the order of law and reason that alone could turn uncivilized creatures into citizens. In contrast, today's conception of citizenship as public practice may even reverse this relationship: by publicly challenging the government, a person becomes a citizen.

The Nation State

The most recent model of citizenship is provided by the nation state. The idea of the nation is not a modern invention, but the nation as the ultimate sovereign actor of politics is, indeed, a decisively modern idea. It emerged in the French Revolution and ascended to the position of an undisputed master-narrative of history and state formation in the first half of the nineteenth century. In the 'spring of nations' these were seen as naturally given collectivities, that—like sleeping giants—could awake, rise, break the chains of foreign domination, and determine their fate by themselves. The revolution against the monarch or foreign rule, the revocation of the political contract, and the return to the state of nature became the foundation myth of the modern democratic nation.

This foundation myth engendered a new notion of citizenship. By emancipating themselves from heteronomous rule and by rebelling against foreign domination, the subjects regained their original autonomy and constituted themselves as citizens of a nation. Thus, the modern concept of the nation merged two different references: the first linked the state to pre-constitutional foundations, i.e. to the state of nature; the other linked individual autonomy and identity to the reflexive determination of the collective self. Both references try to cope with the vacuum after the decapitation of the monarch as the foundation of the state. If people and monarchs change positions as regards the foundation of the state and the authentic source of political action, the contours of the sovereign become unclear, fragile, and shifting. New questions arise: Who is a member of 'the people'? What are the boundaries of the nation? Who is to be excluded from citizenship? The new sovereign has to demarcate its boundaries against outsiders. Its identity and homogeneity had yet to be constructed, its history to be invented and its natural origin to be imagined. Thus, the strong programme of the modern nation state postulated not only the holy trinity of national culture, national economy, and nation state, but also the congruence of nation and citizenry.

One version of this congruence programme reduced the citizenry to the nation that, in turn, was defined by its common history and common culture, and, beyond this, by its common natural origin in distinction to others. The homogeneity of the nation in the state of nature provided the pre-social basis for the legal equality of all citizens. Equality was no longer imposed by the state on the people, rather it was a primordial attribute of the people. The reference to a natural diversity of nations does not inevitably engender a claim for superiority of one nation. Instead the natural diversity of nations as imagined by enlightenment philosophers like Montesquieu or by German romantics like Schlegel is seen as compatible with the coexistence of different nations. This coexistence and territorial separation of different nation states has its ugly side. Those who refuse to join the unified national culture, and those who were marked as different by nature, are excluded from citizenship and frequently even expelled from the territory of the state. Ethnic cleansing and migration seem to be the inevitable consequence of the primordialist version of the strong programme of national citizenship and its insistence on cultural purity and ethnic homogeneity.

Contrary to this reduction of citizenship to the primordial homogeneity of the nation, a second model reversed this relationship. According to this second model, it is not the nation that defines citizenship, but the practice of citizenship that defines the nation. Instead of assuming a natural homogeneity of the nation, this model centred on the idea that the nation constitutes its collective identity by rebelling against the monarch. Here, citizenship is turned into an active practice against the centre. By the very refusal to obey the commands of the ruler, the individuals constitute themselves as citizens and become the authentic and sovereign source of politics. The citizens dissolve the social contract between government and people and open up the space for new collective action.

Citizenship in modern nation states can, as is obvious, no longer be constructed by actual participation in acts of rebellion. Instead, the self-constitution of the nation through revolutions is substituted by an institutionalized mode of disempowering the centre. Critical participation in public discourse would provide such a substitute. The common reading of Renan's famous phrasing '*la nation est le plébiscite de tous les jours*' points in this direction. Here citizenship is not just a legal status, but a practice of participation in public discourse. This shift, however, comes at a price: it excludes implicitly those who cannot or do not want to participate, those who cannot step forward and raise their voice, those who are doomed to be the passive audience.

Notwithstanding whether we opt for the first or the second version of the nation state programme, it seems to be grossly inadequate for the institution of a European citizenship. There is, as we have pointed out before, no history of a European uprising against foreign domination that could provide the

commemorative basis for an all-embracing European demos. Cultural differences impede the development of a European public sphere in which a
European civil society could constitute itself in opposition to the system of
governance in Brussels. Only few can imagine a European national identity to
be based on a natural homogeneity of the European people. Past and present
waves of ethnic cleansing, racism, and genocide have discredited the attempt
to justify the equality of citizens by referring to a natural homogeneity of the
nation. It might even be argued that successful nation-building, when it
occurred, had to disregard the natural heterogeneity of the people, their local
and cultural diversity, their differences in historical memories and actual
merits, and to treat them as if they were equal. Nations are 'imagined communities'—to reiterate Anderson's phrasing—with imagined histories and imagined origins. This imagination of a sovereign collective subject has to blur
internal differences if it is to convince an audience. This process of staging and
imagining the nation cannot dispense with cathectic identification—the
nation emerges because people strive for an image of themselves that they can
fill with hope and pride or fear and hate.

The institutional setting of contemporary Europe may favour the citizenship of enlightened absolutism or early modern city states more than the
conception of national citizenship. But this conception has an undeniable
advantage: it is rooted in the idea of the sovereignty and autonomy of the
people—whoever this people is.

From a constructivist point of view, the project of European citizenship is
not doomed to failure because the current institutions have not yet realized
the normative ideals of national citizenship. No nation has been constructed
within a decade, although collective memory, reaching out for the past, tends
to imagine special events as the birth of the nation. What we argue is that
European citizenship requires a model different from the historical models—
including the nation-state model—discussed so far. There are elements of
each tradition at work in the process of constructing European citizenship.
However, it is not the sum of these elements, but their rearrangement that we
have to look at. In order to understand this logic of rearranging these elements
into a European citizenship we have to come back to the question of what
constitutes the specificity of Europe.

The Social Construction of Europe

Europe as a Cultural Movement

The special tension between inclusion and exclusion, universalism and particularism that is at the core of the project of European citizenship is a consequence

of the fact that modern Europe has never developed a unified political order. The few cases of a clear hegemonic system, e.g. Napoleon's Empire, Hitler's '*Grossdeutsches Europa*', or even the Soviet Empire, have been considered as, mostly short-lived, pathological, and irregular cases. Since its very beginnings Europe has been, above all, a cultural movement, aiming at a transformation of the existing world, contrasting with the fragmentation and polycentrism of political organization, constructing unity, and continuity not by relying on mundane powers, but by referring to a transcendental realm. This cultural idea of Europe was carried by intellectuals and artists, monks and missionaries, crusaders and conquerors, who responded to a challenge from outside or ventured out to spread the message of European culture. This pulsating cultural movement called Europe had no clearly demarcated and continuous centre. In defence or in expansion, it was sharply focused on moving boundaries, on a definition of the other. As a cultural movement Europe claimed the continuity of a cultural heritage that, in fact, was based on ruptures and discontinuity. The project of salvation through European culture consisted of a blend of highly diverse elements, and its claim for unity ignored, in fact, fundamental internal contradictions. To phrase it even more strongly: the power of the European cultural movement emerged mainly from its ability to absorb and to include, to assimilate and to merge seemingly inconsistent symbolic elements into a syncretist unity. What is usually regarded as a more or less continuous tradition from Greek antiquity to contemporary Western civilization is a history of political discontinuity, of cultural hybridization and syncretism, of translations and breakdowns. The invention of descendency and the appropriation of a heritage is central for the construction of Europe. Europe has more than other civilizations—with the possible exception of ancient Egypt and China—insisted on its historical continuity, which could not be based on the continuity of a political organization, but on its capacity to bridge political cleavages and breakdowns through culture. It was based on the translation of a cultural heritage. We will mention only five of these translations.

The first centre of Europe (a Greek term) was the Eastern part of the Mediterranean sea, in what later became known as Asia Minor, the Balkans, the Middle East. Its constitutive boundary ran between Greeks and barbarian outsiders. This first conception of Europe was translated into the Roman Empire by appropriating and assimilating Greek culture. The Roman culture was a field of deliberate hybridization and religious syncretism—the statues of Latin deities were sent as a gift to the temples in the newly conquered colonies and the statues of foreign gods, in their turn, were venerated in Roman temples.

The second major translation occurred in the takeover of the imperial tradition by Frankish and later on Saxon chiefs. After the coronation of Charles the Great by the pope in the year 800 Europe moved westwards. Its constitutive boundary ran between Latin Christianity and the Muslim empires that controlled most of the Mediterranean coast. The political transfer of the imperial tradition from Byzantium to the West was backed by the cultural appropriation of the Christian heritage reflected by the relics of the Christian martyrs that were traded or stolen in Byzantine or Muslim cities in the East and in the crusaders' attempt to conquer the holy places in Palestine. Ironically, it was mainly Muslim and Jewish scholars in the East who continued the tradition of Greek antiquity that was for centuries almost forgotten in the Latin West, but later remembered as the origin of Western culture.

The third major translation of Europe can be seen in the emergence of a Western civilization established by Portuguese and Spanish conquistadors and Dutch and English traders who crossed the Atlantic for the lure of the new world's treasures or for the pursuit of religious perfection. Here, the constitutive boundary did run between the savages of the New World and the Christian conquerors who ventured out from the western shores of the Old World and—despite their internal competition—kept an awareness of their common European identity. Religious mission and trade capitalism transformed the Atlantic ocean into an inland sea of the European colonial empires. In this missionary transformation, the idea of Europe was gradually decoupled from its territorial ties and received a temporal connotation. The 'res publica christiana' could and should finally include every human being. European Christendom reached out to become a universal community.

The fourth major translation of Europe occurred in the process of modernization and secularization that is commonly associated with the rationalization and the enlightenment of the eighteenth century. It gave rise to the idea of universal human rights, the rule of impersonal law, and the constitutional liberties of citizens. It also led to the conception of the world as nature to be described by empirical science and of progress as the guiding principle of history. The constitutive boundary between Europe and the outside other was even more temporalized and decoupled from the ties of descent and territory. It did run between the European vanguard of history and the backward 'races', but could occasionally also hint at the backwardness and decadence of the European centre and the natural innocence of the periphery. The noble savage could be closer to human perfection than the European—in particular if the European opposed the rule of reason and natural order. The enlightenment was a decisively European movement which aimed at the universal community of mankind. Everybody's true identity was European—and it was the task of education and emancipation to further the awareness of this identity. Contemporary criticism frequently accuses the enlightenment of being insensitive to cultural differences. The contrary is true. The enlightenment was strongly interested in all variations of human society. It gave rise to a comparative perspective on human civilizations which was more extensive than had previously been the case. Possibly for the first time, it tried to take the position of the other in order to focus on the peculiarities of European culture. In its refined forms it still remains the most complex intellectual endeavour to account for differences between the others outside of one's own community.

The fifth major translation can be seen in the human rights regime that, starting in the nineteenth century, has ascended to the status of a global ethic of international responsibility. This movement started with the French Revolution and created a unity of discourse which fuelled political movements against traditional forms of domination throughout Europe. The politicized intelligentsia of the nineteenth century created networks whose nodes were equally in Paris, London, or St Petersburg.[5] The defence of human rights was their weapon. Censorship and state persecution have been the answer of the European powers. Such networks created a counter-unity to the Metternich system which tried to remake the old European order. Their success was limited, but taken over by the worker's movement in Europe which in the beginning conceived itself as an international movement, although at that time it was essentially a European movement. The idea of human rights provided the meta-narrative of a better Europe. Transported into the Americas by European settlers and re-imported after two World Wars it became the 'post-war consensus' underlying the restructuration of Europe after World War II.

All these versions of the European cultural movement had a universalist core. They were normative projects that aimed at a transformation of politics, at a change in the mundane sphere of rights and entitlements, and at an inclusive shift of boundary construction. The idea of a transnational order is—contrary to the dominant narrative of the nation state as Europe's modernity—endemic to the idea of Europe. The discourse about citizenship represents the interface between the universalist thrust of the European cultural movement and the political institutions created in Europe. Because of this universalist thrust, European citizenship transcends the nation state as it transcends the other models of political institution building that we find in Europe since early modernity.

European citizenship—we conjecture—does not only define a social status in Europe, but could also become a founding myth for a European collective identity beyond the nation state.

The Organizational Representation of the Cultural Order

Europe has always been more than the sum of its parts. This holds for the feudal era as well as for the early modern territorial states and the modern nation states. It represented an order that mediated between the transcendental realm of the sacred and the mundane realm of politics, between unity and diversity, between the universal and the particular. The tension between these oppositions has always been at the core of the European movement. This European order has been more than a cultural movement. It has also been a social fact. Such a claim is based on a phenomenon that has always puzzled comparative historical research. Europe has been a world of competing feudal estates, principalities, monarchies, and nation states that lacked centralized rule.[6] But despite the heterogeneity of its political centres Europe has developed a homogeneous socio-cultural landscape. It has developed what can be called the *model of coordinated competition and conflict*. It developed an institutional order which has been capable of coordinating competing states and feuding parties.[7]

The '*European puzzle*' in historical analysis is that this centrifugal system has not fallen apart even in times of devastation and defeat. If culture is the basis for the homogeneity of Europe we have to ask for its social and institutional conditions. These conditions have been sought in the dense networks of communication among European intellectuals, among medieval monks and humanist scholars, enlightenment philosophers, and modern scientists. But the networks of intellectuals alone do not provide a firm basis for an institutional system capable of coordinating centrifugal centres of authority. The cultural unity of Europe had to be represented in a mundane organizational form that transcended political particularism and that could serve as an interface between the political and the transcendental realm.[8]

The first of these organizational forms was provided by the centralized Christian Church as it developed at the turn of the millennium in Western Europe. To describe the exceptionality of this institutional form, we have to take into account the structures established by the Church in order to control the emerging European society. The Church provided not only a cultural centre that represented the transcendental realm in this world; it also shaped the system of property rights throughout Europe; it included people into a system in which each individual soul had an equal chance of salvation. The control over the salvation of the soul was the control over the people, and this was enacted through abbeys and parishes. It has been a highly rational system of rule, based on the canonical law. It provided a linguistic idiom that made elite communication possible, the Latin language. And it provided the legitimate interpreters to the extent that Latin was confined to a tiny elite and vernacular languages did not dominate communication. Even the need for interpreters is functional to such an institutional order. The control over interpreters has made it possible to control the process of communication in and between the states and landlords.

Like all institutional forms of cultural orthodoxy, this institutional system, too, provoked heterodoxies which could, mostly, be absorbed, integrated, or defeated. Within its frame new social carriers and institutions could establish international networks: a European aristocracy that was tightly connected by marriage and dynastic filiation; a class of rulers that served as experts in a complicated system balancing conflict (especially inter-ethnic) in Europe; a class of intellectuals that controlled the interpretation of the sacred writings and transnational literary discourse; a system of monasteries and universities, that controlled transnational academic knowledge; and a system of property rights that provided the social structure for trade and production that finally led to rational forms of economic action.

In the sixteenth century, however, this institutional interface between the transcendental order and the realm of political action broke down—the Church was no longer able to integrate or overcome powerful new hetero-doxies. Europe split in the confessional camps of Reformatory Protestantism, Lutheranism, and Catholicism which resulted in a conflation of the political and the religious organization: the famous principle '*cuius regio, eius religio*' that ended the confessional wars put the religious confession under the polit-ical reason of the state. Politics took over the cultural claims of religious confession.

The decline of the all-embracing institutional order of the Christian Church led to the rise of a new secularized institutional order that, like the Church before it, transcended the boundaries of the princely states and embodied a new universalist cultural movement: the public sphere of the enlightenment and the institutional system of modern science. Although orig-inally favoured and supported by the princely powers, modern science, as it emerged in the seventeenth century, as well as its corollary, the enlightenment, had no national flavour. Any attempt to confine the spirit of scholarship and science into the confines of political power were bound to fail. The rationality of science was international and so were its institutional ways of communica-tion. Modern science and enlightenment replaced the universal chance of salvation with the universal chance of education, the universal community of souls with the universal community of mankind based on natural reason and the empirical examination of nature. Here, too, the tension between the tran-scendental principles of reason and morality, on the one hand, and the factual realization of these principles in history, on the other hand, had to be medi-ated by an institutional interface. This institutional interface which replaced the Church was provided by the growing institutional system of science and education. Science and education were not inventions of the seventeenth century. However, the cultural status of modern science and education differed profoundly from those of medieval science and education. From the seventeenth century onwards, they were increasingly regarded as the royal path to settling social and political conflicts, of overcoming the misery of mundane life, to emancipating individuals from the bonds of superstition and tradition. It was the institutions of science and education, the academies and universities, the schools and publishing houses, that provided the transfer between the master narrative of modernity and the factual limitations of everyday life, and it was the institutions of science and education that became the firm basis for the criticism of the narrow-mindedness of politics. The princely courts were the carriers of early modern science, a role that was, from the eighteenth century onwards, taken over by the European bourgeoisie. At the beginning of this century, Latin and French were still the main languages of intellectual publication and scholarly exchange, but even later on, with the rise of the national languages, translations were easily available and most members of the educated classes did speak several languages. The new institutions of science and education were not only a matter for intellectuals and educated cosmopolitans. New groups joined the movement of modernization in Europe: a class of international merchants and entrepreneurs who, originally encouraged by the princely powers but confined by mercantilist policies, increasingly reached out for a European and even global market that crossed territorial boundaries, a class of engineers and technicians promoting the pursuit of technological progress, a class of administrators that reorganized the state according to the impersonal standards of universal rationality.

With the rise of the nation states in the nineteenth century, the transnational space of the modernizing elites aiming at a universal rationality had to give way to the forces of diversity and fragmentation. The nation state aimed, again, at alleviating the tension between the universal range of the cultural institution and the particular boundaries of the state. Culture and politics were to refer to the same social bodies. Cultural movements were increasingly couched in national terms and aimed at a decisively national literature and even science. National languages replaced the traditional coexistence of European elite languages (Latin or French) and a diversity of local and regional dialects. Collective identity was no longer constructed in terms of a universal order but in terms of national distinctions. Still, the European bourgeoisie travelled internationally and boasted of speaking several foreign languages. Science remained, despite of all efforts to constrain it within a particular national culture, a predominantly international endeavour. International economic exchange flourished after the demise of mercantilism as economic policy. The all-embracing cultural unity of the modern order, however, was profoundly challenged.

After World War I at the latest, Europe had become an idea deprived of an organizational basis, a free-floating symbolic device that could be used and misused by anybody. Hitler and his followers could refer to the idea of defending Europe against some alleged Asian barbarism and the Western Allies could refer to the values of Europe pitted against the Fascist barbarism. The big divide between the Western democracies and Socialist Eastern Europe allowed for a revival of this rhetoric thus blurring the fact that Europe, again, consisted of entrenched confessional camps that were at the same time cultural as well as political.

Left with a historically loaded *idée directrice* Europe entered the second half of the twentieth century with an attempt to re-establish its organizational unity. Yet the self-description that accompanied this attempt has, until now, taken place in a situation of cultural discontinuity where the memory of the immediate past dominated the past of Europe. The consequences of such discontinuity have culminated in the idea of Europe as a '*Zweckverband*', as a rational institution for maximizing the interests of nation states through cooperation between nation states. Moral ideas such as peace or well-being were transformed into means to a greater end: a common market for all protected by nation states which for that purpose entered a rational game of cooperation. The cultural aspect of organizing a social and political order in Europe is reduced to the meagre idea of maximizing individual (or national) interests.

This is an insufficient base for organizing Europe, and this becomes more apparent the more the old reference to a foundation myth fades away: namely the construction of a peaceful order among nations after the catastrophe of two world wars. The moral basis of the post-war settlement, peaceful cooperation among nations through contracting mainly economic cooperation between the nations in Europe, is no longer sufficient to serve as a foundation myth for further European integration. The more national sovereignty, defined as the sovereignty of a nationally defined people to rule itself, is given up in favour of a supranational institution, i.e. European institutions of governance, the more the quest for a new narrative foundation beyond the myth of a nationally defined *volonté générale* will arise. It is our central claim that citizenship could serve as a foundation myth for further European integration by providing a model for a collective identity of the people in Europe.

Citizenship as the Foundation Myth of a New European Collective Identity

Citizenship as a Meta-narrative for European Integration

The theory explaining the function of European citizenship in providing a collective identity draws on the constructivist position that has inspired neo-institutionalist theorizing in the social sciences.[9] This theory emphasizes more than what is characteristic for the actual scholarly debate on the 'new Europe', namely the cultural aspect of institution-building in Europe.

The argument is that citizenship emerges as a strong *idée directrice* in the development of a European society. This European development follows a path which is different from the path taken by the nation state. The nation-state model was conceived as a political centre controlling and regulating a society of national citizens. The resulting collective identity was based finally on identifying with the state which represented the nation. This historical model of the nation state is, we claim, misleading when used to understand and explain the dynamics of the political and social integration of Europe. Instead of seeing European institution-building as a continuation of national state-building we propose to see it in two ways: as a continuation of the self-organization of European society as it evolved at the turn of the first millennium through the organizational power of the Church and as a continuation dating back to the seventeenth century and the rise of enlightenment and science in Europe. Such a theoretical perspective takes seriously the general theoretical argument regarding the historical embeddedness of institutional designs for a social order.

Nevertheless, Europe owes a lot to the past of nation-building. The *idée directrice* of a European citizenship cannot be imagined without the tradition of democratic nation-building in Europe. However, Europe provides a different organizational context for such ideas. Our theoretical proposal is that with the turn of the second millennium a new pattern in the history of organizing a European society emerges through the ascending power of citizenship that is decoupled from membership in a nationally defined community. The self-organization by citizens, which we have observed in city states, in empires, in enlightened absolutism and finally in the nation state, serves as the model from which to construct a community of equal persons to be protected regardless of their origins and—if necessary—even against their ethnic origins.

Such a European community of citizens replaces the idea of a Holy Empire of souls that shaped Europe in its beginning. It also replaces the idea of a universal community of reasonable and discursive individuals invented as a model of the cultural unity of Europe. In Europe's institutional design the idea of civic participation takes the vanguard which previously had been salvation and education. The mytho-moteurs of religious transcendence and of inner-worldly transcendence by enlightenment and scientific progress are substituted by the mytho-moteur of collective self-creation through participation in public activities. The mytho-moteur of citizenship transcends the limits of the myth of the nation and decouples the practice of citizenship from being the member of a national community defined by birth or territoriality. It mobilizes the myth of an association of free and equal beings living together in peace, i.e. the myth of a community of citizens brought into existence through the practice of citizens.

Such a myth continues a specific European tradition of framing a social order. The Church provided the frame of a community of souls striving for heaven; whoever failed to be saved was lost to hell. Science and education provided the frame of a society in the pursuit of becoming perfectly rational and reasonable; whoever failed to join progress and rationality was bound to fall back into barbarism. Citizenship provides the frame of a self-creation of a community of citizens;[10] those who take part in this process will be included. The discourse on citizenship has become the transnational master-narrative of democratic self-organization in Europe.[11]

The rise of this *idée directrice* has been prepared and preluded by the great democratic movements and revolutions of the nineteenth century. Although constrained by the horizons of nation and class, the movements of democratic participation in political power and economic welfare established a new master-reference for public debate about conflicts and claims, about the ideal society and its internal order. These debates are no longer patterned by the opposition between religious tradition and legitimacy, on the one side, and the rational perfection of the state, on the other, but increasingly linked to claims for representation, inclusion, and participation, for collective self-determination, and public recognition. The quest for a collective identity through citizenship[12] has come to the fore and become a powerful rival to the quest for a collective identity through salvation or the quest for a collective identity through rationality and enlightenment.

The *idée directrice* of national citizenship is a preparatory and transitory event in this evolution. It mixes salvation and rationality with citizenship by offering objective criteria for citizenship, namely it is open to those engaged in a project of saving a nation. The idea of socialist citizenship is based on a similar fusion of citizenship with objective criteria of who is to be a citizen: those engaged in the project of realizing a rationally planned society. Both experiments in collective identity construction have failed. The quest of a European identity is thus an experiment in leaving such constructions behind.

European Collective Identity as a Precondition of a Democratic Europe

Is is not only because of a secular shift in the master-narratives that the question of a European collective identity is raised. This question is of paramount importance even when we remain within the realist camp and focus on the preconditions of democratic governance in Europe. European society conceived as a mode of self-organization of a civil society requires an exorbitant consensus to serve as an institutional device limiting political power and private interest. Whether the forms of solidarities created through the collective action of engaged citizens are strong enough to provide such consensus, is subject to debate. Liberals would argue in favour of such a scenario. Communitarians would disagree. They would rather argue for a strong notion of collective identity that can exert constraints on power and the free play of interest.

Liberals in fact have problems demonstrating the origins of solidarities that motivate citizens to coordinate interests and define a common good.

Communitarians have a point in saying that interests can only be made compatible by reference to some shared definition of the common good. As long as interests are considered as preferences of citizens that definition will be changed only when it is in the interest of those concerned. There is no reason to expect that the coordination of interests will lead to a common good. By assuming a shared idea of a common good underlying the preferences of citizens, we have a social basis for the coordination of competing interests. This is the same as saying that collective interests are embedded in collective identities. The communitarian theory of citizenship is based on the assumption that a strong collective identity is needed in order to have citizenship in the complex and fluid world of modern societies.

In the debate about a European collective identity three arguments have been put forward to answer the question regarding the origin of such a collective identity. The first argument is to base collective identities on universalist human rights discourses. This is the universalist solution of constituting a community of people doing good, of defending an idea that should be applied to everybody. A second argument is the primordialist one: Europe as an exclusive community with its own unalienable and unshareable cultural roots, a fortress Europe in which this particularity is to be defended against those who are not able to share these roots. The third argument focuses on narrative traditions, but does not assume them to be primordial; through integrating people by shared routines or historical traditions outsiders can join the community if they respect basic routines and agree on participating in the construction and reconstruction of these traditions (Giesen 1998).

Criticism may be levelled against all three arguments. The third type of collective identity might be questioned by pointing out that the political culture of a traditionally organized society contradicts the form of civil society that has already evolved. The second type of collective identity, the idea of a primordial collective identity, is a self-destructive collective identity; it is an exclusionary device of defining a community of citizens which tends towards the implosion of society. The first type of collective identity, based on a strong form of ideological universalism, tends towards explosion; it has turned European nation states into the protagonist of human rights across the globe,[13] thus creating the well-known consequence of missionary zeal in defending the right and the good.

Although European collective identity in a globalized world has to keep its universalist elements it can no longer alleviate and mediate the tension between the universal scope of the transcendental order and the inevitable limitations of political decisions by missionary inclusion. The thrust for the conversion and education of outsiders has to be replaced by the chance of inclusion for those who opt for it and who know about the obligations that are engendered by this option. The post-utopian universalism of postnational citizenship comes close to the third solution: the assumption of a community of civil traditions that balance the implosive forces of primordial exclusion and the explosive forces of missionary inclusion. The boundaries of such a civic European community are shifting and under continuous reconstruction. There is neither a territorial referent such as national borders (there is on the contrary fluidity and heterogeneity) nor a substantive referent such as language or culture or welfare of a nation. There is only the complexity of global problems and the making of a transnational community of citizens.

What Is Left in Europe?

What remains in Europe is the option for a collective identity that allows citizens to permanently question given interests and that encourages them to enter debates about the legitimacy of their interests. Such a collective identity is—we would argue—built into the myth of being a citizen. Citizenship implies a sense of a collective identity created through social action proper. Such a collective identity requires particular spaces for its making: transnational spaces of citizenship practices, transnational legal orders, and transnational discourses. Citizenship in Europe is forced to become transnational since people no longer restrict their space of action to the national realm; since discourses transcend national discourses; since legal rules are no longer contained in the nation state.

Filling such transnational spaces is not a voluntary act. It is embedded in the cultural movement that has shaped European society since its beginning. The European Union can join this movement. It does not have to become a state like the nation state. It has the option to develop an institutional form for coordinating competing centres of (national and regional) power. The dual structure of European society, the existence of an institutional order above the centres of political power can thus be reproduced. The emerging multi-level institutional order in the European Union is a form that has a long tradition in Europe.[14] Such an institutional order needs an idea of a shared world beyond the realm of power. It needs a collective identity. The transformation of the narrative basis of this overarching institutional order from a community of souls via a community of rational subjects educated by an enlightened ruler to a community of citizens provides a foundation myth for the making of a European institutional order.

The Union of the American States was to become the 'first new nation'. Europe must not become the 'second new nation'. Like the USA before it, Europe has to invent and imagine a people beyond the national origins of its component groups and at the same time to recognize the origins of the people. Unlike the United States, Europe has a long tradition of a double-layered and tension-prone structure: a society that is constructed with reference to a transcendental universal order and states that are constructed with reference to the particular interests of territorially or culturally defined people.

Citizenship is the potential basis of the collective identity of Europe. It is based on the modern myth of the free and equal citizen participating in public affairs. Those considered to be good citizens in Europe are included. To be a citizen in Europe is no longer congruent with the mere fact of being the member of a nation state, thus becoming a European citizen by birth or descent. Such a collective identity includes then not only those who are members of Member States. It also includes those who live in other nation states and those who have no membership in a nation state, i.e. the stateless persons, and those who are members of more than one nation state.

Such a collective identity continues the specific tradition of the making of a European society: it once included souls; then it included enlightened people across feudal or national boundaries; it thus provided a sense of collective identity beyond the confines of systems of political domination. It includes in the making of the 'new Europe' nothing but good citizens. European citizenship then becomes more than the sum of citizens defined by national membership. It becomes an idea of an inclusive community beyond the nation state. Up till now a European collective identity that supports a transnational space of equal and free citizens is struggling with a collective identity defined as the sum of its diverse parts and particular interests. The European flag with the stars that equal the sum of the parts manifests its dominant type of collective identity. If democratic governance in Europe is to succeed it will be bound to a transnational order of citizenship which is based on a collective identity beyond the nation. This is the option left for the making of the new Europe.

NOTES

1. This perspective is found in the contribution from von Beyme, Schmitter, and Streeck. The political conclusion is necessarily a plea for the strengthening of the nation state.
2. This is the perspective taken by Soysal and Closa who differ however in the theoretical approach taken on the issue.
3. This issue is at the base of the contributions from Lepsius and Eder.
4. This is not to deny the importance of the regulatory perspective. An excellent example is Majone (1996, 1998a).
5. It is less easy to find such nodes in Germany or Italy where a network of small university towns fulfilled the same function.
6. The emperor did not represent these parts; he represented a holy order beyond the feuding parties. This explains why his function was mainly reduced to a judicial role.

7. This notion follows the paradox of the emergence of such a system which has been called the European miracle (Hall 1988). For the notion of a European puzzle, see also the explanation of the European dynamics by Mann (1988, 1992).

8. John W. Meyer has provided a short but succinct analysis of this phenomenon, where he explained the role of Christendom in terms of the organizational theory that has become the starting point of sociological neo-institutionalism (Meyer 1989).

9. There are several neo-institutionalisms. However, it should have become clear that the neo-institutionalism used here is that which has emerged from organizational sociology (Powell and DiMaggio 1991). Good examples of its macrosociological application can be found in Thomas et al. (1987). The central argument is simply: there is no organizational form that is not linked to some ideal referents that transcend it. Such 'transcendence' can be an illusory, a utopian, or any normative ideal that is used in the making and reproduction of organizational forms. Such a model is analytical, not tied to a specific historical constellation and does not presuppose any empirical assumptions.

10. This idea of societal self-creation emerges at times even in the sociological theories making sense of modernity. An especially instructive example has been Touraine's idea of the self-production of society (Touraine 1973, 1977). He misunderstood this idea as an analytical framework for understanding modern society instead of taking it as an emerging meta-narrative for a modern society beyond the nation state.

11. Somers (1993) has applied narrative analysis to a historical account for the making of the Anglo-Saxon narrative of citizenship. This historical narrative has gained, she argues, the position of a meta-narrative in Western societies.

12. This quest is well grasped by Dolf Sternberger, a German political scientist, who, motivated by a specifically German experience, wrote a book with the title: *Ich wünschte ein Bürger zu sein* [I would want to be a citizen] (Sternberger 1967).

13. Following the model of the European nation states, the modern United States has taken on such a role in the twentieth century.

14. Much of the claim about the originality of the multi-level system of governance in Europe turns out to be part of the specific organizational tradition of Europe for many centuries. For an excellent characterization of the multi-level character of European governance, see Kohler-Koch and Eisinger (1999).

REFERENCES

EDER, K. (1985). *Geschichte als Lernprozeß? Zur Pathogenese politischer Modernität in Deutschland*. Frankfurt am Main: Suhrkamp.

EISENSTADT, S. N. (ed.) (1987). *The Origins and Diversity of Axial Age Civilizations*. Albany, NY: Suny Press.

GIESEN, B. (1998). *The Intellectuals and the Nation: Collective Identity in German Axial Age*. Cambridge: Cambridge University Press.

HALL, J. A. (1988). 'States and Societies: The Miracle in Comparative Perspective', in J.

Baechler, J. A. Hall, and M. Mann (eds.), *Europe and the Rise of Capitalism*. London: Blackwell, 20–38.

KOHLER-KOCH, B., and EISINGER, K. (eds.) (1999). *The Transformation of Governance in Europe*. London: Routledge.

MAJONE, G. (ed.) (1996). *Regulating Europe*. London: Routledge.

—— (1998a). 'Europe's "Democracy Deficit": The Question of Standards'. *European Law Journal*, 4: 5–28.

—— (1998b). *The Regulatory State and its Legitimacy Problems*. Vienna: Institut für Höhere Studien.

MANN, M. (1986). *The Sources of Social Power: A History of Power from the Beginning to A.D. 1760*, Cambridge, Mass.: Cambridge University Press.

—— (1988). 'European Development: Approaching a Historical Explanation', in J. Baechler, J. A. Hall, and M. Mann (eds.), *Europe and the Rise of Capitalism*. Oxford: Blackwell, 8–19.

—— (1992). *The Sources of Political Power, ii*. Cambridge: Cambridge University Press.

MARSHALL, T. H. (1950). *Citizenship and Social Class*. Cambridge, Mass.: Cambridge University Press.

MEYER, J. W. (1989). 'Conceptions of Christendom: Note on the Distinctiveness of the West', in M. L. Kohn (ed.), *Cross-National Research in Sociology*. Newbury Park, Calif.: Sage, 395–413.

POWELL, W. W., and DiMAGGIO, P J. (eds.) (1991). *The New Institutionalism in Organizational Analysis*. Chicago: University of Chicago Press.

SOMERS, M. R. (1993). 'Citizenship and the Place of the Public Sphere: Law, Community, and Political Culture in the Transition to Democracy'. *American Sociological Review*, 58: 587–620.

STERNBERGER, D. (1967). *Ich wünschte ein Bürger zu sein: Neun Versuche über den Staat*. Frankfurt am Main: Suhrkamp.

THOMAS, G. M., MEYER, J. W., RAMIREZ, F. O., and BOLI, J. (eds.) (1987). *Institutional Structure: Constituting State, Society, and the Individual*. Newbury Park, Calif.: Sage.

TOURAINE, A. (1973). *Production de la société*. Paris: Seuil.

—— (1977). *The Self-Production of Society*. Chicago: University of Chicago Press.

INDEX

ÍNDICE

CONTENTS

GERÊNCIA DE PROJETO/PROJECT MANAGEMENT
Teresa Álvarez García
Carol McCann

COLABORADORES/CONTRIBUTORS
John Whitlam
Helen Newstead
Vitoria Davies
Mike Harland
Jane Horwood
Lígia Xavier
Gerard Breslin
Laura Neves
Emma McDade
Daniel Veloso
Orin Hargraves
Maggie Seaton
Cordelia Lilly

PARA A EDITORA/FOR THE PUBLISHER
Lucy Cooper
Kerry Ferguson
Ruth O'Donovan
Elaine Higgleton

INTRODUÇÃO

Ficamos felizes com a sua decisão de comprar o Dicionário Inglês-Português Collins e esperamos que este lhe seja útil na escola, em casa, de férias ou no trabalho.

Esta introdução fornece algumas sugestões de como utilizar da melhor maneira possível o seu dicionário – não somente a partir da ampla lista de palavras mas também a partir das informações fornecidas em cada verbete. Este dicionário visa ajudá-lo a ler e a entender o inglês moderno assim como a exprimir-se corretamente.

No início do Dicionário Collins aparecem as abreviaturas utilizadas, e a ilustração dos sons através de símbolos fonéticos. O suplemento "Inglês em Ação" contém informações práticas sobre tópicos como correspondências, falsos cognatos, frases e expressões úteis, verbos irregulares, datas, horas e números.

COMO UTILIZAR O DICIONÁRIO COLLINS

Um grande número de informações pode ser encontrado neste dicionário. Vários tipos e tamanhos de letras, símbolos, abreviaturas e parênteses foram utilizados. As convenções e símbolos usados são explicados nas seções seguintes.

VERBETES

As palavras que você procurar no dicionário – os verbetes – estão em ordem alfabética. Eles estão impressos em cor para uma rápida identificação. As palavras que aparecem no topo de cada página indicam o primeiro verbete (se for nas páginas pares) ou o último verbete (se for nas páginas ímpares) da página em questão. Informações sobre a utilização ou forma de certos verbetes são dadas entre parênteses e, em geral, aparecem em forma abreviada e em itálico (p. ex. *(fam)*, *(Com)*).

Quando for apropriado, palavras derivadas aparecem agrupadas no mesmo verbete (abade, abadia; produce, producer) num formato ligeiramente menor do que o verbete.

As expressões comuns nas quais o verbete aparece estão impressas em um tamanho diferente de negrito romano. O símbolo '~' usado nas expressões representa o verbete principal no começo de cada parágrafo. Por exemplo, na entrada 'cold', a expressão **'to be ~'** equivale a **'to be cold'**.

SIGNIFICADOS
A tradução para o verbete aparece em letra normal e quando há mais de um significado ou utilização, estes estão separados por um ponto e vírgula. Frequentemente, você encontrará outras palavras em itálico e entre parênteses antes da tradução, sugerindo contextos nos quais o verbete pode aparecer (p. ex. rough *(voice)* ou *(weather)*), ou fornecendo sinônimos (p. ex. rough *(violent)*).

PALAVRAS-CHAVE
Atenção especial foi dada a certas palavras em inglês e em português consideradas 'palavras-chave' em cada língua. Elas podem, por exemplo, ser usadas com muita frequência ou ter muitos tipos de utilização (p. ex. be, get). Verbetes destacados com números ajudam a distinguir as categorias gramaticais e diferentes significados.

Informações complementares são fornecidas entre
parênteses e em itálico na língua relevante para o usuário.

INFORMAÇÃO GRAMATICAL

As categorias gramaticais são dadas em versalete e
abreviadas após a ortografia fonética do verbete (p. ex. VT,
ADJ, VI).

Os adjetivos aparecem em ambos os gêneros quando forem
diferentes (interno, -a). Esta distinção também é feita
quando os adjetivos têm uma forma irregular no feminino
ou no plural (p. ex. ateu, atéia). As formas irregulares de
substantivos feminino ou plural também são indicadas
(p. ex. child (*pl* ~**ren**)).

INTRODUCTION

We are delighted you have decided to buy the Collins Portuguese Dictionary and hope you will enjoy and benefit from using it at school, at home, on holiday or at work.

This introduction gives you a few tips on how to get the most out of your dictionary – not simply from its comprehensive wordlist but also from the information provided in each entry. This will help you to read and understand modern Portuguese, as well as communicate and express yourself in the language.

The Collins Portuguese Dictionary begins by listing the abbreviations used in the text and illustrating the sounds shown by the phonetic symbols. The Portuguese in Action supplement contains useful information on topics such as correspondence, false friends, useful phrases, irregular verbs, dates, time and numbers.

USING YOUR COLLINS DICTIONARY

A wealth of information is presented in the dictionary, using various typefaces, sizes of type, symbols, abbreviations and brackets. The conventions and symbols used are explained in the following sections.

HEADWORDS

The words you look up in the dictionary – 'headwords' – are listed alphabetically. They are printed in **colour** for rapid identification. The headwords appearing at the top of each page indicate the first (if it appears on a left-hand page) and last word (if it appears on a right-hand page) dealt with on the page in question.

Information about the usage or form of certain headwords
is given in brackets after the phonetic spelling. This
usually appears in abbreviated form and in italics.
(e.g. (*fam*), (*Comm*)).

Where appropriate, words related to headwords are
grouped in the same entry (**abade, abadia; produce,
producer**) in a slightly smaller bold type than the
headword. Common expressions in which the headword
appears are shown in a different size of bold roman type.
The swung dash, ~, represents the main headword at the
start of each entry. For example, in the entry for '**caminho**',
the phrase '**pôr-se a ~**' should be read '**pôr-se a caminho**'.

PHONETIC SPELLINGS
The phonetic spelling of each headword (indicating its
pronunciation) is given in square brackets immediately
after the headword (e.g. **grande** ['grɑ̃dʒi]). A list of these
spellings is given on page xiv.

MEANINGS
Headword translations are given in ordinary type and,
where more than one meaning or usage exists, they are
separated by a semicolon. You will often find other words
in italics in brackets before the translations. These offer
suggested contexts in which the headword might appear
(e.g. **intenso** (*emoção*)) or provide synonyms (e.g. **cândido**
(*inocente*)).

Special status is given to certain Portuguese and English words which are considered as 'key' words in each language. They may, for example, occur very frequently or have several types of usage (e.g. bem, ficar). A combination of lozenges and numbers helps you to distinguish different parts of speech and different meanings. Further helpful information is provided in brackets and in italics in the relevant language for the user.

GRAMMATICAL INFORMATION
Parts of speech are given in abbreviated form in small caps after the phonetic spellings of headwords (e.g. VT, ADJ, PREP).

Genders of Portuguese nouns are indicated as follows: *m* for a masculine and *f* for a feminine noun. Feminine and irregular plural forms of nouns are also shown next to the headword (inglês, -esa; material (*pl* **-ais**)). Adjectives are given in both masculine and feminine forms where these forms are different (comilão, -lona).

The gender of the Portuguese translation also appears in *italics* immediately following the key element of the translation, except where there is a regular masculine singular noun ending in 'o', or a regular feminine singular noun ending in 'a'.

ABREVIATURAS

ABBREVIATIONS

abreviatura	AB(B)R	abbreviation
adjetivo	ADJ	adjective
administração	Admin	administration
advérbio, locução adverbial	ADV	adverb, adverbial phrase
aeronáutica	Aer	flying, air travel
agricultura	Agr	agriculture
anatomia	Anat	anatomy
arquitetura	Arq, Arch	architecture
artigo definido	ART DEF	definite article
artigo indefinido	ART INDEF	indefinite article
uso atributivo do substantivo	ATR	compound element
Austrália	Aust	Australia
automobilismo	Aut(o)	the motor car and motoring
auxiliar	AUX	auxiliary
aeronáutica	Aviat	flying, air travel
biologia	Bio	biology
botânica, flores	Bot	botany
português do Brasil	BR	Brazilian Portuguese
inglês britânico	BRIT	British English
química	Chem	chemistry
linguagem coloquial	col	colloquial
comércio, finanças, bancos	Com(m)	commerce, finance, banking
comparativo	compar	comparative
computação	Comput	computing
conjunção	CONJ	conjunction
construção	Constr	building
uso atributivo do substantivo	CPD	compound element
cozinha	Culin	cookery
artigo definido	DEF ART	definite article
economia	Econ	economics
educação, escola e universidade	Educ	schooling, schools and universities
eletricidade, eletrônica	Elet, Elec	electricity, electronics
especialmente	esp	especially
exclamação	excl	exclamation
feminino	f	feminine
ferrovia	Ferro	railways
uso figurado	fig	figurative use
física	Fís	physics

fotografia	*Foto*	photography
(verbo inglês) do qual a partícula é inseparável	FUS	(phrasal verb) where the particle is inseparable
geralmente	*gen*	generally
geografia, geologia	*Geo*	geography, geology
geralmente	*ger*	generally
impessoal	IMPESS, IMPERS	impersonal
artigo indefinido	INDEF ART	indefinite article
linguagem coloquial	*inf*	colloquial
infinitivo	*infin*	infinitive
invariável	INV	invariable
irregular	*irreg*	irregular
jurídico	*Jur*	law
gramática, linguística	*Ling*	grammar, linguistics
masculino	*m*	masculine
matemática	*Mat(h)*	mathematics
medicina	*Med*	medicine
ou masculino ou feminino, dependendo do sexo da pessoa	*m/f*	masculine/feminine
militar, exército	*Mil*	military matters
música	*Mús, Mus*	music
substantivo	N	noun
navegação, náutica	*Náut, Naut*	sailing, navigation
adjetivo ou substantivo numérico	NUM	numeral adjective or noun
	o.s.	oneself
pejorativo	*pej*	pejorative
fotografia	*Phot*	photography
física	*Phys*	physics
fisiologia	*Physiol*	physiology
plural	*pl*	plural
política	*Pol*	politics
particípio passado	PP	past participle
preposição	PREP	preposition
pronome	PRON	pronoun
português de Portugal	*PT*	European Portuguese
pretérito	*pt*	past tense
química	*Quím*	chemistry
religião e cultos	*Rel*	religion, church services
	sb	somebody
educação, escola e universidade	*Sch*	schooling, schools and universities